Controversy

Controversy

Issues for Reading and Writing

THIRD EDITION

Judith J. Pula
Frostburg State University

Audrey T. Edwards
Eastern Illinois University

R. Allan Dermott
*New Hampshire Community Technical College
at Manchester/Stratham*

PEARSON
Prentice
Hall

Upper Saddle River, New Jersey 07458

Library of Congress Cataloging-in-Publication Data

Controversy : Issues for reading and writing / [compiled by] Judith J. Pula, Audrey T.
Edwards, R. Allan Dermott – 3rd ed.
    p. cm.
    Includes bibliographical references and index.
    ISBN 0-13-185096-2
    1. College readers. 2. English language—Rhetoric—Problems, exercises, etc. 3. Report
writing—Problems, exercises, etc. I. Pula, Judith J. II. Edwards, Audrey T. III. Dermott,
R. Allan.

PE1417.C6543 2005
808'.0427—dc22   2003070652

Editor-in-Chief: Leah Jewell
Senior Acquisitions Editor: Craig Campanella
Assistant Editor: Karen Schultz
Editorial Assistant: Joan Polk
Production Liaison: Joanne Hakim
Senior Marketing Manager: Rachel Falk
Marketing Assistant: Adam Laitman
Manufacturing Buyer: Benjamin Smith
Cover Design: Robert Farrar-Wagner
Cover Illustration/Photo: *Shapes,* The Studio Dog / Photodisc Collection / Getty Images, Inc.
Cover Image Specialist: Karen Sanatar
Composition/Full-Service Project Management: Rosaria Cassinese/Prepare Inc.
Printer/Binder: Phoenix Book Tech Park

Pearson Education LTD.   Pearson Education North Asia Ltd
Pearson Education Singapore, Pte. Ltd   Pearson Educación de Mexico, S.A. de C.V.
Pearson Education, Canada, Ltd   Pearson Education Malaysia, Pte. Ltd
Pearson Education–Japan   Pearson Education, Upper Saddle River,
Pearson Education Australia PTY, Limited   New Jersey

10 9 8 7 6 5 4 3 2 1
S·E· ISBN 0-13-185096-2
I·E· ISBN 0-13-189145-6

Contents

Introduction

This book asks you to use what you know to judge an author's ideas and write about them.

You may think you don't know enough to argue with a professional writer. We think you do. For one thing, you have had experiences no one else has had; you and your classmates together have had a great many experiences. For another thing, it's possible to reach different opinions from the same set of facts. In fact, this book gives two opinions on each topic: a short preview article and a longer essay following it. Once you've compared the two, you can draw your own conclusions.

There are 16 major topics in this book, ranging from juvenile justice to the effects of technology. For each topic, the book has four steps: preview, reading, discussion, and composition.

Step One: Preview

During the preview step, you'll be thinking about your own beliefs on the topic, discussing your ideas with your classmates, and reading a short preview article. Then you'll be taking a quick look at the essay—the title, the first and last paragraphs, and the author's background—so you can predict the main idea. You'll also look at some quotations from the essay to figure out the meanings of any new words. (To assist you, we've included a list of common word parts in Appendix A at the back of the book.)

Step Two: Reading

After the preview, you'll be ready to read the essay on your own. Following the essay are some reading questions dealing with the main idea, your reactions to it, and the author's writing techniques. As you read, be sure to write down your answers to these questions so that you'll have notes to speak from when you discuss the essay. If an occasional question seems difficult, do the best you can and be prepared to compare ideas in class.

Step Three: Discussion

Having read the essay and made your notes, you're ready for the discussion. By talking with your classmates, you may find facts you've missed, and you'll certainly hear other people's ideas on the topic. The discussion will help sum up your reading experience and prepare you for writing.

Step Four: Composition

When you write, you'll be giving your opinion on the topic you've discussed. At this point, your short answers to the reading questions should help you collect your thoughts and even try out some of the writing techniques used by the authors. Once you've thought about your own experiences, as well as the beliefs of at least two authors and several classmates, you should have something very worthwhile to say.

Making Discussions Effective

Sometimes you're surprised by what you say: Good ideas pop into your mind while you're talking. And sometimes other people's words will give you a new way of looking at things. Good discussion is truly creative.

In fact, discussion has such a strong effect on reading and writing that it's built into the plan for this book—in two places. First, a preview session allows you to think over a topic with other students before you read. Then, after you read, a second session lets you compare notes on the essays and prepare to write about them.

Of course, this class is not the only place where you'll be taking part in discussions. Over the course of a lifetime, you'll sit through many meetings—in classes, clubs, sororities, business groups. These meetings can be a pleasure or an annoyance, and although you can't entirely control the outcome, you can improve the odds—by improving the content and by helping the group to work together more smoothly.

CONTENT

If you've ever felt that you couldn't get a word in—that the discussion went on to something new before you could get your thoughts in order—try forming some opinions ahead of time. (Naturally, these can change when you hear other people's ideas, but at least you'll have a head start.) Before a meeting, thoroughly read anything that's assigned. Mark the key parts and jot down a word or two to remind you of each point you want to make during the discussion. (In using this book, you probably won't be expected to prepare for the preview discussion, but you probably will be asked to write down your answers to the Reading Questions before class.) Then, just before the discussion, quickly look over your notes to refresh your memory. Having prepared, you'll be moving the session along instead of being dragged in its wake. The next question is how to move things along most effectively.

TASK AND MAINTENANCE ROLES

When you think of discussions, you may picture two people trading facts or opinions. Actually, though, a discussion becomes much more interesting when shared by several people playing a variety of roles. People may play either a "task role," helping the group to deal with the task at hand, or a "maintenance role," maintaining group harmony.

Both task actions and maintenance actions are important to the success of your discussions. Listed below are some task and maintenance roles in the form of self-quizzes. Answers are listed after Matching Exercise 2.

Matching Exercise 1.   To help you learn the task and maintenance roles, match the following terms with their definitions.

Task Roles   ## Actions

__ 1.   Information and Opinion Giver   a. Makes sure all group members under-
                                                stand what each is saying
__ 2.   Information and Opinion Seeker   b. Pulls together related ideas or suggestions
                                                and restates them
__ 3.   Direction and Role Definer   c. Offers facts, opinions, ideas, feelings, and
                                                information
__ 4.   Summarizer   d. Expresses acceptance and liking for group
                                                members
__ 5.   Energizer   e. Uses observations of how the group is
                                                working to help discuss how the group
__ 6.   Comprehension Checker   can improve
                                             f. Lets members know their contributions
Maintenance Roles   are valued
                                             g. Asks for facts, opinions, ideas, feelings,
__ 7.   Encourager of Participation   and information
                                             h. Asks others to summarize discussion to
__ 8.   Communication Facilitator   make sure they understand
                                             i. Encourages group members to work hard
__ 9.   Tension Releaser   to achieve goals
                                             j. Calls attention to tasks that need to be
__ 10. Process Observer   done and assigns responsibilities
                                             k. Helps resolve and mediate conflicts
__ 11. Interpersonal Problem-Solver   l. Tells jokes and increases the group fun

__ 12. Supporter and Praiser

Matching Exercise 2.   Match each statement below with the task or main-tenance role it seems to fit best.

Task Roles   ## Statements

__ 1.   Information and Opinion Giver   a. "Does everyone in the group understand
                                                Helen's idea?"
__ 2.   Information and Opinion Seeker   b. "How about giving our report on yoga
                                                while standing on our heads?"
__ 3.   Direction and Role Definer

Task Roles	**Statements**
__ 4. Summarizer	c. "Edye's idea sounds like Buddy's; I think they could be combined."
__ 5. Energizer	d. "I think we should openly discuss the conflict between Dave and Linda to help resolve it."
__ 6. Comprehension Checker	

Task Roles

__ 4. Summarizer

__ 5. Energizer

__ 6. Comprehension Checker

Maintenance Roles

__ 7. Encourager of Participation

__ 8. Communication Facilitator

__ 9. Tension Releaser

__ 10. Process Observer

__ 11. Interpersonal Problem-Solver

__ 12. Supporter and Praiser

Statements

c. "Edye's idea sounds like Buddy's; I think they could be combined."

d. "I think we should openly discuss the conflict between Dave and Linda to help resolve it."

e. "Before we go on, let me tell you how other groups have solved this task."

f. "We need a time-keeper, Keith. Why don't you do that?"

g. "I really enjoy this group; I especially enjoy Roger's sense of humor."

h. "I think we'd find a good solution if we put a little more work into it."

i. "Frank, tell us what we've said so far to see if you understand it correctly."

j. "We seem to be suggesting solutions before we're ready. Let's define the problem first."

k. "I don't understand. What do you mean?"

l. "Helen, I'd like to hear what you think about this; you have such good ideas."

Answer Key. Exercise 1: 1. c; 2. g; 3. j; 4. b; 5. i; 6. h; 7. f; 8. a; 9. l; 10. e; 11. k; 12. d.
Exercise 2: 1. e; 2. k; 3. j; 4. c; 5. h; 6. a; 7. l; 8. i; 9. b; 10. f; 11. d; 12. g.

Playing Task and Maintenance Roles: Winter Survival Exercise

Now that you've seen how many different roles you can play, you know you can contribute in some way to an actual discussion. (You needn't attempt all these roles, of course, and you needn't stick with any one type. Just contribute your thoughts in a way that suits you and perhaps try a new role once in a while.)

Try testing out some of these roles using the following short discussion exercise, "Winter Survival." We recommend the following plan for its use.

First, break up into groups of four or five people; move a little way apart from the other groups. Each group should choose one person to record group decisions, either in writing or on tape. Next, read "Winter Survival."

(It contains your task and all the information you will need.) As soon as everyone in your small group has finished reading, begin your discussion.

About halfway through the time allowed for discussion, STOP. As a group, consider the following questions. How many people have taken part so far? What went well? How could the discussion be improved during its second half?

Resume your discussion, and try to carry out any suggested improvements.

Once you've concluded the discussion, evaluate it again. What roles did you actually play? Go back over the list of task roles: Check the two or three you found yourself playing most often during the discussion of "Winter Survival." Then pick your two or three most important maintenance roles.

Finally, sum up: How did you help the group—either in getting the job done or in keeping the group going?

What would you like to do differently another time?

WINTER SURVIVAL: THE SITUATION

You have just crash-landed in the woods of northern Minnesota and southern Manitoba. It is 11:32 A.M. in mid-January. The light plane in which you were traveling crashed on a lake. The pilot and copilot were killed. Shortly after the crash, the plane sank completely into the lake with the pilot's and copilot's bodies inside. Miraculously, the rest of you are not seriously injured, and you are all dry.

The crash came suddenly, before the pilot had time to radio for help or inform anyone of your position. Since your pilot was trying to avoid a storm, you know the plane was considerably off course. The pilot announced shortly before the crash that you were 20 miles northwest of a small town that is the nearest known habitation.

You are in a wilderness area made up of thick woods broken by many lakes and streams. The snow depth varies from above the ankles in windswept areas to knee-deep where it has drifted. The last weather report indicated that the temperature would reach minus 25 degrees Fahrenheit in the daytime and minus 40 at night. There is plenty of dead wood and twigs in the immediate area. You are dressed in winter clothing appropriate for city wear—suits, pantsuits, street shoes, and overcoats.

While escaping from the plane, the several members of your group salvaged 12 items. Your task as a group is to rank these items according to their importance to your survival, starting with 1 for the most important item and ending with 12 for the least important one.

You may assume that the number of passengers is the same as the number of persons in your group and that the group has agreed to stick together.

Winter Survival Decision Form.   Rank the following items according to their importance to your survival, starting with 1 for the most important one and proceeding to 12 for the least important one.

_____ Ball of steel wool
_____ Newspapers (one per person)
_____ Compass
_____ Hand ax
_____ Cigarette lighter (without fluid)
_____ Loaded .45-caliber pistol
_____ Sectional air map made of plastic
_____ Twenty-by-twenty-foot piece of heavy-duty canvas
_____ Extra shirt and pants for each survivor
_____ Can of shortening
_____ Quart of 100-proof whiskey
_____ Family-size chocolate bar (one per person)

Differences of opinion will arise in groups.   Try to come to an agreement. If your group can't agree, part of the group may want to agree on a minority opinion and part on a majority opinion.

Essay Questions: Winter Survival.   Choose one of the following questions and answer it in a short essay (about 300 words).

1. Explain why one item on the list created a difficult decision for you. Tell why you finally made the decision you did.

2. Pick one feature (for example, ability to retain heat) that you think is very important in choosing items from the list. Explain what makes that feature so important to your survival.

3. From the items on the list, choose two. Explain why one item is more valuable than the other.

Acknowledgments

Our students contributed many substantive comments to *Controversy,* thereby proving that several heads are better than one at critiquing.

Our teaching colleagues provided advice, information, and warm encouragement.

Our editors at Prentice Hall and their reviewers helped us to see the book clearly as it took shape. Our reviewers were Diane Bosco, Suffolk County Community College; Ronald Burritt, Frostburg State University; Mary Caldwell, El Paso Community College/University of Texas at El Paso; Christine Carter, St. Louis Community College; Elaine Chakonas, Triton College; Beth Childress, Armstrong State College; Janet Cutshall, Sussex Community College; Clare Frost, SUNY at Stony Brook; Andrea Greenbaum, Barry University; Patrick Haas, Glendale Community College; Clarence Hundley, Thomas Nelson Community College; Roberta Panish, Rockland County Community College; Harvey Rubinstein, Hudson County Community College; Nancy Schneider, University of Maine at Augusta; Andrea Shanklin, Howard Community College; Margaret Shaw, Nassau Community College; and William Thelin, University of Akron.

Eastern Illinois University and the Maryland chapter of the Delta Kappa Gamma Society International gave us grants to help defray production costs. Elizabeth Howell, Elysa Friedman, Paula Murray, Heather Wilkinson, and Layni Winston served as editorial assistants. Lynn Dermott, Chris Metz, MaryKate Morse, and Pamela Williams provided library research.

Finally, Sharon Ritchie typed the manuscript. She and Michael Pula formatted it, with precision and patience.

Our heartfelt thanks to all who helped make the book a reality.

Judith J. Pula
Audrey T. Edwards
R. Allan Dermott

Note to Instructors: An instructor's manual is available on line. The instructor's manual resembles the book but includes answers and no reading selections. An instructor's edition of this book is also available. This edition contains all material from the student edition, followed by an instructor's section containing ideas on using the text. Contact your local Prentice Hall representative for copies of these valuable supplements or call Prentice Hall Faculty Services at 1-800-526-0485.

About the Authors

Judith J. Pula, professor of English at Maryland's Frostburg State University, has nearly 20 years of experience as a reading, composition, and learning disabilities specialist in a university setting. She has been recognized at campus and statewide levels for teaching excellence. A recipient of state and international organization scholarships, Pula has also served the Delta Kappa Gamma Society International as a member of its journal's editorial board and as state and chapter research chair.

Audrey T. Edwards taught reading and composition to college freshmen for 11 years; she has won several awards for her teaching, including individualized instruction of students with learning disabilities. Currently a professor in the Department of Secondary Education and Foundations at Eastern Illinois University, she administers a field-oriented program to prepare secondary-school teachers.

R. Allan Dermott, professor emeritus of English at the New Hampshire Community Technical College at Manchester/Stratham, taught English for 28 years, first in the public schools and then at four universities and colleges. He has several published articles and presentations to his credit. His main focus was in teaching developmental reading and composition courses and helping students with learning disabilities.

UNIT

ONE

Overview:
The Processes of Critical
Reading and Writing

The Process of Critical Reading

—————————— ✦ ——————————

Picture a man who has built some bookshelves but now wants to take on something more ambitious. He wants to build kitchen cabinets for his wife. Our inexperienced cabinetmaker can jump in there with his tools and the best of intentions. If he is persistent, he probably will come up with some kind of cabinets. If he is smart, however, he will get together with an experienced cabinetmaker to pick up a few "tricks of the trade." The result will probably be less time wasted, less frustration, and a better finished product. Likewise, a smart student who knows he is inexperienced at reading may check with a better reader. However, many good readers don't know how to explain what they do in any meaningful way. Allow us, the authors, to be your experienced cabinetmakers.

A good reader doesn't just start sawing and hammering chapter one of a piece of nonfiction. A good reader will preview first—that is, check out a few things before beginning. But what things? These are a few "tricks of the trade" to be discussed in this unit.

Second, what do experienced readers do while reading a chapter? "Read," you say? But what is going on in their thought processes? How do they understand what they are reading if they don't look up every unfamiliar word in the dictionary? Again, we have "tricks of the trade."

Third, let's say that you have "read" the assignment. How comfortable do you usually feel in discussing such assignments when the class meets again? In taking a quiz? In writing an essay on the assignment? If any of these questions make you feel uneasy, you might want to visit your friendly cabinetmakers.

In short, we suggest that you break the process of reading into three steps: previewing, reading to answer questions, and discussing your ideas with others. The results should be a clearer understanding of the ideas involved.

PREVIEWING

Before carpenters begin sawing and hammering, they look over the situation. They get out the measuring tape and jot down a few notes and think some more. Most importantly, they call on past experiences and knowledge to get a better perspective on the current circumstances. The more novel the present situation, the more they need to think through where they are heading. When they understand what the owners want and have integrated the two sets of ideas and possibly recommended changes, then they are ready to proceed.

When it comes to reading, too, past experience and knowledge help. The more we readers can pull together our own ideas before looking at an article, the better. In addition, it often helps if we consider ideas from another author. Therefore, this book begins most units with a short selection having an alternate view to the one in the unit's main reading.

Room is provided for you to write your answers to questions. Go through the reading/thinking process and make a clear, written response. If you do, you can be reasonably sure you are on the way to mastering a process that can serve you well for the rest of your life.

In surveying an essay, we as readers prepare ourselves mentally. Before reading the article, we want to know what the writer wants us to get from the paper more than anything else—the main idea, or thesis. Experienced readers predict the main idea through a two-step process. First, they study the title, which is sometimes the main idea itself or perhaps a modification of it. In any case, as readers we expect the title to at least suggest the topic—that is, tell us what the essay is about.

The second step in predicting the main idea is to read the first and last paragraphs. Often the main thrust is in the first paragraph. If not, it is sometimes in the last. In either case, we should now have a better idea of what the essay is going to say.

In writing your statement of a main idea, answer these questions: What does the author want me to believe? What point is the author trying to make? Note that the main idea can be stated in a sentence, unlike the subject matter, topic, or title, which usually is stated in a fragment. Following are some examples of topics and main ideas.

Subject or topic
- Fighter pilots during World War I
- The dangers of flying in World War I

Poor statements of main idea
- It is about fighter pilots during World War I.
- The main idea is about the dangers of flying in World War I.

Good statements of main idea

- Pilots during World War I, who had no parachutes, faced death when their planes were shot down.
- Flying a fighter during the First World War was especially dangerous because the pilots did not have parachutes.

To help you with what might be harder words in each essay, we have added another step to the previewing sections in this book. We could just give you the definitions of words so that you wouldn't have to look them up in the dictionary. Many books like ours do that very thing, but we will be doing something different. In helping you to think the way the very best readers do, we wish to show you how to figure out the meaning of words using a quotation from the essay and Appendix A, Word Parts. You should not have to look up a word in the dictionary unless there are too few meaningful clues. As you learn to use these clues by finding them in the various essays of this book, you should find that increasingly you can use such clues in reading passages in other books.

Now you should be ready to read the preview article. Remember why we included this preview article for you. It presents a point of view different from that of the main essay and thus should help you raise important questions when you read the main selection.

In previewing the unit, you have had a chance to think about the topic and read the preview article. Now it is time to briefly preview the main essay itself. By calling it "the main selection," we do not mean to imply that we think the ideas in the main essay are either more important or better than those in the prereading assignment. It is called that simply because you are going to examine in detail not only what the author says but also how he or she says it. Remember that the way an idea is packaged can greatly influence readers as to the reasonableness of the idea itself.

Once you have a fairly good idea of what the main selection is saying, you then want to turn your attention to the author's background. You may have to check the library for the information. If you already know it or it is given with the article, as in this book, all the better. What you want to determine is what in the author's background may have led him or her to the main idea. Is there anything in the writer's experience that might have influenced him or her? The answer to this question helps you determine what to look at most closely in considering this person's ideas. Even if a writer is qualified, if the essay is subjective—that is, subject to much opinion as with politics—you must proceed with your antennae tuned for detecting prejudices. Equally important, once you know between? Once you have read and rated a few essays, you will have a basis for comparison. Also remember that the ability to judge the tone or style is more important than "getting the right number." Even teachers probably would not agree on the exact number.

"Where do you see the following features of style?"

Here we discuss features such as allusion and metaphor. The terms themselves are not all that important; focus on the writing techniques behind them and the way the author may be using these techniques to communicate something. We have found, however, that these labels make it easier to discuss the essay.

Earlier, we mentioned that an inexperienced reader may want to learn from a "master cabinetmaker" before he or she becomes too frustrated or confused. The last sentence of that paragraph read, "Let us, the authors, be your experienced cabinetmakers." If you recognized the comparison between reading and skillful carpentry, then you can grasp what some people call figurative language. You are well on your way to understanding how experienced writers convey their ideas through special techniques.

The key to success lies in taking on only a few of these concepts at a time until you finally have mastered all of them by the end of the course.

When a new term comes up, you can find its meaning in Appendix B, Guide to Literary Terms, and do the accompanying exercise if there is one. For example, turn to the Guide to Literary Terms on page 289 and check out the term *jargon*.

"Does the author propose any change?"

Here you will find questions about the content of the essay. These will help you to clarify the author's views. Three good questions are "Does the author propose any change?" "What would the result be?" and "Do you agree with the author's main idea?"

READING TO ANSWER QUESTIONS

Let's go back to our carpenter who is redoing someone's kitchen. He now knows what the owner's views are and knows how they relate to his own experience, so he can proceed fairly confidently with the job. The end of the preparation does not mean the end of thinking, however. As the carpenter progresses, he asks questions and reevaluates the situation. Without these questions, he is open to errors that may require some retracing of his steps. Likewise, research shows that people do a better job of understanding what they read if they do it for the purpose of answering questions.

Unlike many other textbooks, this one provides room for you to jot down your answers right after each question. The advantages of these jottings are fourfold. (1) They are all in one place when you study for a quiz. (2) When a teacher calls on you to answer a certain question, you will have notes that can jog your memory. (With a book like this, a teacher is less apt to accept the excuse, "I don't remember.") (3) The spaces after the questions are also good for adding thoughts and examples that occur to you during the class discussion. (4) All these notes are naturally in a well-organized place, ready for you to study for a large exam or to refer to when writing your own essay on the subject.

In explaining the ideas of others, try to sum up briefly instead of quoting. One way to summarize a paragraph: read it, close your book with your finger marking the page, state the main idea in your own words, and then open the book to check your accuracy. Try this method with the first essay you read: Sum up the main idea and then check your answer with your instructor.

You should now be ready to read the main essay. As you read it, be certain to keep the preview questions and your responses to them in mind. Read to answer the Reading Questions you just finished looking over. These Reading Questions are reproduced right after the essay itself with space to write your answers in the book.

FOLLOWING UP ON READING: DISCUSSING YOUR IDEAS

Throughout this unit, we have compared reading to building kitchen cabinets. Reading, you see, is more than getting the main idea. It also involves reconstructing the author's plan, the methods of presenting that plan, and, most importantly, the ways these methods help establish the main point. What if a homeowner asks a carpenter to build kitchen cabinets for her? The carpenter now knows the main point: The owner wants new cabinets in her kitchen. But is that all the carpenter needs to know in order to understand what the owner has in mind? Hardly. He also wants to know her plan: when she wants them done and just where and how high she wants them. Furthermore, he must consider the style she has in mind. Does she want a rustic old barnboard look, a sleek shine with fancy hinges and knobs, or something in between? Likewise, understanding the plan and tone of an essay can help you enter the writer's mind to better understand his or her style and personality. And often it's an aid to finding the meaning. Discussing the essay with your classmates will help you see the reading from different angles.

Once you have read many essays and noticed other people's plans and techniques, you will have a collection of such resources to call on in presenting your own ideas. Here is the point where we experienced carpenters can help you. The more you know about various organizational plans and writing techniques, the more easily you can pull together those that best fit your own personality and ideas.

The notes you take in the reading stage will help you to recall the author's facts and writing techniques, as well as your reactions to them. These notes will help you during class discussion. Furthermore, notes on your classmates' reactions, combined with your notes made while reading, should aid you in the writing stages. The more time you spend on reading and analyzing, the easier it should be for you to develop your own ideas and to present them effectively.

The Writing Process

For most people, writing isn't difficult. It's torture. Yet they do it—to keep up a friendship, to get a job, to pass a course. And if a person must write, there are ways to make the work bearable and the results actually satisfying.

When a task seems to be too much for you, you may be able to manage it by breaking it into parts. One way to break up writing is to set aside a short time for it each day. Your instructor may set aside some class or lab time for writing so you can get help as you go along. Even so, you probably will need to work outside of class, too. Many professional writers schedule morning sessions: Even for them, writing is difficult enough that it requires a clear head. (The best time for you may be different, though.) And it's good to have a place free of tempting distractions: One well-known author goes to the garage and locks herself in the car. This book was written at school, where the authors couldn't develop a sudden interest in washing the dishes, the clothes, the car, and so forth.

Another way of breaking the task into manageable parts is to attack it in stages. A nightmare known to all writers is "The Terror of the Blank Page": They feel that the beautiful white page before them deserves a perfect composition—or at least a composition of some sort, since that's the result they're supposed to produce. But an oil painting may begin as a pencil sketch (or several sketches); a football play may begin as Xs on a chalkboard. Writing, too, can be attacked in stages.

As with painting and football—and, not surprisingly, reading—writing proceeds most easily when you go from large to small, when you try to see the major outlines before worrying about the details. In the case of reading, you can move from previewing to reading to discussing; in composing, you can move from planning to writing to revising and editing. The process isn't that neat, of course: You may go back and forth between stages. In addition, after using a writing procedure for a while, you add the touches that make it your own. (Some people can think only in tiny, penciled words; you may prefer to use a computer.) Working in stages does help, however.

As you read about each stage below, try it out to see how it works and how important it is to the success of your writing.

PLANNING

The first stage, planning, involves getting ideas together before writing a message. Where to begin? In many real-life writing situations, you are responding to someone else's ideas. In this book, you'll be given a reading selection and some questions to discuss after you read. If you jot down your own answers to these questions at the time, you'll have some good notes to work from when you plan your writing. These notes will show what the author says about the subject and whether you agree.

You will also be given a composition question or will choose one from a list. (In some cases, with instructor approval, you may write your own question.) Your reply will be your essay. Before looking at these composition questions, try to guess what they'll be. Write down your guesses and then compare them to the questions given. If you can learn to predict, you'll have a useful test-taking skill—and if you come up with a question you like better than what's given, your instructor may prefer it, too.

If you have a choice of questions, take your time deciding; jot down a few words under each one. Which one do you know the most about? Which do you feel most strongly about?

Once you've settled on a single composition question, you have your work cut out for you. You also have quite a few notes on the reading selection, but they won't all help with your particular question. Go back to these notes and copy the few words or phrases that will help answer this one question.

Now you probably will need to make some more notes to plan your answer. Here you have a choice: Some people work from the top down—from main ideas to details—whereas others work from the bottom up. (If you've always done it one way, why not try the other?) The "top-down" method is to list—far apart—three or four key words showing your main idea, or thesis, and a few supporting points that will help sell that idea to your reader. Then fill in the space beside each word with details from your notes and ideas that occur to you. The more ideas and connections you think of, the more changes you will probably make in the original plan—and that's fine.

Example: For Composition Question 4 in Unit Two, The Juvenile Justice System (about whether to treat juveniles as adults), here are some sample notes made in "top-down" style. The first section is partly filled in. Try completing the second section ("Size of crime?") with your own ideas.

Treat some juveniles as adults? Depends on two things:

Points	**Notes**
1. Going straight?	How often in trouble? Getting worse/better?
	Any sign that problem is due to temporary upset (death, etc.)?
	Whole pattern of life strange?
	Court psychologist talk with kid—not hired by lawyer
	Look at number of past crimes
	Secrecy is to help kid go straight—if he isn't going to go straight, name him!
2. Size of crime?	

Another method, the "bottom-up" strategy, is to jot down whatever comes to mind, quickly, without stopping to polish or discard anything. From this wealth of detail, you can decide on the key points that you want to make. If you use this method, try folding your paper lengthwise and writing on only one side. This should help you to write single words or phrases, not "The Perfect Sentence." And it will leave some space to write comments on your ideas when you later sort them.

Example: For the same composition question on guilty juveniles, here are some partly-finished sample notes made in "bottom-up" style. Point 1 is already filled in. For point 2, read the detailed notes at the right. Then, at the left, list the major points the student could make in his or her essay.

Points	**Notes**
1. Not all kids alike	Sheindlin sounds like my neighbor—"kids rotten these days"—all kids? Sour—trusted wrong kids and got burned?—failure as a parent?
2. _____	H.F. in 1st grade—nice valentine 3rd grade—broke windows 5th grade—shooting Not bad to start with—wish he'd gotten help—mother dead What kind of help, when? Don't know—but Sheindlin says send 'em to prison—no second chances

A third method, mapping, is to jot down a mixture of main ideas and details, circling them and connecting them with lines to show their relationship.

Example: For the same composition question, here are some sample notes mapped out with boxes and lines. Try filling in the blank boxes or adding some that will connect to those already shown.

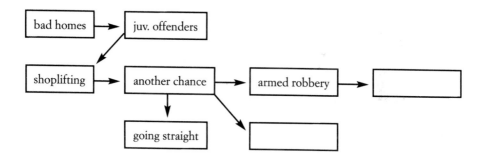

Now that you have thought of a few points you could make in reply to your composition question, you are ready to organize them into an essay. (If, however, you are assigned to write a single-paragraph response instead of a long essay, narrow the topic: You may have two or three points you could use to answer a question, but choose just one of these points to address in your paragraph.)

WRITING

Now for the actual writing. It should proceed more easily once you have notes and a plan, but now that it's time to write the real composition, "The Terror of the Blank Page" may hit with full force. Try to create a situation that allows you to experiment and make changes. One student, José, composes on a computer so he can easily add words or change the order of paragraphs. Another student, Amy, leaves large blanks when she's hung up on a point and then comes back to it later. If Sean has questions about how clear or correct something is, he marks the spot but keeps on writing. Many people write on every other line; that way, whenever they can't choose the right word or sentence, they write both (one above the other) and make a choice later. Either way, try to write fairly quickly so as not to lose your train of thought, knowing that you can always make changes later.

If you are writing a paper about other people's essays, your introduction should give the first and last names of the authors (and anyone featured), as well as the titles of what they have written. The introduction also gives the authors' main ideas and the question you plan to discuss. (You can give the answer, too, or choose to leave us in suspense for now. Either way will work.)

As you begin writing, you may think of new ideas—ones that didn't occur to you during the planning stage. These may be some of your best ideas. Go ahead and use them. Just look over your plan to see where they fit best or change your whole plan.

The other part of the paper that calls for special handling is the conclusion. Just as when you're saying good-bye to someone, don't start the conversation up again with new ideas or details. Instead, tell the reader—briefly—what you really want him or her to remember.

REVISING

Once your paper has been written all the way through to the end, it still is not finished. Now—as with reading—you need to see other points of view. To do this, you should find at least two readers who are friendly but honest.

The first reader can be you—but to really see what you've written, you must first go away from it, preferably overnight. Then return to it, putting yourself in the reader's shoes, and ask yourself following questions.

REVISION QUESTIONS

1. Is there any statement the reader might not understand?
   (Explain it.)
2. Is there any statement that might offend the reader?
   (See if you can make it more acceptable.)
3. Is there anything that's not very convincing?
   (Maybe you can add a sentence to strengthen your case.)
4. Have I changed the subject and then changed it back again?
   (Possibly you should rearrange paragraphs so that one idea leads into another.)
5. Have I said the same thing twice?
   (Cross out words or combine sentences where you can.)
6. Do I want to try using any feature of style I've seen in the reading selection?
   (Consider any features discussed in the Reading Questions under style.)

Even after you've made these changes, of course, you still won't know for sure how your composition strikes another person, so mark any places you still have questions about. Then find someone else to read what you've written. This person can be your instructor as long as you make it clear that the composition is not ready for grading. Or your reader may be a classmate. Do not ask any questions at first. Just ask the other person to read the whole essay silently. (If you were to read it aloud, your expression would add clues that aren't available on the page itself. Hold back on the explanations, too.) Your reader could mark the page, placing a "+" beside any sentence that seems especially convincing and a "?" beside any sentence that is unclear or seems to be of questionable value. Then let the other person tell you what message he or she got. Do not argue. If it's not what you meant, the misunderstanding tells you where to strengthen your writing. Then go over any parts either of you has marked. Ask questions about these parts, and make notes as you go along.

Finally, consider your reader's reactions and decide what changes to make. (Even though another person's ideas can be useful, you have the final say.) Add, subtract, rearrange, and combine to make your paper as clear and convincing as possible.

EDITING

Now that you've decided on your ideas and have put them in order, you are finally ready to edit your writing—to polish it. By leaving the editing until last, you probably have been able to see the overall picture better. And you've saved yourself work: You don't need to worry about correcting or polishing any words or sentences you've discarded.

To make sure your composition is as clear and easy to read as possible, read each sentence out loud, pause, and ask yourself the following questions.

EDITING QUESTIONS

1. Does the sentence make sense?
   (Do its parts fit together? Or does it begin as one sentence and change to another in the middle?)
2. Does the sentence use the kind of language that most people consider "good English" these days?
   (*Hint:* Imagine a TV announcer reading it.)
3. Do the periods, commas, and other punctuation show the reader how to interpret what I am writing? Does the use of each punctuation mark conform to the rules that readers expect me to follow?
   (A handbook can help you with basic rules, but the more willing you are to try something new, the more questions you'll have that the book can't answer. When in doubt, ask your instructor for an opinion.)
4. Are the words spelled right?
   (Spelling the words right helps you look like an authority. Here again, reading out loud helps: Listen to make sure you've written a group of letters for each syllable—each beat, if you're a musician. Then use a spell check, consult the dictionary, or ask your instructor. You may want to reread your paper backward, word by word, so as to really see each word. But if many of your spelling errors are real words in the wrong place, such as *there* for *they're,* you might do better reading backward, sentence by sentence.)

Once all these changes have been made, your paper should be easy to read—if you have been using a computer. If you have been writing by hand, your paper is probably full of crossouts, extra words wedged in at the end of a line, and arrows where you've decided to move a paragraph. And the more improvements you make, the harder it is to read. Should you copy it over?

If another person can't read the paper, copy the worst parts over; cut and tape paragraphs in the order you want. To produce finished copy, of course, you would type or neatly rewrite; find out whether your instructor wants this. If your instructor asks you to make a clean copy, proofread again for errors before you hand it in.

Some people like to do the whole thing over just to help themselves remember new rules they've learned. Consider this, however: You could, instead, make a separate list of the sentences that gave you trouble, all neatly corrected, with the troublesome parts circled. That way, you'd have the practice and you'd have a personal "handbook" for use in editing your next paper.

You could also make a list of any spelling words you were unsure of so you'd have them for next time; a list is quicker to use than a dictionary. Our student Mike suggested grouping the *a* words and so forth by dividing a sheet of paper into squares—twelve on each side, since very few words start with *x* or *z*. We have included such a form for your use as Appendix K, Spelling List, on page 311.

Now you have a finished paper. Do professional writers really go through all these stages? Do they plan, write, revise, edit? Basically, yes. It really is helpful to work on the main points before worrying about the details; it's important not to rush on to the next stage too soon or to skip stages. But sometimes it is necessary to backtrack—you might, for instance, stop editing and go back to add ideas you've just thought of.

It's also important to make the process your own. Some people like to write in pencil so that they can write wherever they are. Many people who are all thumbs prefer a typewriter or computer; it's easier for them to think about ideas when they're not struggling with a pencil. Others dictate to a tape recorder and then play the tape and write out their words.

You may find, after trying out several methods, that you prefer to type instead of write by hand. You'll also know whether you like to plan your writing from the top down (main ideas to details) or from the bottom up. And you'll probably find someone who's a really helpful reader. Whatever methods you use, writing won't suddenly become easy. It can become a little more pleasant, however—and the products can become much more rewarding—if you attack the task by stages: planning, writing, revising, and editing.

The Juvenile Justice System: Does It Work?

PREVIEW STEPS FOR UNIT TWO

In response to questions 1 and 2, try these steps: Write your answers, talk them over with three or four classmates, and then discuss them with the whole class.

1. Have you ever known or heard of a teenager in your neighborhood who was involved in some kind of crime? If so, do you know why the teenager acted as he or she did?

2. In the right-hand column below, check any reason(s) that you think might be a cause for juvenile delinquency. (Leave the columns at left under **S** and **J** blank for now.)

Possible Causes

S. J.
☐ ☐ ☐ a. lack of jobs (to fill time as well as to get money)
☐ ☐ ☐ b. boredom: desire for excitement
☐ ☐ ☐ c. neglect or abuse
☐ ☐ ☐ d. lack of parental love
☐ ☐ ☐ e. lack of purpose in life
☐ ☐ ☐ f. feeling that society is against them
☐ ☐ ☐ g. disillusionment about benefits of education
☐ ☐ ☐ h. feeling of being trapped in poverty or ignorance
☐ ☐ ☐ i. peer pressure
☐ ☐ ☐ j. peer comradeship
☐ ☐ ☐ k. experimentation
☐ ☐ ☐ l. need for food, shelter, etc.
☐ ☐ ☐ m. drug abuse
☐ ☐ ☐ n. desire to defy authority
☐ ☐ ☐ o. viewing crime on TV
☐ ☐ ☐ p. other: _____

3. In light of the causes of juvenile delinquency, look at some possible solutions below. Check any that seem to be good ways of solving the problem. (Leave columns at left blank for now.)

Possible Solutions

S.　J.

☐　☐　☐　a. imprisonment

☐　☐　☐　b. detention halls

☐　☐　☐　c. court-administered reprimands

☐　☐　☐　d. court-administered spanking

☐　☐　☐　e. punishment of parents for teen crimes

☐　☐　☐　f. roughing up of delinquents in dark alleys

☐　☐　☐　g. other punishment by members of the community

☐　☐　☐　h. release of names to press as with adults

☐　☐　☐　i. probation

☐　☐　☐　j. ignoring the incident; problem will go away as teenagers become adults

☐　☐　☐　k. education

☐　☐　☐　l. not giving extra chances to young offenders

☐　☐　☐　m. part-time jobs

☐　☐　☐　n. legally imposed curfews

☐　☐　☐　o. drug rehab programs

☐　☐　☐　p. other: _____

4. a. Read the title of the first essay (page 23). Name the topic. (Who or what is this essay about?)

   b. Now predict the main idea. (What is the main point the author wants to make about this topic?)

   c. Read the first and last paragraphs. Revise your prediction if necessary. (*Note:* The main idea should sum up the smaller ideas of the essay.)

5. Some words from the essay are listed below, accompanied by quotations. Mark any words you do not know and make an educated guess about their meanings using the context supplied by the quotations—and possibly Appendix A, Word Parts, on page 285. You may want to work with a small group of classmates.

anthropologist "Sullivan is an *anthropologist* who, instead of heading off to the South Seas, has [been] . . . studying youth crime . . . [in] Brooklyn."

scavenging "homes . . . , victims of *scavenging* junkies"

ethnic "In a Hispanic neighborhood. . . . In another *ethnic enclave* he listened to the grandsons of Polish immigrants . . ."

enclave See above quotation.

irony ". . . grandsons of Polish immigrants boast, without [seeing] *irony,* how they preyed on new refugees"

predatory "lots of poor teenagers commit *predatory* street crimes."

incapacitation "the *incapacitation* strategy would . . . *incarcerate* offenders."

incarcerate See above quotation.

intramural "they . . . moved from *intramural mayhem* to muggings."

mayhem See above quotation.

abstract "If local residents tolerated burglaries, they drew the line at muggings. . . . [This] was a hard lesson for the young offenders to learn in the *abstract.*"

saturated "Zap . . . had *saturated* his market."

implicit "The big question *implicit* in Sullivan's work is how [juvenile delinquents] can learn their lessons sooner."

6. Now read the following essay. As you read, jot down any questions that occur to you.

(*Note:* Questions 7–10 appear after the essay.)

Mapping the Streets of Crime

from *Newsweek*

Mercer Sullivan is an anthropologist who, instead of heading off to the   1
South Seas, has spent the last four years studying youth crime on the
streets of Brooklyn. In housing projects, he hung out with gold-chain
snatchers. In a Hispanic neighborhood, he watched a row of three-
story homes slowly disappear, victims of scavenging junkies and arson-
ists. In another ethnic enclave he listened to the grandsons of Polish immigrants boast without irony how they preyed on new refugees who got
drunk on payday and became easy marks. From these field studies Sullivan has emerged with a picture of juvenile crime that any graduate of
a tough urban neighborhood will instantly recognize: Lots of poor
teenagers commit predatory street crimes for a few years—then most
stop, reformed by a combination of jail, growing fear and, most importantly, jobs. . . . What Sullivan's work suggests is that since most teen
crime careers are short, the incapacitation strategy would needlessly
incarcerate offenders who are on the verge of going straight.

Sullivan's research grew out of a Vera Institute of Justice project   2
aimed at testing links between crime and employment. . . . Vera's researchers, . . . armed with a federal grant, . . . surveyed 900 criminal
defendants and dispatched Sullivan and a team of field workers to
track small groups of young men through three low-income neighborhoods in Brooklyn.

Sullivan found that the youths in the white, black, and Hispanic   3
neighborhoods all began their crime careers as street brawlers, dangerous only to each other. As they grew older, however, they followed
markedly different paths. The white teenagers tended to get part-time

---

jobs through family connections, which filled their time and provided spending money. The few who experimented with street robberies quickly found themselves confronted by angry neighbors or businessmen who were prepared either to go to the police or whip the youngsters into line themselves—a form of what anthropologists call local social control.

In contrast, few of the black and Hispanic youths managed to find part-time work. Instead, they took to street corners where most moved from intramural mayhem to muggings. . . . If local residents tolerated burglaries, they drew the line at muggings. "No community will stand for random street attacks," says Sullivan. But he found that was a hard lesson for the young offenders to learn in the abstract. Many of the boys progressed to muggings as they grew bigger. Typically, they struck close to home because they knew the turf. Their victims, however, soon knew them and many were able to identify them to police. Eventually almost all the muggers were arrested, or if they weren't, they knew someone who was. Some, like Zap Andrews, weighed the odds and changed course. His specialty was elevator robberies in housing projects. Not long after one incident, he discovered that his victim was his new girlfriend's mother, who could easily have identified him. Zap, as Sullivan says, had saturated his market. Later he lost more of his bravado after being arrested for assault and landing in jail. Then he turned 17 and found a job in a drycleaning shop, where the money was steady and the risks were few. "Hey," he told Sullivan, "I learned before I got my 20 years." 4

The big question implicit in Sullivan's work is how Zap Andrews and his friends can learn their lessons sooner. There are no easy answers; but they are more apt to emerge from research that focuses—as the Vera study did—on the processes of crime, and not just on its results. Ignoring those processes may itself be delinquent. 5

7. State the essay's main idea in your own words. Compare it to your prediction of the main idea. (*Note:* The main idea should sum up the smaller ideas of the essay.)

8. Return to the Unit Preview, question 2, on page 20, and make check-marks in the **S** column to show Mercer Sullivan's explanations for the causes of the juvenile crime problem.

9. Return to the Unit Preview, question 3, on page 21, and make check-marks in the **S** column to show Mercer Sullivan's suggestions for solving the juvenile crime problem.

10. What are Sullivan's views on sending juvenile offenders to jail?

PREVIEW STEPS FOR "Enough Is Enough"

1. a. Read the title of the second essay (page 27). Name the topic. (Who or what is this essay about?)

   b. Now predict the main idea. (What is the main point the author wants to make about this topic?)

   c. Read the first and last paragraphs of the essay. Revise your predic-tion if necessary. (*Note:* The main idea should sum up the smaller ideas of the essay.)

2. What in the author's background may have led her to the main idea? (See author's background, below title.)

3. Some words from the essay are listed below, accompanied by quotations. Mark any words you do not know and make an educated guess about their meanings using the context supplied by the quotations—and possibly Appendix A, Word Parts, on page 285. You may want to work with a small group of classmates.

ferocity "the incidence and *ferocity* of juvenile crime accelerated."

post-traumatic stress "Tito's older brother has just been sent to prison. . . . the boy's lawyer insists . . . [Tito's] crime was a result of *post-traumatic stress.*"

inversion "This *inversion* of priorities. . . . [Contrast] a state-of-the-art gymnasium . . . at a state-detention facility . . . [with] an over-crowded, deteriorating school with . . . broken windows."

expunged "If a youngster turns his or her life around, those records can be sealed or *expunged* at age 25."

reimburse "We must demand that parents *reimburse* the state for housing their failures."

exemption "If a middle-class kid drops out of school, the $2750 tax break that his parents claim for him should be eliminated. . . . [P]arents should lose the *exemption.*"

accountability "Self-discipline, individual *accountability* and responsible conduct are the answer."

4. At the end of the Preview, you may want to go over any new features of style that occur in the following reading selection. You will need to know the term *metaphor.* For help, see Appendix B, Guide to Literary Terms (page 288), with accompanying exercises on individual features.

5. Before reading "Enough Is Enough," turn to pages 30–32 and skim the Reading Questions. Then read the essay to find answers to these questions. As you read, jot down any questions that occur to you.

Enough Is Enough

Judy Sheindlin, with Josh Getlin

Judy Sheindlin (1942–) stars in the television show Judge Judy, *based on real court cases. In 1972 she began a career in the New York City Family Court system, first as a prosecutor and 10 years later as a judge. In her book* Don't Pee on My Leg and Tell Me It's Raining *(1996), she bills herself as "America's toughest family court judge," saying she practiced "tough love" with juvenile offenders she dealt with in court, just as she did with her own children. The daughter of a dentist and a housewife, she is married to a New York State Supreme Court judge.*

As a family court judge, I looked down daily on a pageant of dysfunc- 1
tion that would curl your hair. After 24 years on the bench, I came to
realize that these are not legal problems: They mirror what is wrong
with our society, reflecting just how far we have strayed from personal
responsibility and old-fashioned discipline.

Most of the kids I prosecuted during my early years in court 2
were involved in petty thefts, but as the 70's passed into the 80's, both
the incidence and the ferocity of juvenile crime accelerated. A new
breed of delinquents was born, and the system did not have a clue
how to treat them. We still don't.

To show you the price we pay, let me share some of my experi- 3
ences in family court.

The first case is heard at 9:30 A.M. A boy I'll call Elmo, 15, has 4
been charged for a second time with selling crack cocaine. His lawyer
argues that Elmo's troubles started when his grandmother died: In his
grief, he had no choice but to deal the hard stuff.

"Get a better story," I fire back, startling the boy, who is looking 5
smug. "Nobody goes out and sells drugs because Grandma died."

Next is a youth I'll call Tito, a delinquent who confesses to mug- 6
ging an 80-year-old man in broad daylight. Tito's older brother has just

been sent to prison for murder. Tito was very close to his brother, the boy's lawyer insists, and his crime was a result of post-traumatic stress.

"You'll have to do better than that," I snap.   7

Then comes a woman who is addicted to crack. She's already   8
given birth to two crack-addicted babies, and she didn't report to her drug-rehab program as promised. Her excuse: She lost the address.

"What do you want, a road map?" I exclaim.   9

Welcome to my world.   10

I believe that you deal with these problems the way you would   11
deal with any crisis in a family: by setting strict limits and by showing compassion. As the mother of five children, I know that you have to get tough at the same time that you show love. Family court should be no different.

I think we should send a tough message to first-time offenders   12
every chance we get, in the hopes that perhaps there will not be a second offense. A male delinquent should find his time in court one of the worst experiences of his life.

The primary obligation of any civilized society is to preserve the   13
peace and protect its citizens. Only after that should you worry about the lawbreakers and their rehabilitation.

This might be our last chance to do something about the future   14
of these delinquents—and our own safety. Here are my suggestions for improving our juvenile system.

Spend Public Moneys on Good Kids

The vast majority of the children who suffer from poverty, neglect,   15
and even abuse do not commit crimes. They struggle in their chaotic environments, with little or no support. But for years our concerns have been with those who break the law.

A recent set of photographs in my local newspaper illustrated   16
this inversion of priorities. In one picture was a state-of-the-art gymnasium, with Nautilus equipment and gleaming free weights—part of the recreational complex at a state-detention facility. The other photo was of an overcrowded, deteriorating inner-city junior high school with peeling paint and broken windows.

What kind of insanity is this? We should offer offenders food,   17
clothing, and a bed, plus vocational and academic training. Period. The money we save by not dressing up our detention facilities should be spent on the good kids who struggle just to get by.

No Rules of Confidentiality for Juvenile Offenders

It is impossible for judges to sentence intelligently if they do not know 18
the offender's criminal history. If a youngster turns his or her life
around, those records can be sealed or expunged at age 25. If he does
not, that record should follow him to the grave.

Make Them Earn Early Release

Convicted juveniles, like adult offenders, often gain early and unde- 19
served release from jail. In my opinion, early release should be earned:
Juveniles should qualify only if they complete an academic or vocational course of study. The rest should stay behind bars their full term.

Enact a National Curfew

Most lawbreaking by youngsters takes place at a time when these kids 20
should be at home. I recommend a national curfew for kids under 18.
If parents cannot or will not set limits, then society must do it for
them, for their protection and its own.

Control Career Criminals

Judges should have the option of imposing consecutive sentences on 21
particularly violent juveniles, those who rape, maim, and kill, just as
they do on adults. For second offenders, there should be the option of
a fixed sentence until age 25 followed by conditional release. The conditions would be simple: There must be no arrests. They must be
employed full time or be in school. And they must check in weekly
with the local police precinct.

Make the Parents Pay

Too many people treat the juvenile system as a joke. That would 22
change overnight if we required parents to pay for their children's defense attorneys according to their means, even if it is a percentage of
their welfare benefits.

Furthermore, in too many states, welfare keeps flowing while the   23
kids are in jail, or middle-class parents continue to claim children as
tax deductions even as the state pays for their upkeep in detention facilities. We must demand that parents reimburse the state for housing
their failures.

No Public Assistance for Parents of Dropouts

Kids need an education to have hope for the future. It makes sense to   24
insist that children stay in school or go off welfare. Our message
should be clear to everyone: If you want to eat, you have to work. If
you stay in school, we'll support you. Otherwise, support yourself. No
exceptions. Does it sound like I'm cracking down on the poor? Far
from it. If a middle-class kid drops out of school, the $2750 tax break
that his parents claim for him should be eliminated. Without proof
that a child is attending school, parents should lose the exemption.

If I had to boil my message down to one sentence, it would be   25
that people create their own opportunities. As a woman, a mother,
and a judge who has seen our criminal system deteriorate for nearly a
quarter of a century, I have had it with the victim game. A delinquent
is responsible for his crime. Parents are responsible for their children.

The prescription so far has been to give them more social pro-   26
grams, and that remedy has failed. Self-discipline, individual accountability, and responsible conduct are the answer. They have always
been the answer, but America got lost. It is time to get back on course.

READING QUESTIONS FOR "Enough Is Enough"

Main Idea

1. State the essay's main idea in your own words. Compare it to your
   prediction of the main idea. (*Note:* The main idea should sum up the
   smaller ideas of the essay.)

Organization

2. a. Where in the essay is the main idea found?

b. Why has the author placed the main idea there?

3. In what order are the paragraphs arranged? (Underline one.)
Time/Least to most important/Most to least important/Simple listing/
Logic: cause and effect/Other logic/Other

Style

4. How formal is the essay? (Circle your choice.)

[Informal—1—2—3—4—5—6—7—8—9—10—Formal]

What indicators convinced you? (For a list of possible indicators and
two benchmark essays, see Appendix F, The Formality Spectrum, on
page 298.)

5. Where do you see the following feature of style? List one or two examples with their paragraph numbers.

Feature (For a definition, see Appendix B, page 288.)

metaphor

Content

6. Return to the Unit Preview, question 2, on page 20, and place check-marks in the **J** column beside Judge Judy Sheindlin's explanations for the causes of juvenile delinquency.
7. Return also to Unit Preview, question 3, on page 21, and place check-marks in the **J** column beside Judge Judy Sheindlin's suggestions for the solutions to juvenile delinquency.
8. Are Mercer Sullivan and Judy Sheindlin discussing the same kind of juveniles?

9. According to Mercer Sullivan, to what extent should the courts give youngsters time to change before imposing harsh adult sentences? Does Judy Sheindlin agree? What are their reasons?

10. How much are Sullivan and Sheindlin concerned with the right of society to be protected from becoming victims of teenage crimes?

11. To what degree would you agree with Judge Judy Sheindlin? Why?

COMPOSITION QUESTIONS

Listed below are the writing questions. Choose one and write an essay that answers it. (If your instructor is willing, try adapting one of these questions or even writing your own. Be sure to get your instructor's approval—and possibly suggestions for change—before answering your question.)

Whichever question you choose, think of the person who will read your answer. The question may tell who your audience is. If not, think of a person you know and respect—preferably your instructor or a fellow student who will read your essay. Try to convince that person to believe you.

Bring in useful details from the selection(s) you have read and perhaps other incidents you know of. For ideas, review your answers to questions in the Preview and Reading Steps. When you first refer to a reading, give its title (in quotation marks) and the author's full name. Also, give the full name of anyone featured in the article the first time you mention that person. In making any later references, use only the person's last name.

Note: If you are assigned to write one paragraph, think of your answer to the question, and list several key points you could make to support your answer. Then choose just one of the points and explain it in detail.

1. Judy Sheindlin and Mercer Sullivan are responding to different aspects of the overall problem of juvenile justice. Sheindlin is calling for more severe penalties and punishments; Sullivan suggests that when society understands "the process of crime," the new-found understanding could be translated into solutions that attack some of the root causes of juvenile crime. Which of these two authorities offers a better starting point for reducing the problem? Why?

2. Judy Sheindlin and Mercer Sullivan both argue that fear is an effective means of reducing juvenile crime. Sheindlin suggests treating young first offenders harshly so they will fear returning to court (paragraph 12). Sullivan, on the other hand, suggests that fear of harsh adult prison sentences causes teens to straighten up before they reach 18 but still gives them time to straighten out without being imprisoned needlessly (paragraph 4). Argue that one use of fear is wiser than the other.

3. Some people may feel that Judy Sheindlin's attitude toward juvenile offenders is too harsh or that Mercer Sullivan's ideas are too weak and unrealistic. Analyze the issues involved; agree and/or disagree with either point.

4. Judy Sheindlin's essay comes from her book *Don't Pee on My Leg and Tell Me It's Raining.* In this book, she suggests that many juvenile offenders will not straighten out. By contrast, Mercer Sullivan indicates that juvenile offenders often do reform. Consider the range of juveniles and offenses discussed in the two readings. Under what circumstances, if any, should juveniles be treated and tried as adults, with no secrecy and no second chances?

5. Judy Sheindlin explains that current laws maintain secrecy and give second chances. She argues that such special treatment overprotects

juvenile offenders at the expense of society. Mercer Sullivan says that most juvenile offenders will go straight, so they deserve secrecy and second chances. How can the juvenile justice system meet the needs of society and still protect juveniles who may reform?

6. According to an African saying, "It takes a village to raise a child." After reading Mercer Sullivan's and Judy Sheindlin's views, we might take "a village" to mean either the juvenile's neighborhood or the justice system. Which one has the greater influence in reforming juveniles? Explain.

7. Judy Sheindlin suggests that punishing parents would prod them to control their children (paragraphs 22–24). Yet in paragraph 20, she suggests that many parents cannot or will not set limits, so the government should step in. To what extent can parents control teenagers who are already in trouble?

REVISION QUESTIONS

Once you have finished writing your essay, ask yourself the following questions.

1. Is there any statement the reader might not understand?
2. Is there any statement that might offend the reader?
3. Is there anything that's not very convincing?
4. Have I changed the subject and then changed it back again?
5. Have I said the same thing twice?
6. Do I want to try using any feature of style I've seen in the reading selection?

EDITING QUESTIONS

Once you've made changes, ask someone else to read your essay. Change it again as needed. Then read your essay out loud and answer the following questions.

1. Does every sentence make sense?
2. Does every sentence use the kind of language that most people consider "good English" these days? (*Hint:* Imagine a TV announcer reading it.)
3. Do the periods, commas, and other punctuation show the reader how to interpret what I am writing? Does the use of each punctuation mark conform to the rules that readers expect me to follow?
4. Are the words spelled right?

Note that good grammar, punctuation, and spelling usually make your writing clearer—and always improve your image as a competent, educated writer.

If you make changes in your paper, proofread it again!

UNIT
THREE

Should Witnesses Become Involved?

PREVIEW STEPS FOR UNIT THREE

1. Have you seen or heard of incidents in which someone needed help right away? What did bystanders do? Why did they act as they did?

2. a. If you saw a murder being committed, what are some things you might do?

   b. What do you think most people would do?
      - ☐ run to the victim's rescue
      - ☐ shout or throw things to scare off the murderer
      - ☐ call the police
      - ☐ do nothing, assuming other witnesses would act
      - ☐ choose not to act, fearing the killer might harm them—then or later
      - ☐ choose not to get involved for fear of police or public notice
      - ☐ choose not to get involved to avoid the bother of going to court
      - ☐ freeze from indecision
      - ☐ other: _____

   c. Why might some people act differently than others do?

   d. Do you think people's decisions are affected by whether they live in a city?

3. a. Read the title of the first essay (page 39). Name the topic. (Who or what is this essay about?)

b. Now predict the main idea. (What is the main point the author wants to make about this topic?)

c. Read the first and last paragraphs. Revise your prediction if necessary. (*Note:* The main idea should sum up the smaller ideas of the essay.)

4. Some words from the essay are listed below, accompanied by quotations. Mark any words you do not know and make an educated guess about their meanings using the context supplied by the quotations—and possibly Appendix A, Word Parts, on page 285. You may want to work with a small group of classmates.

abduction "It was a massacre," said [the police commissioner], adding that the victims had come upon an "*abduction* or *altercation.*"

altercation See above quotation.

5. Now read the following essay. As you read, jot down any questions that occur to you.

(*Note:* Question 6 appears after the essay.)

Triple Slaying Probed

from The Associated Press

New York (AP)—A man trying to force a woman into a van shouted   1
"What did you see?" at three men picking up their cars in a parking lot, then chased them down one by one and shot them in the head at close range, killing them, police said.

Reprinted with permission of The Associated Press.

With the woman slumped inside, the gunman drove the van   2
down a winding ramp and left the lot, police said, quoting a witness
who hid under a car. Police were searching for the van early today.

"It was a massacre," said Deputy Police Commissioner Alice   3
McGillion, adding that the victims had come upon an "abduction or
altercation."

The witness said the three men, all technicians at a nearby CBS   4
television network studio, were heading to their cars at dusk Monday
when they saw a man struggling with a woman in the parking lot,
which is atop a pier that juts into the Hudson River, Chief of Detectives James T. Sullivan said Monday.

The three approached and the man asked what they had seen,   5
but without waiting for an answer, he drew a pistol and shot the first
victim in the back of the head as the man started to flee, the witness,
also a CBS employee, said.

The gunman chased the other two around parked cars and   6
across the lot and killed them by shooting each behind the right ear.

"It appears as though they were coming to the assistance of the   7
woman who was being accosted," Sullivan said of the three victims—
Leo A. Kuranuki of Great Neck, N.Y., and Edward M. Benford of
Clifton, N.J., both managers of studio maintenance, and Robert W.
Schulze of Bergen County, N.J., a technician.

One of the victims lay with his car keys clutched in his hand, the   8
detective said.

Police said the woman, whom they could not identify, may have   9
been injured. There was blood near the spot where the van had stood,
Sullivan said, and the witness, who escaped unnoticed by the gunman,
reported seeing her slumped inside the late-model van.

A scarf, sunglasses, a plastic headband, and a pair of high-heeled   10
shoes were found, left behind after the woman's struggle with the
gunman, police said.

The victims had just left work at the CBS Broadcast Center a few   11
blocks away and were approaching their own cars at about 6 P.M. on
the roof of Pier 92, which stands in a waterfront area where cruise
ships dock.

After the gunman shot the first victim, the gunman chased the   12
two other CBS employees as they fled toward the river end of the pier,
which is 75 feet wide and has spaces for 700 cars. It was not known
why the victims fled toward the lot's river end, which has no exit.

The gunman caught up with the second victim and shot him, ap- 13
parently also at point-blank range, about 30 feet from the first victim.
The gunman caught the third man near a waist-high concrete wall at
the end of the pier, about 100 feet from the first victim. The third
victim also was believed to have been shot at close range.

Police also found three .22-caliber shell casings near the bodies, 14
apparently from the handgun used to kill the men.

6. State the essay's main idea in your own words. Compare it to your
   prediction of the main idea. (*Note:* The main idea should sum up the
   smaller ideas of the essay.)

PREVIEW STEPS FOR "37 Who Saw Murder Didn't Call the Police"

1. a. Read the title of the second essay (page 42). Name the topic. (Who
      or what is this essay about?)

   b. Now predict the main idea. (What is the main point the author
      wants to make about this topic?)

   c. Read the first and last paragraphs of the essay. Revise your predic-
      tion if necessary. (*Note:* The main idea should sum up the smaller
      ideas of the essay.)

2. What in the author's background may have led him to the main idea?
   (See author's background, below title.)

3. Some words from the essay are listed below, accompanied by quotations. Mark any words you do not know and make an educated guess

about their meanings using the context supplied by the quotations—
and possibly Appendix A, Word Parts, on page 285. You may want to
work with a small group of classmates.

shrouded "At night the quiet neighborhood is *shrouded* in the slumbering darkness. . . ."

distraught "Today witnesses . . . find it difficult to explain why they
didn't call the police. . . . A *distraught* woman, wiping her hands on
her apron, said, 'I didn't want my husband to get involved.'"

4. At the end of the Preview, you may want to go over any new features
of style that occur in the following reading selection. You will need to
know the terms *connotation, irony of situation, irony of wording,
metaphor, restraint,* and *symbol.* For help, see Appendix B, Guide to
Literary Terms (page 288), with accompanying exercises on individual
features.

5. Before reading "37 Who Saw Murder Didn't Call Police," turn to
pages 46–48 and skim the Reading Questions. Then read the essay to
find answers to these questions. As you read, jot down any questions
that occur to you.

---

37 Who Saw Murder Didn't Call the Police

Martin Gansberg

*Martin Gansberg (1920–1995) lived in the New York area all his
life except for a three-year assignment in Paris. After receiving a
bachelor of social sciences degree, he joined* The New York Times,
*where he served as a reporter and later as assistant managing
editor. He also taught journalism at Fairleigh Dickinson University for more than 20 years and wrote for several magazines, including* Catholic Digest, Diplomat, *and* Facts. *The article below
won wide recognition, including three special awards.*

Apathy at Stabbing of Queens Woman Shocks Inspector

For more than half an hour 38 respectable, law-abiding citizens in   1
Queens watched a killer stalk and stab a woman in three separate
attacks in Kew Gardens.

Twice the sound of their voices and the sudden glow of their   2
bedroom lights interrupted him and frightened him off. Each time he
returned, sought her out and stabbed her again. Not one person tele-
phoned the police during the assault; one witness called after the
woman was dead.

That was two weeks ago today. But Assistant Chief Inspector   3
Frederick M. Lussen, in charge of the borough's detectives and a veteran of 25 years of homicide investigations, is still shocked.

He can give a matter-of-fact recitation of many murders. But the   4
Kew Gardens slaying baffles him—not because it is a murder, but because the "good people" failed to call the police.

"As we have reconstructed the crime," he said, "the assailant   5
had three chances to kill this woman during a 35-minute period. He
returned twice to complete the job. If we had been called when he
first attacked, the woman might not be dead now."

This is what the police say happened beginning at 3:20 A.M. in   6
the staid, middle-class, tree-lined Austin Street area:

Twenty-eight-year-old Catherine Genovese, who was called   7
Kitty by almost everyone in the neighborhood, was returning home
from her job as manager of a bar in Hollis. She parked her red Fiat in
a lot adjacent to the Kew Gardens Long Island Rail Road Station, facing Mowbray Place. Like many residents of the neighborhood, she
had parked there day after day since her arrival from Connecticut a
year ago, although the railroad frowns on the practice.

She turned off the lights of her car, locked the door and started   8
to walk the 100 feet to the entrance of her apartment at 82-70 Austin
Street, which is in a Tudor building, with stores on the first floor and
apartments on the second.

The entrance to the apartment is in the rear of the building   9
because the front is rented to retail stores. At night the quiet neighborhood is shrouded in the slumbering darkness that marks most
residential areas.

Miss Genovese noticed a man at the far end of the lot, near a   10
seven-story apartment house at 82-40 Austin Street. She halted. Then,

nervously, she headed up Austin Street toward Lefferts Boulevard, where there is a call box to the 102d Police Precinct in nearby Richmond Hill.

"He Stabbed Me!"

She got as far as a street light in front of a bookstore before the man grabbed her. She screamed. Lights went on in the 10-story apartment house at 82-67 Austin Street, which faces the bookstore. Windows slid open and voices punctured the early-morning stillness. **11**

Miss Genovese screamed: "Oh, my God, he stabbed me! Please help me! Please help me!" **12**

From one of the upper windows, in the apartment house, a man called down: "Let that girl alone!" **13**

The assailant looked up at him, shrugged and walked down Austin Street toward a white sedan parked a short distance away. Miss Genovese struggled to her feet. **14**

Lights went out. The killer returned to Miss Genovese, now trying to make her way around the side of the building by the parking lot to get to her apartment. The assailant stabbed her again. **15**

"I'm dying!" she shrieked. "I'm dying!" **16**

A City Bus Passed

Windows were opened again, and lights went on in many apartments. The assailant got into his car and drove away. Miss Genovese staggered to her feet. A city bus, Q-10, the Lefferts Boulevard line to Kennedy International Airport, passed. It was 3:35 A.M. **17**

The assailant returned. By then, Miss Genovese had crawled to the back of the building, where the freshly painted brown doors to the apartment house held out hope of safety. The killer tried the first door; she wasn't there. At the second door, 82-62 Austin Street, he saw her slumped on the floor at the foot of the stairs. He stabbed her a third time—fatally. **18**

It was 3:50 by the time the police received their first call, from a man who was a neighbor of Miss Genovese. In two minutes they were at the scene. The neighbor, a 70-year-old woman and another woman were the only persons on the street. Nobody else came forward. **19**

The man explained that he had called the police after much de- 20
liberation. He had phoned a friend in Nassau County for advice and
then he had crossed the roof of the building to the apartment of the
elderly woman to get her to make the call.

"I didn't want to get involved," he sheepishly told the police. 21

Suspect Is Arrested

Six days later, the police arrested Winston Moseley, a 29-year-old 22
business-machine operator, and charged him with the homicide.
Moseley had no previous record. He is married, has two children and
owns a home at 13319 Sutter Avenue, South Ozone Park, Queens. On
Wednesday, a court committed him to Kings County Hospital for psy-
chiatric observation.

When questioned by the police, Moseley also said that he had 23
slain Mrs. Annie May Johnson, 24, of 146-12 133rd Avenue, Jamaica,
on Feb. 29 and Barbara Kralik, 15, of 174-17 140th Avenue, Spring-
field Gardens, last July. In the Kralik case, the police are holding Alvin
L. Mitchell, who is said to have confessed to that slaying.

The police stressed how simple it would have been to have got- 24
ten in touch with them. "A phone call," said one of the detectives,
"would have done it." The police may be reached by dialing "0" for
operator or SPring 7-3100.

Today witnesses from the neighborhood, which is made up of 25
one-family homes in the $35,000 to $60,000 range with the exception
of the two apartment houses near the railroad station, find it difficult
to explain why they didn't call the police.

A housewife, knowingly if quite casually, said, "We thought it 26
was a lover's quarrel." A husband and wife both said, "Frankly, we
were afraid." They seemed aware of the fact that events might have
been different. A distraught woman, wiping her hands on her apron,
said, "I didn't want my husband to get involved."

One couple, now willing to talk about that night, said they heard 27
the first screams. The husband looked thoughtfully at the bookstore
where the killer first grabbed Miss Genovese.

"We went to the window to see what was happening," he said, 28
"but the light from our bedroom made it difficult to see the street."
The wife, still apprehensive, added: "I put out the light and we were
able to see better."

Asked why they hadn't called the police, she shrugged and   29
replied: "I don't know."

A man peeked out from a slight opening in the doorway to his   30
apartment and rattled off an account of the killer's second attack.
Why hadn't he called the police at the time? "I was tired," he said
without emotion. "I went back to bed."

It was 4:25 A.M. when the ambulance arrived for the body of   31
Miss Genovese. It drove off. "Then," a solemn police detective said,
"the people came out."

READING QUESTIONS FOR "37 Who Saw
Murder Didn't Call the Police"

Main Idea

1. State the essay's main idea in your own words. Compare it to your prediction of the main idea. (*Note:* The main idea should sum up the
   smaller ideas of the essay.)

Organization

2. a. Where in the essay is the main idea found?

   b. Why has the author placed the main idea there?

3. In what order are the paragraphs arranged? (Underline one.) Time/
   Least to most important/Most to least important/Simple listing/ Logic:
   cause and effect/Other logic/Other

Style

4. How formal is the essay? (Circle your choice.)

   [Informal—1—2—3—4—5—6—7—8—9—10—Formal]

What indicators convinced you? (For a list of possible indicators and two benchmark essays, see Appendix F, The Formality Spectrum, on page 298.)

5. Where do you see the following features of style? List one or two examples of each with their paragraph numbers.

Features (For definitions, see Appendix B, page 288.)

a. connotation

b. irony of situation

c. irony of wording

d. metaphor

e. restraint

f. symbol

Content

6. Does the author propose any change? If so, what do you think would be the result of such a change?

7. Do you agree with the author's main idea? Why or why not?

If you have not already read the essay and answered the Reading Questions, be sure to do so before you proceed.

COMPOSITION QUESTIONS

by Mon, segol.
next Wed, pick thesis
3-5 pg

Listed below are the writing questions. Choose one and write an essay that answers it. (If your instructor is willing, try adapting one of these questions or even writing your own. Be sure to get your instructor's approval—and possibly suggestions for change—before answering your question.)

Whichever question you choose, think of the person who will read your answer. The question may tell who your audience is. If not, think of a person you know and respect—preferably your instructor or a fellow student who will read your essay. Try to convince that person to believe you.

Bring in useful details from the selection(s) you have read and perhaps other incidents you know of. For ideas, review your answers to questions in the Preview and Reading Steps. When you first refer to a reading, give its title (in quotation marks) and the author's full name. Also, give the full name of anyone featured in the article the first time you mention that person. In making any later references, use only the person's last name.

Note: If you are assigned to write one paragraph, think of your answer to the question, and list several key points you could make to support your answer. Then choose just one of the points and explain it in detail.

1. Why is it that some people, like the 37 witnesses, don't get involved and others, like the thirty-eighth, do? Consider some of the following: emotional stability; physical strength; background (upbringing, education, and training); previous experience in a crisis, either as a victim or as a rescuer; seeing or hearing of someone else's experience; reasons to avoid the police; and anything else you think is important.

2. If you had been Kitty's neighbor and knew her slightly, do you think you would have acted differently from the 37 witnesses who did not act? Consider some of the variables in question 1.

③ Keep objections in mind

When did you decide that an interference in your life was worth more than the loss of another's?

3. Write to a person who would choose not to assist someone else in distress. Imagine his reasons. Argue that he should become a more involved sort of person. Remember that he may be on the defensive; if you suggest, for example, that he is a bad person, he may tune you out. What reasoning would appeal to this person?

4. Write to a person who would choose to help someone else in distress. Consider her reasons. Using evidence from "Triple Slaying Probed," argue that she should become more cautious and more self-protective. Remember that her beliefs may be part of her sense of who she is (a strong person or a moral person). Your appeal will have to fit her self-concept.

5. Imagine that Kitty Genovese's relatives are suing the 37 witnesses for "wrongful death," saying she would be alive today if they had intervened. You are defending one of the witnesses. Argue that he had good reasons not to get involved. You may want to use evidence from "Triple Slaying Probed."

6. Propose a plan for bystanders to use in responding to violence. The plan should offer a balance between risk to the bystander and risk to the victim. Show how your plan would fit the situations in both "Triple Slaying Probed" and "37 Who Saw Murder Didn't Call the Police."

7. Explain what psychologists call the "bystander effect," in which people's sense of responsibility is diluted in a crowd. Discuss ways of reducing the bystander effect.

REVISION QUESTIONS

Once you have finished writing your essay, ask yourself the following questions.

1. Is there any statement the reader might not understand?
2. Is there any statement that might offend the reader?
3. Is there anything that's not very convincing?
4. Have I changed the subject and then changed it back again?
5. Have I said the same thing twice?
6. Do I want to try using any feature of style I've seen in the reading selection?

EDITING QUESTIONS

Once you've made changes, ask someone else to read your essay. Change it again as needed. Then read your essay out loud and answer the following questions.

1. Does every sentence make sense?
2. Does every sentence use the kind of language that most people consider "good English" these days? (*Hint:* Imagine a TV announcer reading it.)
3. Do the periods, commas, and other punctuation show the reader how to interpret what I am writing? Does the use of each punctuation mark conform to the rules that readers expect me to follow?
4. Are the words spelled right?

Note that good grammar, punctuation, and spelling usually make your writing clearer—and always improve your image as a competent, educated writer.

If you make changes in your paper, proofread it again!

UNIT
FOUR

Keeping Secrets:
Should Adoption Records
Be Confidential?

PREVIEW STEPS FOR UNIT FOUR

In response to questions 1 and 2, try these steps: Write your answers, talk them over with three or four classmates, and then discuss them with the whole class.

People disagree on whether adoption records should be kept secret. Some adopted children say they have a right to know their family history, but many birth parents don't want it known that they have had a child and given up the child for adoption. Consider how you would feel if you were involved.

1. a. Have you ever asked your relatives about family members you never knew? If so, why?

   b. How would you feel if this information were denied to you?

2. Are there things about you that you would prefer to keep secret? If so, do you think you have a right to keep them secret?

3. Have you ever known anyone who was adopted? If so, did this person find his or her birth parent(s)? Was the outcome a happy one?

4. a. The report "Do Adopted Children Have the Right to Know About Their Birth Parents?" [*Glamour,* May 1999, p. 188] presents two interviews on whether adoptees should have full access to their adoption records. The first interview, on pages 53–54, is entitled "I Have a Right to Know." Name the topic. Who or what is this interview about?

   b. Now predict the main idea. (What is the main point the interviewee wants to make about this topic?)

   c. Read the first and last paragraphs. Revise your prediction if necessary. *(Note:* The main idea should sum up the smaller ideas of the essay.

5. In the following reading selection, mark any words you do not know and make an educated guess about their meanings using the surrounding sentences—and possibly Appendix A, Word Parts, on page 285. You may want to work with a small group of classmates.

6. Now read the following interview. As you read, jot down any questions that occur to you.

(Note: Question 7 appears after the reading.)

I Have a Right to Know

by Jessica Branch, featuring an interview of Shanna Wells

Shanna Wells, 21, of Fort Smith, Arkansas, plans to study law. She was adopted at 22 days old and is seeking her birth parents.

I've always known I was adopted, and I've always wanted to know   1
where I came from. Who gave me my naturally curly hair and other characteristics and little quirks? How did my parents meet? Basic things most people wonder about their families, the difference being that they can ask, and I've never been able to.

    When I turned 18, I started searching for answers. All I've   2
managed to find out is my birth name—Christina Marie White—and that I was born in Little Rock, Arkansas. I've pored over yearbooks

from before I was born, looking for a face similar to mine. I've spent weekends in Little Rock going through phone directories, calling people named White. I've e-mailed total strangers, saying, "Hey, this is probably not you, but . . . ." And my name is plastered all over the Internet.

In December, I got a call from a lady who said, "Hi, Shanna, this is your mom." We talked for hours. But ultimately we learned that she's not my mom, after all. I was disappointed but not surprised. She'd only been searching for two days; I'd been looking for three years. Why should it be so easy?   3

I feel like I've searched all I can with the information I have, so now I'm fighting for open-records legislation. With the help of Bastard Nation, a national adoptees' rights group, I organized a Rush for the Records rally at the county courthouse in Fort Smith. We walked in and said, "We want our records" (knowing full well we wouldn't get them). We had to leave, but people on the street were really interested. They'd assumed you could just see your records when you turned 18. Point me to that line!   4

I have nothing but love for my adopted family, and they know that and support my search. I'd understand if, once I found her, my birth mother didn't want me in her life—I don't want to break up anyone's marriage or be a nuisance. What I'm after is a medical history, and then . . . not exactly an explanation—that sounds too harsh—but an idea of what kind of life my birth parents have had. Because everyone has a right to know where they came from, a right to know who brought them into this world.   5

7. State the interview's main idea in your own words. Compare it to your prediction of the main idea. (*Note:* The main idea should sum up the smaller ideas of the essay.)

PREVIEW STEPS FOR "I Have a Right to My Privacy"

1. a. Read the title of the second interview (page 56). Name the topic. (Who or what is this interview about?)

   b. Now predict the main idea. (What is the main point the interviewee wants to make about this topic?)

   c. Read the first and last paragraphs of the selection. Revise your prediction if necessary. (*Note:* The main idea should sum up the smaller ideas of the reading.)

2. What in the interviewee's background may have led her to the main idea? (See interviewee's background, below title.)

3. One word from the reading is listed below, accompanied by a quotation. If you do not know the word, make an educated guess about its meaning using the context supplied by the quotation—and possibly Appendix A, Word Parts, on page 285.

spouse "My *spouse* knows about the adoption and is understanding, but most people in my life, including my children, don't know."

4. At the end of the Preview, you may want to go over any new features of style that occur in the following reading selection. You will need to know the term *cliché*. For help, see Appendix B, Guide to Literary Terms (page 288), with accompanying exercises on individual features.

5. Before reading "I Have a Right to My Privacy," turn to pages 57–58 and skim the Reading Questions. Then read the selection to find answers to these questions. As you read, jot down any questions that occur to you.

I Have a Right to My Privacy

by Jessica Branch, featuring an interview of an anonymous
birth mother

To maintain her anonymity, this birth mother asked that the author not reveal any identifying information about her or her child.

I gave my baby up about 20 years ago when I was in my twenties. I was single, I was in college, I was pregnant and I didn't want to be. Marriage was out—the father and I didn't love each other. I'd always been opposed to abortion, but when you're desperate, it can seem like an option. I thought long and hard, and with the help of counseling, I decided that adoption would be best for my child. I don't know what I would have done if I hadn't believed that my identity would always be confidential. It was a *large* part of the reason I opted for adoption.

In the hospital, someone said it might be better if I never saw my newborn, but I insisted and spent three wonderful, bittersweet days with my baby. The hardest thing I ever did was to put my child down and say goodbye. It's haunting, knowing your kid's out there, but time heals all wounds. I finished school, became a professional and got married.

Now a few states are trying to change the rules so that adoptees can find their records [and track down their parents], and I think that's wrong. Changing the law now is going back on a promise that was made to me. My spouse knows about the adoption and is understanding, but most people in my life, including my other children, don't know, and to force me to tell them is unfair and disruptive. I've built my life on the expectation that this very private chapter of my past will remain confidential. And what about a rape victim who gave up her child—why would she want to revisit the rape? How do we speak up, approach the legislature, without losing the privacy we've protected so long?

I don't think it's my child's right to know me. I'd happily provide medical records—anonymously. You may think that's cold, but the adoptive parents raised my child; I've moved on with my life. I don't want someone shoving openness down my throat.

I hope my child will understand and believe me when I say, 5
thank you for respecting my privacy and please appreciate the sacrifice I made to give you life and a family. I remember you and will love
you always.

READING QUESTIONS FOR "I Have a Right to My Privacy"

Main Idea

1. State the interview's main idea in your own words. Compare it to your
   prediction of the main idea. (*Note:* The main idea should sum up the
   smaller ideas of the reading.)

Organization

2. a. Where in the reading is the main idea found?

   b. Why has the interviewee placed the main idea there?

3. In what order are the paragraphs arranged? (Underline one.) Time/
   Least to most important/Most to least important/Simple listing/Logic:
   cause and effect/Other logic/Other

Style

4. How formal is the reading? (Circle your choice.)

   [Informal—1—2—3—4—5—6—7—8—9—10—Formal]

   What indicators convinced you? (For a list of possible indicators and
   two benchmark essays, see Appendix F, The Formality Spectrum, on
   page 298.)

5. Where do you see the following feature of style? List one or two examples with their paragraph numbers.

Feature (For a definition, see Appendix B, page 288.)

cliché

Content

6. Does the interviewee propose any change? If so, what do you think would be the result of such change?

7. Do you agree with the interviewee's main idea? Why or why not?

8. The anonymous interviewee says that only her husband knows her secret. She says it would be unfair and disruptive if her identity were revealed. Whose lives would be disrupted by revealing the secret?

If you have not already read the selection and answered the Reading Questions, be sure to do so before you proceed.

COMPOSITION QUESTIONS

Listed below are the writing questions. Choose one and write an essay that answers it. (If your instructor is willing, try adapting one of these questions or even writing your own. Be sure to get your instructor's approval—and possibly suggestions for change—before answering your question.)

Whichever question you choose, think of the person who will read your answer. The question may tell who your audience is. If not, think of a person you know and respect—preferably your instructor or a fellow student who will read your essay. Try to convince that person to believe you.

Bring in useful details from the selection(s) you have read and perhaps other incidents you know of. For ideas, review your answers to questions in the Preview and Reading Steps. When you first refer to a reading, give its title (in quotation marks) and the author's full name. Also, give the full name of anyone featured in the article the first time you mention that person. In making any later references, use only the person's last name.

Note: If you are assigned to write one paragraph, think of your answer to the question, and list several key points you could make to support your answer. Then choose just one of the points and explain it in detail.

1. The anonymous birth mother gives two major reasons for keeping adoption records closed: Opening the records would be "unfair" and "disruptive." Of the two reasons she gives (and possibly other reasons that she does not state), which one may be the most important to her and others who want closed records? How valid is that reason?

2. Shanna Wells and others give three basic arguments for opening adoption records: that they have a right to a complete birth certificate just as other citizens do; that they need their medical histories in order to take care of their health; and that they need a sense of identity. (In terms of identity, Wells mentions that she wants to know what relatives she looks like, what her family history is, and what kind of life her birth parents had, which might include why she was given up for adoption.) Of all the reasons Wells gives, which one may be the most important to her and others who want open records? How valid is that reason?

3. According to Wells, adopted children need to know their medical history in order to take care of their health. According to the anonymous birth mother, she would be willing to give medical history anonymously. Is this a good compromise that would balance the needs of the adopted child and the birth mother?

4. Wells argues that adopted children have a right to a complete birth certificate just as other citizens do. Yet even knowing one's original last name and place of birth may reveal the birth mother's identity. Does the birth mother also have rights in this situation—in this case, a right to privacy—as the anonymous birth mother argues? If so, which right is more important, the right to a complete birth certificate or the right to privacy?

5. Many childless couples want to adopt but cannot do so. Abortions can be kept private, but opening adoption records would deny privacy to the birth mother. If adoption records are made public, will these mothers be more apt to choose abortion over adoption?

REVISION QUESTIONS

Once you have finished writing your essay, ask yourself the following questions.

1. Is there any statement the reader might not understand?
2. Is there any statement that might offend the reader?
3. Is there anything that's not very convincing?
4. Have I changed the subject and then changed back again?
5. Have I said the same thing twice?
6. Do I want to try any feature of style I've seen in the reading selection?

EDITING QUESTIONS

Once you've made changes, ask someone else to read your essay. Change it again as needed. Then read your essay out loud and answer the following questions.

1. Does the sentence make sense?
2. Does every sentence use the kind of language that most people consider "good English" these days? (*Hint:* Imagine a TV announcer reading it.)
3. Do the periods, commas, and other punctuation show the reader how to interpret what I am writing? Does the use of each punctuation mark conform to the rules that readers expect me to follow?
4. Are the words spelled right?

Note that good grammar, punctuation, and spelling usually make your writing clearer—and always improve your image as a competent, educated writer.

If you make changes in your paper, proofread it again!

UNIT
FIVE

Aggression in Sports

PREVIEW STEPS FOR UNIT FIVE

In response to questions 1 and 2, try these steps: Write your answers, talk them over with three or four classmates, and then discuss them with the whole class.

1. List at least three sports in each of the following areas.

Contact Sports	Sports That Are Supposed to Be Noncontact but Often Involve Contact	Noncontact Sports

2. a. Read the title of the first essay (page 63). Name the topic. (Who or what is this essay about?)

   b. Now predict the main idea. (What is the main point the author wants to make about this topic?)

   c. Read the first five short paragraphs and the last paragraph. Revise your prediction if necessary. (*Note:* The main idea should sum up the smaller ideas of the essay.)

3. One word from the essay is listed below, accompanied by a quotation. If you do not know the word, make an educated guess about its meaning using the context supplied by the quotation—and possibly Appendix A, Word Parts, on page 285. You may want to work with a small group of classmates.

resignation "to break down the protection and reach the quarterback, to loom over him, seeing the last quick frantic turns of the passer's helmet before it ducks in *resignation*"

4. Now read the following essay. As you read, jot down any questions that occur to you.

(*Note:* Questions 5–8 appear after the essay.)

Mr. Hyde and Dr. Jekyll

George Plimpton

[Ed. note: Following are two excerpts from George Plimpton's book Paper Lion. *Plimpton is the "paper" football player who tells how he was given permission to practice with the Detroit Lions a number of years ago and then go through a few plays during a game so that he could experience the life of a pro football player. The headings below and the title above Plimpton's name are ours; the title was taken from one of the passages below.]*

Big Daddy Lipscomb

They were watching the rookies substituting at their positions. "That's   1
crud," one of them said, gauging his replacement. "Look at that!" he
said scornfully. Their attention was completely taken up by it. He
pointed at some maneuver the rookie had made which was too subtle
for me to catch.

I asked, "Will you straighten him out—whatever it is he did   2
wrong?"

"You must be kidding," Brettschneider said. "They're after our   3
jobs, boy."

"But they're your teammates—common cause," I said tenta-   4
tively. I was startled.

"Crap," one of them said.   5

Wayne Walker pointed at the rookie who had taken over at his   6
position. "Look at Clark's stance," he said. "It's wrong for a linebacker. He's got his arms hanging down as he waits. When the lineman busts through to him he's got to bring those hands up to stave
him off, which loses him half a second or so of motion. He should wait
with those hands up—all set to fend. . . ."

"But you won't tell him?" I asked.   7

"Hell no," said Schmidt. "He'll learn quick enough. He'll get hit   8
on his ass and he'll learn."

"That's the damnedest thing," I said.   9

Schmidt looked across. He could sense my disillusionment, par-   10
ticularly after the display of the regulars coming into the scrimmage to
help me. "I'll tell you," he said. "When I came up in 1953 the team was
hot off the 1952 championship. But it was a team getting on, long in the
tooth, and Buddy Parker traded some of the regulars to put in rookies
and first-year men. When he traded Flanagan, the middle linebacker, a
lot of the regulars broke down and cried, I want to tell you, and when I
took over his position they took it out on me as if I was responsible.
They wouldn't have anything to do with me. I went through six league
games as a regular and no one talked to me. I played the game, dressed,
and then I went home to my apartment and looked at the wall.

"Veterans don't love rookies," he went on. "It's as simple as that.   11
You always read in the paper that some young rookie coming up says
he couldn't've done it if it hadn't been for some ol' pappy-guy veteran
who took him aside and said: 'No, son, up here we do it this way,' and
then showing him. Well, that's crap, you'd better believe it. A regular,
particularly an old-timer, will do almost anything to hold on to his position short of murder. They say that Big Daddy Lipscomb used to get
into these horrible fights, close to kill these guys during the training
season when he was with Los Angeles, really beat up on them, and
everybody'd say, 'Boy, Big Daddy's got a mean temper this year.' Then
the coaches look around and find that cooler than hell he'd been beating up on the guys trying for his position so that finally there wasn't
anybody at his position but Big Daddy."

Roger Brown

That provides the highest satisfaction—to break down the protection   12
and reach the quarterback, to loom over him, seeing the last quick
frantic turns of the passer's helmet before it ducks in resignation, and

the quarterback's body begin to jackknife over the ball tucked in the belly for protection as Brown enfolds and drops him. Brown does not feel he has had a good game unless he has been able to do this once or twice during the afternoon.

"Well, what sort of pleasure is it?" I asked him. The Dinah   13
Washington records were going and Night Train Lane was lying on his belly on the next bed, watching them turn.

Brown shrugged.   14

"Well, what about rage?" I asked.   15

He blinked behind his spectacles. It was strange to think that his   16
vision was poor. I remembered him one night trying to slap a big moth that was hammering around the overhead light. He shouted, "Fly still," flailing at the moth with a big towel so wildly that he drove Night Train out of the room.

"No," he said. "I don't go around growling. But the feeling's   17
there. You know what I feel, Train," he said to Lane. "I think back on all the guys I know who have been injured, and I say to myself those guys across the line are trying to do it to me. Well, they aren't going to do it," he said.

Night Train nodded. "You got . . . er . . . a great communion to   18
get to the Hall of Fame," he said.

Brown stared briefly at him, and continued: "It's not hatred. You   19
feel deep you want to win. It feels good to get to the quarterback, but you never want to disjoint him. Mind, you want to let him know you're there. For sure. So I get plenty worked up. Home with the wife and then on the field, I'm two different people—like Mr. Hyde and Dr. Jekyll. On the field"—he began laughing—"I don't know that I'd like to meet myself on the field. . . . I mean I can think of other folks around that I'd prefer meeting."

5. State the essay's main idea in your own words. Compare it to your prediction of the main idea. (*Note:* The main idea should sum up the smaller ideas of the essay.)

6. The title of this essay is an allusion to a nineteenth-century book by Robert Louis Stevenson, *The Strange Case of Dr. Jekyll and Mr. Hyde*, about a man who was sometimes gentle but was at other times a monster. Which of the two players is described as both a Mr. Hyde and a Dr. Jekyll?

7. a. What evidence does Plimpton give that a good football player must see his opponent as an opponent, not as a fellow sportsman?

   b. What statements of Plimpton's players show that they enjoy treating their opponents as opponents?

8. Pro football is a contact sport. How much roughness do you think is needed in order to keep pro football interesting to its fans?

PREVIEW STEPS FOR "A Humanistic Approach to Sports"

1. a. Read the title of the second essay (page 68). Name the topic. (Who or what is this essay about?)

   b. Now predict the main idea. (What is the main point the author wants to make about this topic?)

   c. Read the first and last paragraphs of the essay. Revise your prediction if necessary. (*Note:* The main idea should sum up the smaller ideas of the essay.)

2. What in the author's background may have led him to the main idea? (See author's background, below title.)

3. Some words from the essay are listed below, accompanied by quotations. Mark any words you do not know and make an educated guess about their meanings using the context supplied by the quotations—and possibly Appendix A, Word Parts, on page 285. You may want to work with a small group of classmates.

mayhem "[Negative remarks can] influence behavior in such a way as to lead to bloodshed and *mayhem*."

humanistic "Words having certain connotations may cause us to react in ways quite foreign to what we consider to be our usual *humanistic* behavior."

mutual "It is possible to experience this new dimension when players enter the court with a set of values based on *mutual* trust."

supersede "In the fun dimension the enjoyment of playing would *supersede* the strong desire to win at any cost, but the desire to win would not *wane*."

wane See above quotation.

antagonistic "Avoid *antagonistic* counterattacks."

disparaging "In the fun dimension . . . participants are enjoying themselves. No harsh words are spoken. No *disparaging* remarks are voiced—about yourself or your *colleague*."

colleague See above quotation.

deleterious "To grow from a level at which the *deleterious* effects of anger, frustration, and regret ran rampant to the level of the fun dimension"

aesthetic "As you play for fun . . . , a . . . more subtle transformation takes place . . . in what I call the '*aesthetic* dimension.'"

repertoire "You try things you never tried before. . . . Your *repertoire* [pronounced *rep'* er twar'] of choices increases. You develop techniques and strategies."

innovation "Spectators . . . delight in seeing the unexpected emerge . . . and at that time *innovation* is applauded."

dexterity "a player's *dexterity* on the handball court and his execution of plays as 'poetry in motion.'"

4. At the end of the Preview, you may want to go over any new features of style that occur in the following reading selection. You will need to know the terms *cliché* and *jargon*. For help, see Appendix B, Guide to Literary Terms (page 288), with accompanying exercises on individual features.

5. Before reading "A Humanistic Approach to Sports," turn to pages 72–74 and skim the Reading Questions. Then read the essay to find answers to these questions. As you read, jot down any questions that occur to you.

A Humanistic Approach to Sports

Irving Simon

Irving Simon (1920–) graduated from UCLA in 1978 at the age of 58 with a B.A. in philosophy. Simon grew up in Brooklyn playing handball on any available wall. He did not compete at the national level until he was 40. As a handball player, he has, with the help of nine different partners, won 15 national doubles championships. In 1980 he won the National Invitational singles for ages 60 to 64. In 1982 he won the Super Golden doubles, partnered with his brother (also over 60). Simon is in the Handball Hall of Fame. He no longer plays handball, although he continues to teach the sport.

"Tear 'em apart!" "Kill the bum!" "Murder the umpire!"   1

These are common remarks one may hear at various sporting   2
events. At the time they are made, they may seem innocent enough.
But let's not kid ourselves. They have been known to influence behavior in such a way as to lead to bloodshed and mayhem. Volumes have
been written about the way words affect us. It has been shown that
words having certain connotations may cause us to react in ways quite
foreign to what we consider to be our usual humanistic behavior. I see

---

Reprinted by permission of Irving Simon.

the term *opponent* as one of those words. Perhaps the time has come to delete it from sports terminology.

The dictionary meaning of the term *opponent* is "adversary"; "enemy"; "one who opposes your interests." Thus, when a player meets an opponent, he or she may tend to treat that opponent as an adversary, and therefore beating the enemy becomes the foremost purpose for playing the game. At such times, winning may dominate one's intellect, and every action, no matter how gross, may be considered justifiable. For example, in my favorite sport, handball, intentional hinders become routine, skip-balls and two-bounce plays are argued, efforts are made to emotionally upset one's opponent, and using every method possible to stall a game becomes a pastime. I recall an incident when a referee refused a player's request for a time out for a glove change because he did not deem them wet enough. The player proceeded to rub his gloves across his wet tee shirt and then exclaimed, "Are they wet enough now?" 3

In the heat of battle, players have been observed to hurl themselves across the court without considering the consequences that such a move might have on anyone in their way. I have also witnessed a player reacting to his opponent's intentional and illegal blocking by deliberately hitting him with the ball as hard as he could during the course of play. Off the court, they are good friends. Does that make any sense? It certainly gives proof of a court attitude which is alien to normal behavior. 4

The Fun Dimension

In this age of "concerned awareness," I believe that it is time we elevated the game of handball to the level where it belongs, thereby setting an example to the rest of the sporting world. Replacing the term *opponent* with *associate* could be an ideal way to start. 5

The dictionary meaning of the term *associate* is "colleague"; "friend"; "companion." Reflect a moment! You may soon see and possibly feel the difference in your reaction to the term *associate* rather than *opponent*. When you realize that your associate is the most important aspect of the game, because without him or her there is no game, it is no longer possible to think in terms of "one who is opposing your interests." 6

When you see yourself and your opponent as associates, a new dimension to the game emerges. I like to think of it as the "fun 7 dimension." All of us who are involved in the game know that there is something more one derives when playing than just the benefits associated with a physical workout. When referring to "fun," I am referring to that something which at times we may vaguely sense but which in actuality is the essence of what we look forward to when we suit up to play.

It is possible to experience this new dimension when players 8
enter the court with a set of values based on mutual trust. At that time a number of things will become evident. Bickering will not take up valuable time. Referees will be given every possible assistance in determining the accuracy of their calls so that the part they play will become more meaningful. Avoidable hinders will be at a minimum, and there will no longer be any need for the intentional hinder to remain part of the rules.

Friendly competition makes it possible to develop our skill and 9
improve our game in general without creating up-tight feelings. This is what may happen when playing for fun in a relaxed and trusting atmosphere. But many players believe that it is necessary to evoke the "killer instinct" in order to bring out one's best, and anything short of a psyched-up feeling would lead to a what's-the-difference-who-wins attitude. It is assumed that competitiveness would diminish. On the contrary, I maintain that mutual trust will heighten competitiveness. It puts responsibility on all players to do their best. Since your associate is dependent on you for the opportunity to compare and improve his or her game, you would be betraying a trust if you should "dog it." One would sense a hollow victory knowing that his or her associate was intentionally not playing up to par.

In the fun dimension the enjoyment of playing would supersede 10
the strong desire to win at any cost, but the desire to win would not wane. Every good play and volley would be pleasing to all players and spectators, who, in a way, are also participating. Sensing the "felt-relatedness" of the players, they may no longer feel a need to take sides. They may find themselves completely involved in watching the game for the game's sake.

You may ask, "How can I put myself in a position of trust when 11
it may not be mutual?" "How can I overcome the bad habits of those who do not read articles like this or who just don't give a damn?" I say, "Take a chance! Avoid antagonistic counterattacks." It may take time, but I sincerely believe that playing in the fun dimension is contagious.

Your attitude will eventually be noticed by your associate, and he or she will want to join with you in making the new experience a joint adventure.

The Game as Art

When people play in the fun dimension, it is understood that the participants are enjoying themselves. No harsh words are spoken. No disparaging remarks are voiced—about yourself or your colleague. Smiles on the part of the participants acknowledge the use of a clever strategy. Jests are made about goofs, and even hearty laughter can be heard after associates end a long volley of trying to "out-fox" one another. 12

The underlying desire to play has more meaning now. Competition is seen as the basis for measuring your ability as a player, an opportunity to improve your skill, and a fundamental requirement for the additional pleasure one derives from winning. 13

To grow from a level at which the deleterious effects of anger, frustration, and regret ran rampant to the level of the fun dimension may have required a transformation. As you play for fun in an atmosphere of mutual trust, a similar but more subtle transformation takes place, and you may soon find yourself in what I call the "aesthetic dimension." You will realize that you are playing at this new level when, among other things, some of the following are noted: 14

1. You find that you do not dwell on misses or so-called "bad plays," but accept mistakes as part of the game. You consider them non-learning experiences.

2. You do reflect on good plays—momentarily or for a longer period of time after the game. You do not take for granted specific (possibly lucky) plays which you rarely execute. You consider them learning experiences. Eventually those plays will become routine.

3. You realize that becoming skillful at the game takes time. But since time is being spent on having fun, you won't mind how long it takes.

4. You become aware that you can improve your game by participating fully as a player, referee, or spectator. As a referee or

spectator, you have a neutral opportunity to learn by watching others play the game.

Playing for the sheer enjoyment of participating with your col-   15
leagues at the level of aesthetics brings to light the aspect of novelty.
Just for the fun of it, you try things you never tried before. Your obvious pattern of playing disappears. Your repertoire of choices
increases. You develop techniques and strategies that test the ingenu-
ity of your associate and vice versa. Spectators as well as players delight in seeing the unexpected emerge from a difficult situation, and at
that time innovation is applauded.

I have heard others remark and I have also referred to a player's   16
dexterity on the handball court and his execution of plays as "poetry
in motion." I compare it to the movements executed by a ballet
dancer. In such a context, playing handball or any other sport can be
as artistic as any other art form, and the more expert one becomes, the
better his or her performance of the art.

It may take a great deal of devotion to the game before one can   17
play as an expert. However, even while we are learning we can direct
our creative talent toward newness, and newness in this context
implies artistry.

Yet how have the spectators changed who used to yell, "Kill the   18
bum!"? In the fun dimension, they have learned to enjoy every play
as it unfolds and no longer find the need to take sides. In the fun dimension, they have given up the need to cast disparaging remarks at
the players or the referee. At the esthetic level, they sense their involvement with the game. At this level we may find the players, the
referee, and the spectators participating in the production of a work
of art.

READING QUESTIONS FOR "A Humanistic Approach to Sports"

Main Idea

1. State the essay's main idea in your own words. Compare it to your
   prediction of the main idea. (*Note:* The main idea should sum up the
   smaller ideas of the essay.)

Organization

2. a. Where in the essay is the main idea found?

b. Why has the author placed the main idea there?

3. In what order are the paragraphs arranged? (Underline one.) Time/ Least to most important/Most to least important/Simple listing/ Logic: cause and effect/Other logic/Other

Style

4. How formal is the essay? (Circle your choice.)

[Informal—1—2—3—4—5—6—7—8—9—10—Formal]

What indicators convinced you? (For a list of possible indicators and two benchmark essays, see Appendix F, The Formality Spectrum, on page 298.)

5. Where do you see the following features of style? List one or two examples of each with their paragraph numbers.

Features (For definitions, see Appendix B, page 288.)

a. cliché

b. jargon

Content

6. Does the author propose any change? If so, what do you think would be the result of such change?

7. Do you agree with the author's main idea? Why or why not?

8. To what extent can Simon's ideas be applied to pro football or boxing? Explain your reasoning.

If you have not already read the essay and answered the Reading Questions, be sure to do so before you proceed.

COMPOSITION QUESTIONS

Listed below are the writing questions. Choose one and write an essay that answers it. (If your instructor is willing, try adapting one of these questions or even writing your own. Be sure to get your instructor's approval—and possibly suggestions for change—before answering your question.)

Whichever question you choose, think of the person who will read your answer. The question may tell who your audience is. If not, think of a person you know and respect—preferably your instructor or a fellow student who will read your essay. Try to convince that person to believe you.

Bring in useful details from the selection(s) you have read and perhaps other incidents you know of. For ideas, review your answers to questions in the Preview and Reading Steps. When you first refer to a reading, give its title (in quotation marks) and the author's full name. Also, give the full name of anyone featured in the article the first time you mention that person. In making any later references, use only the person's last name.

Note: If you are assigned to write one paragraph, think of your answer to the question, and list several key points you could make to support your answer. Then choose just one of the points and explain it in detail.

1. Irving Simon proposes that we take part in sports with a new attitude. Does either of the two football players in the Plimpton selection have a personality that might make him more likely to accept at least some of Simon's humanistic concepts concerning sports? Why? Why would the other player be less likely to agree with Simon?

2. Can you think of any football players' nicknames (such as "Monsters of the Midway" and "Bulldog" Turner) that suggest violence? Simon discusses at some length the connotations of certain terms such as *opponent.* Just how much do our words influence our attitudes and in turn our behavior? Or are our words just symptoms of our attitudes?

3. You may have seen one of the movies in the *Rocky* series, starring Sylvester Stallone. If Rocky had embraced Simon's philosophy, would his career have been the same? Can boxers accept such a philosophy and still be champions? Why or why not?

4. In the first Preview Step, you were asked to list three sports in each of three areas: (a) contact sports, (b) sports that are supposed to be non-contact but often involve contact, and (c) noncontact sports. Consider one or more of these divisions. What would it take for players to live by Simon's philosophy? Would the results be favorable or unfavorable? Why?

5. Plimpton suggests that some football players have a split personality. Discuss some traits of typical football players' personalities. Could such players follow Simon's philosophy?

6. Can players or spectators find psychological relief by expressing aggression under controlled conditions? If Simon's ideas were put into practice, would society be losing a useful safety valve?

7. According to Simon, would competition decrease if his proposal went into effect? Why or why not?

8. Compare amateur players, such as Simon, to professional players, such as those in the Plimpton article. Would one type of player have more trouble than the other in carrying out Simon's philosophy?

REVISION QUESTIONS

Once you have finished writing your essay, ask yourself the following questions.

1. Is there any statement the reader might not understand?
2. Is there any statement that might offend the reader?
3. Is there anything that's not very convincing?
4. Have I changed the subject and then changed back again?
5. Have I said the same thing twice?
6. Do I want to try using any feature of style I've seen in the reading selection?

EDITING QUESTIONS

Once you've made changes, ask someone else to read your essay. Change it again as needed. Then read your essay out loud and answer the following questions.

1. Does every sentence make sense?
2. Does every sentence use the kind of language that most people consider "good English" these days? (*Hint:* Imagine a TV announcer reading it.)
3. Do the periods, commas, and other punctuation show the reader how to interpret what I am writing? Does the use of each punctuation mark conform to the rules that readers expect me to follow?
4. Are the words spelled right?

Note that good grammar, punctuation, and spelling usually make your writing clearer—and always improve your image as a competent, educated writer.

If you make changes in your paper, proofread it again!

Affirmative Action in College Admissions: Essential or Unfair?

PREVIEW STEPS FOR UNIT SIX

In response to questions 1 and 2, try these steps: Write your answers, talk them over with three or four classmates, and then discuss them with the whole class.

1. Former President Lyndon Johnson, when speaking of African Americans, said: "You do not take a person who for years has been hobbled by chains and liberate him, bringing him up to the starting line of a race and then say, 'You are free to compete with all the others' and still justly believe that you have been completely fair." Thus, trying to be fairer, college admissions have introduced affirmative action to admit more minorities. The debate is over what would be the fairest solution for both whites and minorities. As Shakespeare would say, "There's the rub."

   Do you know anyone who feels that he or she was treated unfairly when applying for college? If not, do you know of any such person in your community or in the news? What does the person say was the basis for his or her discrimination?

2. a. For the next couple of minutes, briefly list some advantages and disadvantages of students having daily contact with people of other cultures.

   Advantages   **Disadvantages**

   b. When you review your lists, which of the two would you say is more important? Why?

3. a. Read the title of the first essay (page 80). Name the topic. (Who or what is this essay about?)

    b. Now predict the main idea. (What is the main point the author wants to make about this topic?)

    c. Read the first and last paragraphs. Revise your prediction if necessary. (*Note:* The main idea should sum up the smaller ideas of the essay.)

4. Some words from the essay are listed below, accompanied by quotations. Mark any words you do not know and make an educated guess about their meanings using the context supplied by the quotations—and possibly Appendix A, Word Parts, on page 285. You may want to work with a small group of classmates.

diversity "*Diversity* is essential."

siege "Affirmative action in higher education was under *siege* from the *right.*"

right See above quotation.

buoyed "*Buoyed* by a successful lawsuit . . . and by ballot initiatives . . . , the opponents set their sights on affirmative-action programs at colleges across the country."

ethnicity "There are many misperceptions about how race and *ethnicity* are considered in college admissions."

immersed "They must be *immersed* in a campus culture that allows them to study with, argue with, and become friends with students who may be different from them."

5. Now read the following essay. As you read, jot down any questions that occur to you.

(*Note:* Question 6 appears after the essay.)

Diversity Is Essential

Lee C. Bollinger

When I became president of the University of Michigan in 1997, af- 1
firmative action in higher education was under siege from the right.
Buoyed by a successful lawsuit against the University of Texas Law
School's admissions policy and by ballot initiatives such as California's
Proposition 209, which outlawed race as a factor in college admissions, the opponents set their sights on affirmative-action programs at
colleges across the country.

The rumor that Michigan would be the next target in this cam- 2
paign turned out to be correct. I believed strongly that we had no
choice but to mount the best legal defense ever for diversity in higher
education and take special efforts to explain this complex issue, in simple and direct language, to the American public. There are many misperceptions about how race and ethnicity are considered in college
admissions. Competitive colleges and universities are always looking
for a mix of students with different experiences and backgrounds—
academic, geographic, international, socioeconomic, athletic, public-
service oriented, and, yes, racial and ethnic.

It is true that in sorting the initial rush of applications, large uni- 3
versities will give "points" for various factors in the selection process
in order to ensure fairness as various officers review applicants. Opponents of Michigan's undergraduate system complain that an appli-
cant is assigned more points for being black, Hispanic, or Native
American than for having a perfect SAT score. This is true, but it
trivializes the real issue: whether, in principle, race and ethnicity are
appropriate considerations. The simple fact about the Michigan

---

undergraduate policy is that it gives overwhelming weight to traditional academic factors—some 110 out of a total of 150 points. After that, there are some 40 points left for other factors, of which 20 can be allocated for race or socioeconomic status.

Race has been a defining element of the American experience.   4 The historic *Brown v. Board of Education** decision is almost 50 years old, yet metropolitan Detroit is more segregated now than it was in 1960. The majority of students who each year arrive on a campus like Michigan's graduated from virtually all-white or all-black high schools. The campus is their first experience living in an integrated environment.

This is vital. Diversity is not merely a desirable addition to a well-   5 rounded education. It is as essential as the study of the Middle Ages, of international politics, and of Shakespeare. For our students to better understand the diverse country and world they inhabit, they must be immersed in a campus culture that allows them to study with, argue with, and become friends with students who may be different from them. It broadens the mind and the intellect—essential goals of education.

Reasonable people can disagree about affirmative action. But it   6 is important that we do not lose the sense of history, the compassion, and the largeness of vision that defined the best of the civil-rights era, which has given rise to so much of what is good about America today.

   6. State the essay's main idea in your own words. Compare it to your prediction of the main idea. (*Note:* The main idea should sum up the smaller ideas of the essay.)

PREVIEW STEPS FOR "But Not at This Cost"

   1. a. Read the title of the second essay (page 83). Name the topic. (Who or what is this essay about?)

---

*In *Brown v. Board of Education* (1954) the U.S. Supreme Court unanimously decided that separating children in public schools on the basis of race was unconstitutional, violating the Fourteenth Amendment.

b. Now predict the main idea. (What is the main point the author wants to make about this topic?)

c. Read the first and last paragraphs of the essay. Revise your prediction if necessary. (*Note:* The main idea should sum up the smaller ideas of the essay.)

2. What in the author's background may have led him to the main idea? (See author's background, below title.)

3. Some words from the essay are listed below, accompanied by quotations. Mark any words you do not know and make an educated guess about their meanings using the context supplied by the quotations— and possibly Appendix A, Word Parts, on page 285. You may want to work with a small group of classmates.

prestigious "I received scholarship offers to attend *prestigious* colleges."

rousing "Sadly, this *rousing* point seems lost on the admissions board."

quota system "Supporters maintain that the *quota system* is essential to creating a diverse student body."

ingrained "A shared history of slavery and discimination has *ingrained* racial *hierarchies* into our national identity, divisions that need to be erased."

hierarchies See above quotation.

inertia "Because of this victim status, the logic goes, [African Americans] are owed special treatment. But that isn't progress. It's *inertia*."

lever "I was taught that personal responsibility was the *lever* that moved the world."

4. At the end of the Preview, you may want to go over any new features of style that occur in the following reading selection. You will need to know the term *metaphor.* For help, see Appendix B, Guide to Literary Terms (page 288), with accompanying exercises on individual features.

5. Before reading "But Not at This Cost," turn to pages 85–86 and skim the Reading Questions. Then read the essay to find answers to these questions. As you read, jot down any questions that occur to you.

But Not at This Cost

Armstrong Williams

Armstrong Williams (1959-) is an African American syndicated columnist featured in many newspapers, such as New York Amsterdam News, Washington Afro-American, Washington Times, USA Today, Detroit Free Press, *and* Los Angeles Times. *His book,* Beyond Blame *(1995), gives advice to a misguided young man. He is contributing editor to three magazines:* Charisma, New Man, *and* Savoy. *Besides hosting his own nationally syndicated television show,* The Right Side with Armstrong Williams, *he also contributes regularly to a number of national TV news programs. The issues that concern him most are work ethic, personal responsibility, and the need to restore morality in today's society.*

Back in 1977, when I was a senior in high school, I received scholar- 1
ship offers to attend prestigious colleges. The schools wanted me in part because of my good academic record—but also because affirmative action mandates required them to encourage more black students to enroll. My father wouldn't let me take any of the enticements. His

reasoning was straightforward: Scholarship money should go to the economically deprived. And since he could pay for my schooling, he would. In the end, I chose a historically black college—South Carolina State.

What I think my father meant, but was perhaps too stern to say,   2 was that one should always rely on hard work and personal achievement to carry the day—every day. Sadly, this rousing point seems lost on the admissions board at the University of Michigan, which wrongly and unapologetically discriminates on the basis of skin color. The university ranks applicants on a scale that awards points for SAT scores, high school grades, and race. For example, a perfect SAT score is worth 12 points. Being black gets you 20 points. Is there anyone who can look at those two numbers and think they are fair?

Supporters maintain that the quota system is essential to creating   3 a diverse student body. And, indeed, there is some validity to this sort of thinking. A shared history of slavery and discrimination has ingrained racial hierarchies into our national identity, divisions that need to be erased. There is, however, a very real danger that we are merely reinforcing the idea that minorities are first and foremost victims. Because of this victim status, the logic goes, they are owed special treatment. But that isn't progress; it's inertia.

If the goal of affirmative action is to create a more equitable so-   4 ciety, it should be need-based. Instead, affirmative action is defined by its tendency to reduce people to fixed categories: At many universities, it seems, admissions officers look less at who you are than *what* you are. As a result, affirmative-action programs rarely help the least among us. Instead, they often benefit the children of middle- and upper-class black Americans who have been conditioned to feel they are owed something.

This is alarming. We have finally, after far too long, reached a   5 point where black Americans have pushed into the mainstream—and not just in entertainment and sports. From politics to corporate finance, blacks succeed. Yet many of us still feel entitled to special benefits—in school, in jobs, in government contracts.

It is time to stop. We must reach a point where we expect to rise   6 or fall on our own merits. We just can't continue to base opportunities on race while the needs of the poor fall by the wayside. As a child growing up on a farm, I was taught that personal responsibility was the lever that moved the world. That is why it pains me to see my peers rest their heads upon the warm pillow of victim status.

READING QUESTIONS FOR "But Not at This Cost"

Main Idea

1. State the essay's main idea in your own words. Compare it to your prediction of the main idea. (*Note:* The main idea should sum up the smaller ideas of the essay.)

Organization

2. a. Where in the essay is the main idea found?

   b. Why has the author placed the main idea there?

3. In what order are the paragraphs arranged? (Underline one.) Time/ Least to most important/Most to least important/Simple listing/ Logic: cause and effect/Other logic/Other

Style

4. How formal is the essay? (Circle your choice.)

   [Informal—1—2—3—4—5—6—7—8—9—10—Formal]

   What indicators convinced you? (For a list of possible indicators and two benchmark essays, see Appendix F, The Formality Spectrum, on page 298.)

5. Where do you see the following feature of style? List one or two examples with their paragraph numbers.

Feature (For a definition, see Appendix B, page 288.)

metaphor

Content

6. Does the author propose any change? If so, what do you think would be the result of such change?

7. Do you agree with the author's main idea? Why or why not?

If you have not already read the essay and answered the Reading Questions, be sure to do so before you proceed.

COMPOSITION QUESTIONS

Listed below are the writing questions. Choose one and write an essay that answers it. (If your instructor is willing, try adapting one of these questions or even writing your own. Be sure to get your instructor's approval—and possibly suggestions for change—before answering your question.)

Whichever question you answer, think of the person who will read your answer. The question may tell who your audience is. If not, think of a person you know and respect—preferably your instructor or a fellow student who will read your essay. Try to convince that person to believe you.

Bring in useful details from the selection(s) you have read and perhaps other incidents you know of. For ideas, review your answers to questions in the Preview and Reading Steps. When you first refer to a reading, give its title (in quotation marks) and the author's full name. Also, give the full name of anyone featured in the article the first time you mention that person. In making any later references, use only the person's last name.

Note: If you are assigned to write one paragraph, think of your answer to the question and list several key points you could make to support your answer. Then choose just one of the points and explain it in detail.

1. Lee Bollinger, a former president of the University of Michigan, writes that diversity "is vital. [It] is not merely a desirable addition to a well-rounded education. It is as essential as the study of [any subject area]" (paragraph 5). Is diversity vital enough to the college experience that we should accept the possible disadvantages of affirmative action? Why or why not?

2. In 2003, the Supreme Court foresaw an end to affirmative action. Yet most statistics show that if affirmative action is done away with, fewer members of some minority groups will gain entry to college. If affirmative action is eliminated, what can be done to assure cultural diversity at U.S. colleges and universities? Choose one possible action and argue for it.

3. Armstrong Williams writes that modern admission policies based on affirmative action may generate "a very real danger that we are merely reinforcing the idea that minorities are first and foremost victims" (paragraph 3). In *The Content of Our Character,* an African-American college professor, Shelby Steele, words the case even more forcefully: "I think the most troubling effect of racial preferences for blacks is a kind of demoralization. . . . Under affirmative action, the quality that earns [blacks] preferential treatment is an implied inferiority." Does affirmative action imply racial inferiority? Why or why not?

4. Robyn E. Blumner, a liberal lawyer, writes in the *St. Petersburg Times:* "Any advantage granted me due to my sex demeans my individuality, reducing me to a walking immutable characteristic. In fact, the very suggestion that I need extra help because I am female, in order to compete with men in college admissions, is not only discriminatory but insulting." Should women take advantage of affirmative action to get into those programs mostly dominated by men?

5. A student pointed out that "admissions at some colleges take race, but not income or educational deprivation, into account. Also, tuition waivers for minorities are the norm, while poor whites must apply for

loans." Yet, as this student also notes, Dr. Martin Luther King, Jr., himself recognized the needs of poor whites: "'[T]he freedom of white labor, especially in the South, was little more than a myth. . . . To this day the white poor also suffer the deprivation and humiliation of poverty. . . .' King insisted that comprehensive efforts to uplift disadvantaged blacks should include poor whites: 'It is a simple matter of justice that America, in dealing creatively with the task of raising the Negro from backwardness, should also be rescuing a large stratum of the forgotten white poor.'" Does affirmative action discriminate against poor white students? Why or why not? What suggestions on this matter, if any, would you make to college admission offices?

6. Armstrong Williams says that "if the goal of affirmative action is to create a more equitable society, it should be need-based" (paragraph 4). Lee Bollinger, however, points out another goal of affirmative action—to assure diversity (paragraph 5). Should Congress amend the affirmative action law to substitute *economic need* for *race* or *minority*? Explain.

7. A white parent writes in the *New York Daily News* that black preference in college admission policies leads to white resentment: "That's what can be bred when a kid is rejected because of race: white. And that's what some parents can carry around after they realize their children have no shot at an Ivy League school because they are not black." Do whites feel resentment over black preference in college admission policies? Should whites view discrimination against them as a just sacrifice in order to assure cultural diversity on a college campus?

8. Dr. Bessie Delany was the second African American woman in New York City to become a dentist. In the book *Having Our Say*, coauthored with her sister, she says African Americans face discrimination, so they need affirmative action. However, she also says she would actually prefer to see people get jobs based strictly on merit. Suppose an African American student agrees with her. Should the student forgo the advantages of affirmative action when applying for admission to college?

9. Consider that a liberal is someone who favors civil liberties, political reforms, and the use of government to advance social progress. A conservative, on the other hand, is cautious, favoring traditional views and values. Lee Bollinger says in paragraph 1 that "affirmative action in higher education was under siege from the right" (those with

conservative views) and praises "the best of the civil-rights era" (paragraph 6), a typical response from someone who tends to be more liberal. Armstrong Williams, on the other hand, is probably more conservative than Bollinger, judging from the name of his syndicated television show, *The Right Side with Armstrong Williams.* Is the main difference of opinion on affirmative action one of degree between liberal and conservative thinking? Why or why not?

10. In 2003, the Supreme Court foresaw an end to affirmative action. In the Court's view, this country still needs affirmative action to make up for unequal opportunities before students go to college. Yet, the Court says, once those opportunities become more nearly equal, colleges and universities should drop affirmative action. How many years are likely to pass before this country gives minorities and whites equal preparation for college? Explain.

REVISION QUESTIONS

Once you have finished writing your essay, ask yourself the following questions.

1. Is there any statement the reader might not understand?
2. Is there any statement that might offend the reader?
3. Is there anything that's not very convincing?
4. Have I changed the subject and then changed back again?
5. Have I said the same thing twice?
6. Do I want to try any feature of style I've seen in the reading selection?

EDITING QUESTIONS

Once you've made changes, ask someone else to read your essay. Change it again as needed. Then read your essay out loud and answer the following questions.

1. Does the sentence make sense?
2. Does every sentence use the kind of language that most people consider "good English" these days? (*Hint:* Imagine a TV announcer reading it.)

3. Do the periods, commas, and other punctuation show the reader how to interpret what I am writing? Does the use of each punctuation mark conform to the rules that readers expect me to follow?
4. Are the words spelled right?

Note that good grammar, punctuation, and spelling usually make your writing clearer—and always improve your image as a competent, educated writer.

If you make changes in your paper, proofread it again!

UNIT
SEVEN

Obedience:
A Good Quality?

PREVIEW STEPS FOR UNIT SEVEN

1. Think back to your early days (10 years old or younger) and your relationship then with your parent(s) or guardian(s). How did you view them? (Indicate by a check in the appropriate blanks.)

guardian 1   guardian 2
☐   ☐   a. authority figure
☐   ☐   b. teacher
☐   ☐   c. role model
☐   ☐   d. friend
☐   ☐   e. other or combination of above: _____

2. Consider the alternatives in question 1. What role(s) should adults take when relating to children? Why?

3. a. Read the title of the first essay (page 93). Name the topic. (Who or what is this essay about?)

   b. Now predict the main idea. (What is the main point the author wants to make about this topic?)

   c. Read the first and last paragraphs. Revise your prediction if necessary. (*Note:* The main idea should sum up the smaller ideas of the essay.)

4. Some words from the essay are listed below, accompanied by quotations. Mark any words you do not know and make an educated guess about their meanings using the context supplied by the quotations—and possibly Appendix A, Word Parts, on page 285. You may want to work with a small group of classmates.

contemporaries "The last thought that would have entered my parents' minds was to ask their children what was good or bad for children. We were not their *contemporaries,* nor their equals, and they were not concerned with our ideas on how to raise a family."

Bar Mitzvah "When I got to thirteen (*Bar Mitzvah* and manhood), I took a chance."

token "Most of the time we got only *token* punishments—small pinches, twists and pokes."

5. Now read the following essay. As you read, jot down any questions that occur to you.

(*Note:* Question 6 appears after the essay.)

"When I Need Your Opinion I'll Give It to You"

Sam Levenson

Although there were eight of us children, we were outnumbered by two parents. Ours was a decidedly parent-centered home. Since respect for age was a cornerstone of our tradition, it followed that Mama and Papa had the right to lead, and we had the right to be led by them. We had very few other rights. We had lots of wrongs which were going to be corrected by any methods our parents saw fit. The last thought that would have entered my parents' minds was to ask their children what was good or bad for children. We were not their contemporaries, nor their equals, and they were not concerned with our ideas on how to raise a family. "When I need your opinion I'll give it to you." 1

We had to wait our turn to speak our minds. It was not clear to us when that turn would come, but I knew that I would have to 2

---

become a little older and a little wiser before I would be called in as a consultant by my parents. If I offered a suggestion, Mama would say, "Wait, Papa is talking." When I got to be thirteen (Bar Mitzvah and manhood), I took a chance. "Now, Ma?"

"Not yet."   3

Most things were "none of my business"—even when they were   4
talking about having my tonsils out. I got the idea finally that my mind was to be used to mind: to mind Papa, mind your teacher, mind your manners, mind your shoes. My shoes were my brother's, my hat was my father's, my bed was anybody's, so I didn't really feel entitled to a mind of my own.

They did not have to explain the basis for their actions, nor did   5
they say, "This hurts me more than it hurts you." If you pressed them for a reason they quoted some authority known as "Because!" If Mama said No to something I wanted to do, and I used the argument that "Louie is doing it, and Georgie is doing it, and Benny . . ." she would cut in with "When I tell you No, don't tell me Who."

It is not as difficult as it seems to explain the common use of cor-   6
poral punishment in those days. Anything, animate or inanimate, that did not respond to reason was hit with the palm of the hand: gas burners, radio, drawers, windows, or children. With the latter a combination of couch therapy and corporal punishment worked best. The kid was told to stretch out on the lounge. He then pulled down his pants and "voluntarily" exposed his psyche for the shock treatment. Most of the time we got only token punishments—small pinches, twists and pokes.

Did we end up hating our parents? No. Why? Because we un-   7
derstood the dogma involved. It was the dogma of parental responsibility, of preventive therapy, of virtue being its own reward and evil bringing punishment. Did we enjoy the practice? Of course not. We understood that a world as tough as ours required tough parents and tough teachers. They had to fight fire with fire. The fight against individual corruption was part of the fight against the environment. The moral standard of the home had to be higher than that of the street. "You are not on the street; you are in our home. This is not a cellar nor a poolroom. Here we act like human beings, not like animals." I remember the speech well. Like royalty, Mama said "we." "We have been put to shame by what you did." Did it make me feel guilty? It sure did. Did I feel I had let the family down? I sure did. Was it worth

a quick sharp pain in the rear end to be reminded of my obligations? It sure was. Better one stabbing moment of truth at home than a stabbing in the street.

6. State the essay's main idea in your own words. Compare it to your prediction of the main idea. (*Note:* The main idea should sum up the smaller ideas of the essay.)

PREVIEW STEPS FOR "Would You Obey a Hitler?"

1. a. Read the title of the second essay (page 97). Name the topic. (Who or what is this essay about?)

   b. Now predict the main idea. (What is the main point the author wants to make about this topic?)

   c. Read the first and last paragraphs of the essay. Revise your prediction if necessary. (*Note:* The main idea should sum up the smaller ideas of the essay.)

2. What in the author's background may have led her to the main idea? (See author's background, below title.)

3. Some words from the essay are listed below, accompanied by quotations. Mark any words you do not know and make an educated guess about their meanings using the context supplied by the quotations— and possibly Appendix A, Word Parts, on page 285. You may want to work with a small group of classmates.

qualms "The drama of the clear-cut choice between obeying orders or *qualms* of conscience seems clearest for the man in uniform. He must decide to pull the trigger."

subject "Imagine yourself as a *subject* in Dr. Milgram's setup. You walk into a laboratory on the Yale campus."

negative reinforcement "Jack Williams . . . explains that if punishment makes you learn faster, that's *negative reinforcement*—as opposed to learning faster when rewarded (*positive reinforcement*)."

positive reinforcement See above quotation.

electrode "'This *electrode* . . . is connected to the shock generator in the next room.'"

hoaxed "The learner is not being shocked: in fact, he is in cahoots with the experimenter. He is part of a play, and you are the only person *hoaxed* in the setup."

blithely "Dr. Milgram had thought that the labels [such as 'intense shock' and 'danger: severe shock'] and voltage designations would stop the teachers [from pulling switches on a board to give electric shocks to someone]. But instead virtually everyone 'went *blithely* to the end of the board, seemingly indifferent to the verbal designations.'"

appalled "Dr. Milgram was *appalled* that many subjects . . . went to the end of the board, giving the harshest punishment."

dubious "The sign on the door said, 'Research Associates of Bridgeport,' a deliberately vague title. . . . Yet, even with this *dubious* authority, the levels of obedience were high, although not as high as on the Yale campus."

callous "'With numbing regularity good people were seen to knuckle under the demands of authority and perform actions that were *callous* and severe.'"

4. At the end of the Preview, you may wish to go over any new features of style that occur in the following reading selection. You will need to know the terms *cliché, jargon,* and *metaphor.* For help, see Appendix B, Guide to Literary Terms (page 288), with accompanying exercises on individual features.

5. Before reading "Would You Obey a Hitler?" turn to pages 102–103 and skim the Reading Questions. Then read the essay to find answers to these questions. As you read, jot down any questions that occur to you.

Would You Obey a Hitler?

Jeanne Reinert

Jeanne Reinert (1941–) earned her bachelor's degree in journalism from the University of Texas. After working briefly as a newspaper editor, she spent nine years as a writer and editor at Science Digest. *Reinert served as an officer of the League of Women Voters for six years and has been active in other civic and professional organizations.*

Who looks in the mirror and sees a person ready and willing to inflict pain and suffering on another in his mercy? Even if commanded? All of our senses revolt against the idea.   1

The drama of a clear-cut choice between obeying orders or qualms of conscience seems clearest for a man in uniform. He must decide to pull the trigger.   2

Being behind the trigger is very dramatic, but obeying orders is an everyday event for all of us. Seldom do we have a chance to test our actions when confronted with a clear-cut choice between hurting a person and [disobeying] orders.   3

In the early 1960s, Stanley Milgram, a psychologist at Yale University, devised an experimental setup to give that choice to subjects. He wanted to measure obedience. He had been taken with the historian's thesis that the Germans shared an extreme trait—a willingness to obey orders. This character flaw was, the theory goes, responsible for the Germans' carrying out Hitler's mad plan against the Jews. Dr. Milgram wanted to test this theory by comparing obedience in America and in Germany. He disguised his obedience tests as experiments in learning.   4

Imagine yourself as a subject in Dr. Milgram's setup. You walk into   5
a laboratory on the Yale campus after answering an ad that asked for
paid volunteers ($4.50 per hour) for an educational experiment.

At your appointment, you and another volunteer, a nervous man   6
in his 50s, are told that the experiment in which you will participate is
set up to test the effect of negative reinforcement on the human learning process. Jack Williams, the experimenter conducting the tests,
explains that if punishment makes you learn faster, that's negative
reinforcement—as opposed to learning faster when rewarded (positive reinforcement). In this experiment the punishment is an electric
shock.

Williams also states, "The money is yours for coming to the lab-   7
oratory. It's yours no matter what happens."

Then Williams takes two pieces of paper, shakes them together   8
in a hat and each of you draw one to see who will be the teacher and
who the learner. The nervous volunteer announces he is the learner;
your slip of paper says "teacher."

The experimenter seats the learner in a chair and explains the   9
procedure. "We have to strap down your arms to avoid excessive
movement during the experiment.

"This electrode," he continues, "is connected to the shock gen-   10
erator in the next room. Does either of you have any questions before
we go into the next room?"

"Are these shocks strong, are they dangerous?" asks the learner.   11

"No," replies Williams, "although they may be extremely   12
painful, they cause no permanent tissue damage."

The experiment involves word pairing (e.g., nice–day, fat–pig,   13
etc.). You, the teacher, read a word to the learner and ask him to
match it with one of four other words. The learner pushes one of four
switches to indicate which of the four answers he believes is correct. If
he is right, you go on to the next set of words. If he is wrong, you push
a switch that buzzes and gives him an electric shock. Then you go to
the next group of words.

Your position is before the electric shock generator, 30 levers   14
in a row across the instrument panel. Each lever is clearly labeled in
15-volt jumps from 15 to 450 volts. When a lever is pushed down, a
pilot light turns bright red, a buzzer sounds, a blue light flashes under
the label "voltage energizer," the dial on the meter swings about and
mechanical clicks are heard.

To be sure you know what is going on, you are given a sample shock, activated by the third switch, on the wrist. This 45-volt shock lets you know how the shock feels. 15

You are instructed to call out the voltage level before pressing the lever each time the learner merits a shock. You note that the levers are marked from left to right in broad categories, "slight shock, moderate shock, strong shock, very strong shock, intensity shock, danger: severe shock," and the two switches on the far right are simply marked "XXX." 16

When the lesson begins, the learner makes a lot of mistakes. In fact, he answers about three wrong answers to one right one. As the shocks get stronger, you are, of course, unhappy about their level. It quickly is apparent that the learner is going to give a lot more wrong answers. So you appeal to Williams, who responds, "Please go on." You protest and he says, "The experiment requires that you continue." 17

The learner is strapped in, he cannot get free. You have already been assured that the money is yours regardless. The experimenter has no actual authority over you. But he is requesting you to obey his commands. Would you do it? Would you injure the learner just because someone told you to do so? You know from your own experience that the shocks are painful. What you do not know is that the experiment is rigged. The learner is not being shocked: in fact, he is in cahoots with the experimenter. He is part of a play, and you are the only person hoaxed in the setup. 18

Before the pilot study, Dr. Milgram took the idea to a class of senior Yale psychology students and asked them to predict the distribution of behavior among 100 subjects. The entire class predicted that only a very small number of people would go to the extreme 450-volt shock. They predicted from none to three percent of any 100 people. Dr. Milgram's colleagues also thought few, if any, subjects would go beyond the shock labeled "very strong shock." 19

But they did go beyond. In fact, Dr. Milgram got such complete obedience that there was nothing to measure. He was, after all, interested in getting people to disobey. His first 40 people went beyond the expected breakoff point. Not one stopped before 300 volts. Only 14 persons stopped shocking the strapped-in learner before going to the very end of the shocks. 20

In the pilot studies, no noise was heard from the strapped-in learner. Dr. Milgram had thought that the labels and voltage 21 designations would stop the teachers. But instead virtually everyone "went blithely to the end of the board, seemingly indifferent to the verbal designations."

Dr. Milgram never expected such obedience. So he began to vary the props and scripts in his private play to see what changes would encourage the teacher to rebel.   22

The first change was to add protests from the victim. Mild protests did no good. Then the victim began to put up a vigorous fight. Dr. Milgram was appalled that many subjects, nonetheless, went to the end of the board, giving the harshest punishment. But at least some subjects did break off and give the experimenters something to measure. It also proved that obedience was much, much stronger than suspected. The victim's cries were tape-recorded so all subjects heard the same protests.   23

Finding in pilot studies that the teacher turned his eyes away from the victim, who could be seen dimly behind a silvered glass, Dr. Milgram devised various ways to make it more difficult for the teacher to ignore his victim.   24

Voice protests were heard. The victim was in another room, but the door was left ajar. At 75 volts, the learner grunted when shocked, also at 90 and 105 volts. At 120 volts, he shouted that the shocks were painful. At 135 volts he groaned, and at 150 he screamed, "Get me out of here! I won't be in the experiment anymore! I refuse to go on!" At 180 volts, he screamed, "I can't stand the pain." Still, 37.5 percent of the teachers went to 450 volts.   25

Each successive scheme brought the teacher and learner into more personal contact until in the final scheme the victim received a shock only when his hand rested on the shockplate. The experimenter then ordered the teacher to push the subject's hand down on the plate. The teacher actually had to physically subdue the victim against his will to give him the shock. No one was more surprised than Milgram that the very first person so commanded reached over and fell upon the victim's arm. Thirty out of every 100 were still willing to go all the way with the shock level when commanded.   26

Dumbfounded by this high compliance, Dr. Milgram then decided the prestige of Yale was causing his subjects to be especially obedient. So the experiment was moved to Bridgeport, 20 miles away. There a modest suite of offices was rented in a run-down section. The sign on the door said, "Research Associates of Bridgeport,"   27 a deliberately vague title. If anyone asked what the work was for, they were told, "for industry."

Yet, even with this dubious authority, the levels of obedience were high, although not as high as on the Yale campus. Forty-eight percent of the people were totally obedient to the commands versus 65 percent under the same conditions at Yale. 28

What these scores do not show is the torment that accompanied the teacher's task. Subjects would sweat, tremble, stutter, bite their lips, and groan as they were caught up in the web of conflict—to obey the calm experimenter's commands or the call of the poor man being shocked. The teachers often broke out in hysterical laughter. 29

Persons would argue with the experimenter, asking if he would take the responsibility. They wondered aloud if the victim had a heart condition. Some would exclaim, "You keep the money," but many times they kept on pulling the levers, despite all of their words to the contrary. They would complain that the other guy was suffering, that it was a hell of an experiment. Some got angry. Some just stood up and proceeded to leave the laboratory. 30

No teacher was kept at the controls once they had reached 450 volts. People either stopped before 350 volts, or carried on to the end, proving there was no limit to their obedience. Hateful as they found it to obey, it must have seemed better for them than to break off. 31

When those who pressed the levers to the end finished their task, the experimenter called a halt. The obedient teachers were relieved. They would mop their brows. Some fumbled for cigarettes. 32

Then Mr. Williams rushed to assure the teachers that it wasn't as bad as it seemed. Most important, the teachers met their screaming victim and had a reconciliation. The real purposes of the experiment were explained, and the participants were promised that the full results of the experiment would be sent to them when it was complete. They were asked to describe how they felt and how painful they believed the shocks to be. Also they were to rate on a scale how tense they were during the experiment. Dr. Milgram wanted to be sure that the persons understood that they had been hoaxed and that the man was only acting as he screamed in agony. 33

Dr. Milgram never imagined that it would be so hard to get people to defy the commands. As he explains, "With numbing regularity good people were seen to knuckle under the demands of authority and perform actions that were callous and severe. Men who in everyday life are responsible and decent were seduced by the trappings of authority. . . ." 34

To date, Dr. Milgram has tested 1,000 people with the steady   35
results—very, very obedient. Of course, if people were not willing to
conform to the many rules that link us in a broader society, chaos
would prevail. But Milgram's results suggest quite the opposite, that
perhaps we have forgotten the formula for saying no. It looks as
though few outrages are so grand as to force us to be defiant. "I was
only following orders" is going to be with us for a long time.

READING QUESTIONS FOR "Would You Obey a Hitler?"

Main Idea

①. State the essay's main idea in your own words. Compare it to your prediction of the main idea. (*Note:* The main idea should sum up the
smaller ideas of the essay.)

Organization

2. a. Where in the essay is the main idea found?

   b. Why has the author placed the main idea there?

3. In what order are the paragraphs arranged? (Underline one.) Time/
   Least to most important/Most to least important/Simple listing/
   Logic: cause and effect/Other logic/Other

Style

4. How formal is the essay? (Circle your choice.)

   [Informal—1—2—3—4—5—6—7—8—9—10—Formal]

What indicators convinced you? (For a list of possible indicators and two benchmark essays, see Appendix F, The Formality Spectrum, on page 298.)

5. Where do you see the following features of style? List one or two examples of each with their paragraph numbers.

   Features (For definitions, see Appendix B, page 288.)

   a. cliché

   b. jargon

   c. metaphor

   Content

6. Does the author propose any change? If so, what do you think would be the result of such a change?

7. Do you agree with the author's main idea? Why or why not?

If you have not already read the essay and answered the Reading Questions, be sure to do so before you proceed.

COMPOSITION QUESTIONS

Listed below are the writing questions. Choose one and write an essay that answers it. (If your instructor is willing, try adapting one of these questions or even writing your own. Be sure to get your instructor's approval—and possibly suggestions for change—before answering your question.)

Whichever question you choose, think of the person who will read your answer. The question may tell who your audience is. If not, think of a person you know and respect—preferably your instructor or a fellow student who will read your essay. Try to convince that person to believe you.

Bring in useful details from the selection(s) you have read and perhaps other incidents you know of. For ideas, review your answers to questions in the Preview and Reading Steps. When you first refer to a reading, give its title (in quotation marks) and the author's full name. Also, give the full name of anyone featured in the article the first time you mention that person. In making any later references, use only the person's last name.

Note: If you are assigned to write one paragraph, think of your answer to the question, and list several key points you could make to support your answer. Then choose just one of the points and explain it in detail.

1. No one really knows why people react the way those in the Milgram study did. Offer some possible explanations for such behavior. In developing your hypotheses, consider how your parents related to you—as authority figures, teachers, role models—and how you want to relate to your children. (Since these hypotheses need to be proven through investigation, be certain not to state them as facts.)

2. Can one expect absolute obedience in rearing children and then, when they are adults, expect them to be selective about obeying? If so, how do they make the transition? (For insights, you might research the developmental stages outlined by psychologist Erik Erikson.)

3. Compare and/or contrast the way your parents reared you with the way Sam Levenson was reared. Evaluate these approaches, indicating what you feel are their pros and cons. Consider Milgram's findings in making your evaluation.

4. What do children need to learn about authority and about various situations they may find themselves in? Do children need to learn principles or assertiveness or both in order to avoid obeying blindly as the Milgram subjects did? In answering this question, you may find it useful to imagine that you are a parent or a high school principal.

5. Do you think a typical nurse would disobey a doctor's order if it seemed morally wrong? (For example, the order might be to stop or to continue life support.) Why? Consider some of the pressures mentioned by Reinert and any other pressures you can think of. (For

insights, you might research the stages of moral development outlined by psychologist Lawrence Kohlberg.)

6. Milgram observed that his subjects acted remarkably alike regardless of the experimental conditions he created. Yet the article does reveal important differences. What situational factors appear to affect people's levels of obedience?

7. Both Milgram's study and the story of Kitty Genovese, recounted in "37 Who Saw Murder Didn't Call the Police" (Unit Three), are analyzed in a collection entitled *Doing Unto Others: Joining, Molding, Conforming, Helping, Loving* (edited by Z. Rubin, Prentice Hall, 1974). Consider why both events might appear in the same text.

REVISION QUESTIONS

Once you have finished writing your essay, ask yourself the following questions.

1. Is there any statement the reader might not understand?
2. Is there any statement that might offend the reader?
3. Is there anything that's not very convincing?
4. Have I changed the subject and then changed it back again?
5. Have I said the same thing twice?
6. Do I want to try using any feature of style I've seen in the reading selection?

EDITING QUESTIONS

Once you've made changes, ask someone else to read your essay. Change it again as needed. Then read your essay out loud and answer the following questions.

1. Does every sentence make sense?
2. Does every sentence use the kind of language that most people consider "good English" these days? (*Hint:* Imagine a TV announcer reading it.)

3. Do the periods, commas, and other punctuation show the reader how to interpret what I am writing? Does the use of each punctuation mark conform to the rules that readers expect me to follow?

4. Are the words spelled right?

Note that good grammar, punctuation, and spelling usually make your writing clearer—and always improve your image as a competent, educated writer.

If you make changes in your paper, proofread it again!

UNIT
E I G H T

Controlling Our
Own Fates

107

PREVIEW STEPS FOR UNIT EIGHT

In response to questions 1 and 2, try these steps: Write your answers, talk them over with three or four classmates, and then discuss them with the whole class.

1. When something bad happens to you—illness, an accident, a rejection—what do you usually tell yourself? (Check one or two.)

☐ a. It must be something I did.
☐ b. It was my attitude.
☐ c. There must be something wrong with me.
☐ d. Somebody was out to get me.
☐ e. Somebody made a mistake.
☐ f. It was meant to be.
☐ g. These things just happen at random.
☐ h. Other: _____

2. a. Of the above possibilities, what is the most useful way for you to look at a situation when something bad happens to you? That is, what will help you most in the long run?

   b. Do you think people can change their attitudes to more useful ones? Explain.

3. a. Read the title of the first essay (page 109). Name the topic. (Who or what is this essay about?)

   b. Now predict the main idea. (What is the main point the author wants to make about this topic?)

   c. Read the first and last paragraphs. Revise your prediction if necessary. (*Note:* The main idea should sum up the smaller ideas of the essay.)

4. Some words from the essay are listed below, accompanied by quotations. Mark any words you do not know and make an educated guess about their meanings using the context supplied by the quotations— and possibly Appendix A, Word Parts, on page 285. You may want to work with a small group of classmates.

omnipotence "Psychologists speak of the infantile myth of *omnipotence*. A baby comes to think that the world exists to meet his needs, and that he makes everything happen in it."

gratuitous "It is *gratuitous*, even cruel, to tell the person who has been hurt. . . . 'Maybe if you had acted differently, things would not have turned out so badly.'"

5. Now read the following essay. As you read, jot down any questions that occur to you.

(*Note:* Question 6 appears after the essay.)

God Helps Those Who Stop Hurting Themselves

Harold Kushner

I had an experience some years ago which taught me something about   1
the ways in which people make a bad situation worse by blaming themselves. One January, I had to officiate at two funerals on successive

---

days for two elderly women in my community. Both had died "full of years," as the Bible would say; both succumbed to the normal wearing out of the body after a long and full life. Their homes happened to be near each other, so I paid condolence calls on the two families on the same afternoon.

At the first home, the son of the deceased woman said to me, "If   2
only I had sent my mother to Florida and gotten her out of this cold and snow, she would be alive today. It's my fault that she died." At the second home, the son of the other deceased woman said, "If only I hadn't insisted on my mother's going to Florida, she would be alive today. That long airplane ride, the abrupt change of climate, was more than she could take. It's my fault that she's dead."

When things don't turn out as we would like them to, it is very   3
tempting to assume that had we done things differently, the story would have had a happier ending. Clergymen know that any time there is a death, the survivors will feel guilty. Because the course of action they took turned out badly, they believe that the opposite course—keeping Mother at home, deferring the operation—would have turned out better. After all, how could it have turned out any worse?

There seem to be two elements involved in our readiness to feel   4
guilt. The first is our strenuous need to believe that the world makes sense, that there is a cause for every effect and a reason for everything that happens. That leads us to find patterns and connections both where they really exist (smoking leads to lung cancer; people who wash their hands have fewer contagious diseases) and where they exist only in our minds (the Red Sox win every time I wear my lucky sweater; that boy I like talks to me on odd-numbered days, but not on even-numbered ones, except where there has been a holiday to throw the pattern off). How many public and personal superstitions are based on something good or bad having happened right after we did something, and our assuming that the same thing will follow the same pattern every time?

The second element is the notion that we are the cause of what   5
happens, especially the bad things that happen. It seems to be a short step from believing that every event has a cause to believing that every disaster is our fault. The roots of this feeling may lie in our childhood. Psychologists speak of the infantile myth of omnipotence. A baby comes to think that the world exists to meet his needs, and that he

makes everything happen in it. He wakes up in the morning and summons the rest of the world to its tasks. He cries, and someone comes to attend to him. When he is hungry, people feed him, and when he is wet, people change him. Very often, we do not completely outgrow that infantile notion that our wishes cause things to happen. A part of our mind continues to believe that people get sick because we hate them.

Our parents, in fact, often feed this notion. Not realizing how 6 vulnerable our childhood egos are, they snap at us when they are tired or frustrated for reasons that have nothing to do with us. They bawl us out for being in the way, for leaving toys around or having the television set on too loud, and we in our childhood innocence assume that they are justified and we are the problem. Their anger may pass in a moment, but we continue to bear the scars of feeling at fault, thinking that whenever something goes wrong, we are to blame for it. Years later, should something bad happen to us or around us, feelings from our childhood re-emerge and we instinctively assume that we have messed things up again.

It is gratuitous, even cruel, to tell the person who has been 7 hurt, whether by divorce or death or other disaster, "Maybe if you had acted differently, things would not have turned out so badly." When we say that, all we are really telling them is, "This is your fault for having chosen as you did." Sometimes marriages fail because people are immature, or because expectations are unrealistic on both sides. Sometimes people die because they have incurable diseases, not because their families turned to the wrong doctor or waited too long to go to the hospital. Sometimes businesses fail because economic conditions or powerful competition dooms them, not because one person in charge made a wrong decision in a crucial moment. If we want to be able to pick up the pieces of our lives and go on living, we have to get over the irrational feeling that every misfortune is our fault, the direct result of our mistakes or misbehavior. We are really not that powerful. Not everything that happens in the world is our doing.

6. State the essay's main idea in your own words. Compare it to your prediction of the main idea. (*Note:* The main idea should sum up the smaller ideas of the essay.)

PREVIEW STEPS FOR "Heart Attack!"

1. a. Read the title of the second essay (page 113). Name the topic. (Who or what is this essay about?)

    b. Now predict the main idea. (What is the main point the author wants to make about this topic?)

    c. Read the first and last paragraphs of the essay. Revise your prediction if necessary. (*Note:* The main idea should sum up the smaller ideas of the essay.)

2. What in the author's background may have led him to the main idea? (See author's background, below title.)

3. Some words from the essay are listed below, accompanied by quotations. Mark any words you do not know and make an educated guess about their meanings using the context supplied by the quotations— and possibly Appendix A, Word Parts, on page 285. You may want to work with a small group of classmates.

Note: This essay contains several medical words, but only a few are needed to understand the major ideas. Only key terms are listed here. If you see other words you don't know, just keep on reading.

impending mortality "The patients were mostly men in their forties and fifties, and the meaning of this illness was clear to them—they were getting older; this was a reminder of their *impending mortality.*"

data "All this information interested me enormously. . . . Now I was getting these *data* from the heart attack patients."

manifesting "How would medicine be different if we considered all these people . . . to be *manifesting* mental processes through their physical bodies?"

medieval "At the farther reaches of this idea, you came uncomfortably close to *medieval* notions that a pregnant woman who suffered a fright would later produce a deformed child."

retrogressive "So this idea that mental processes caused disease seemed to have *retrogressive* aspects."

abdicate "Of course it isn't helpful to blame ourselves for an illness. . . . But that doesn't mean we should *abdicate* all responsibility as well."

ameliorate "We are better able to focus on what we can do now to *ameliorate* the illness."

4. At the end of the Preview, you may want to go over any new features of style that occur in the following reading selection. You will need to know the terms *jargon, metaphor, overstatement,* and *simile.* For help, see Appendix B, Guide to Literary Terms (page 288), with accompanying exercises on individual features.

5. Before reading "Heart Attack!" turn to pages 119–121 and skim the Reading Questions. Then read the essay to find answers to these questions. As you read, jot down any questions that occur to you.

Heart Attack!

Michael Crichton

Michael Crichton (1942–) began writing as a student at Harvard Medical School during the late 1960s. Some of his more popular works, such as Rising Sun *and* Jurassic Park, *have been made into major motion pictures.* Jurassic Park *is one of the top grossing films of all time. He is the creator and an executive producer of the NBC emergency room drama series* ER. *Crichton also writes under the pseudonyms Michael Douglas, Jeffrey Hudson, and John Lange.*

A major disaster befell the medical wards of the Beth Israel Hospital. 1
All the interns and residents went around shaking their heads. The
disaster was that, by some quirk of fate or statistics, two-thirds of the
patients on the ward had the same illness. Heart attack.

The residents acted as if all the theaters in town were playing the 2
same movie, and they'd seen it. Furthermore, most of these patients
would be here for two weeks, so the movie wasn't going to change soon.
The home staff was gloomy and bored, because, from a medical standpoint, heart attacks aren't terribly interesting. They are dangerous and
life-threatening, and you worry about your patients, because they may
die suddenly. But the diagnostic procedures were well worked out, and
there were clear methods for following the progress of recovery.

By now I was in my final year of medical school, and I had de- 3
cided I would quit at the end of the year. So my three months at the
Beth Israel were going to be all the internal medicine I would ever
learn; I had to make the best of this time.

I decided to learn something about the feelings the patients had 4
about their disease. Because, although doctors were bored by myocardial infarcts, the patients certainly weren't. The patients were
mostly men in their forties and fifties, and the meaning of this illness
was clear to them—they were getting older; this was a reminder of
their impending mortality and they would have to change their lives:
work habits, diets, perhaps even their pattern of sexual relations.

So there was plenty of interest for me in these patients. But how 5
to approach them?

Some time earlier, I had read about the experiences of a Swiss 6
physician who, in the 1930s, had taken a medical post in the Alps because it allowed him to ski, which was his great passion. Naturally, this
doctor ended up treating many skiing accidents. The cause of the
accidents interested him, since he was himself a skier. He asked his patients why they had had their accidents, expecting to hear that they
had taken a turn too quickly, or hit a patch of rock, or some other skiing explanation. To his surprise, everyone gave a psychological reason
for the accident. They were upset about something, they were distracted, and so on. This doctor learned that the bald question "Why
did you break your leg?" yielded interesting answers.

So I decided to try that. I went around and asked patients, "Why 7
did you have a heart attack?"

From a medical standpoint, the question was not so nonsensical 8
as it sounded. During the Korean War, post-mortems on young men

had shown that the American diet produced advanced arteriosclerosis by the age of seventeen. You had to assume that all these patients had been walking around with severely clogged arteries since they were teenagers. A heart attack could happen any time. Why had they waited twenty or thirty years to develop a heart attack? Why had their heart attack happened this year and not next, this week and not last week?

But my question "Why did you have a heart attack?" also im-   9
plied that the patients had some choice in the matter, and therefore some control over their disease. I feared they might respond with anger. So I started with the most easygoing patient on the ward, a man in his forties who had had a mild attack.

"Why did you have a heart attack?"   10

"You really want to know?"   11

"Yes, I do."   12

"I got a promotion. The company wants me to move to Cincin-   13
nati. But my wife doesn't want to go. She has all her family here in Boston, and she doesn't want to go with me. That's why."

He reported this in a completely straightforward manner, with-   14
out a trace of anger. Encouraged, I asked other patients.

"My wife is talking about leaving me."   15

"My daughter wants to marry a Negro man."   16

"My son won't go to law school."   17

"I didn't get the raise."   18

"I want to get a divorce and feel guilty."   19

"My wife wants another baby, and I don't think we can afford it."   20

No one was ever angry that I had asked the question. On the   21
contrary, most nodded and said, "You know, I've been thinking about that. . . ." And no one ever mentioned the standard medical causes of arteriosclerosis, such as smoking or diet or getting too little exercise.

Now, I hesitated to jump to conclusions. I knew all patients   22
tended to review their lives when they got really sick, and to draw some conclusion about why the illness had happened. Sometimes the explanations seemed pretty irrelevant. I'd seen a cancer patient who blamed her disease on a lifelong fondness for Boston cream pie, and an arthritis patient who blamed his mother-in-law.

On the other hand, it was accepted in a vague way that there was   23
a relationship between mental processes and disease. One clue came from timing of certain illnesses. For example, the traditional season for duodenal ulcers was mid-January, just after the Christmas

holidays. No one knew why this should be, but a psychological factor in the timing of the disease seemed likely.

Another clue came from the association of some physical ill-   24
nesses with a characteristic personality. For example, a significant percentage of patients with ulcerative bowel disease had extremely irritating personalities. Since the disease itself was hard to live with, some doctors wondered if the disease caused the personality. But many suspected that it was the other way around: the personality caused the disease. Or at least whatever caused the bowel disease also caused the personality.

Third, there was a small group of physical diseases that could be   25
successfully treated with psychotherapy. Warts, goiter, and parathyroid disease responded to both surgery and psychotherapy, suggesting that these illnesses might have direct mental causes.

And, finally, it was everybody's ordinary experience that the   26
minor illnesses in our own lives—colds, sore throats—occurred at times of stress, times when we felt generally weak. This suggested that the ability of the body to resist infection varied with mental attitude.

All this information interested me enormously, but it was pretty   27
fringe stuff in the 1960s in Boston. Curious, yes. Worthy of note, yes. But nothing to pursue in a serious way. The great march of medicine was headed in another direction entirely.

Now, I was getting these data from the heart attack patients. And   28
what I was seeing was that their explanations made sense from the standpoint of the whole organism, as a kind of physical acting-out. These patients were telling me stories of events that had affected their hearts in a metaphorical sense. They were telling me love stories. Sad love stories, which had pained their hearts. Their wives and families and bosses didn't care for them. Their hearts were attacked.

And pretty soon their hearts were literally attacked. And they ex-   29
perienced physical pain. And that pain, that attack, was going to force a change in their lives, and the lives of those around them. These were men in late middle life, all undergoing a transformation that was signaled by this illness event.

It made almost too much sense.   30

Finally I brought it up with Herman Gardner. Dr. Gardner was   31
then chief of medicine at the hospital, and a remarkable, extremely thoughtful man. As it happened, he was the attending physician who made rounds with us each day. I said to him that I had been talking with the patients, and I told him their stories.

He listened carefully. 32

"Yes," he said. "You know, once I was admitted to the hospital 33
for a slipped disc, and sitting in bed I began to wonder why this had
happened to me. And I realized that I had a paper from a colleague
that I had to reject, and I didn't want to face up to it. To postpone it,
I got a slipped disc. At the time, I thought it was as good an explanation as any for what had happened to me."

Here was the chief of medicine himself reporting the same kind of 34
experience. And it opened up all sorts of possibilities. Were psychological factors more important than we were acknowledging? Was it even
possible that psychological factors were the most important causes of
disease? If so, how far could you push that idea? Could you consider
myocardial infarctions to be a brain disease? How would medicine be
different if we considered all these people, in all these beds, to be manifesting mental processes through their physical bodies?

Because at the moment we were treating their physical bodies. 35
We acted as if the heart was sick and the brain had nothing to do with
it. We treated the heart. Were all these people being treated for the
wrong organs?

Such errors were known. For example, some patients with 36
severe abdominal pain actually had glaucoma, a disease of the eye. If
you operated on their abdomens, you didn't cure the disease. But if
you treated their eyes, the abdominal pains disappeared.

But to extend that idea more broadly to the brain suggested 37
something quite alarming. It suggested a new conception of medicine,
a whole new view of patients and disease.

To take the simplest example, we all believed implicitly the germ 38
theory of disease. Pasteur proposed it one hundred years before, and
it had stood the test of time. There were germs—micro-organisms,
viruses, parasites—that got into the body and caused infectious disease. That was how it worked.

We all knew that you were more likely to get infected at some 39
times than others, but the basic cause and effect—germs caused
disease—was not questioned. To suggest that germs were always out
there, a constant factor in the environment, and that the disease
process therefore reflected our mental state, was to say something else.

It was to say mental states caused disease. 40

And if you accepted that concept for infectious disease, where did 41
you draw the line? Did mental states also cause cancer? Did mental
states cause heart attacks? Did mental states cause arthritis? What

about diseases of old age? Did mental states cause Alzheimer's? What about children? Did mental states cause leukemia in young children? What about birth defects? Did mental states cause mongolism at birth? If so, whose mental state—the mother's or the child's? Or both?

It became clear that at the farther reaches of this idea, you came   42 uncomfortably close to medieval notions that a pregnant woman who suffered a fright would later produce a deformed child. And any consideration of mental states automatically raised the idea of blame. If you caused your illness, weren't you also to blame? Much medical attention had been devoted to removing ideas of blame from disease. Only a few illnesses, such as alcoholism and other addictions, still had notions of blame attached.

So this idea that mental processes caused disease seemed to have   43 retrogressive aspects. No wonder doctors hesitated to pursue it. I myself backed away from it for many years.

It was Dr. Gardner's view that both the physical and the mental   44 aspects were important. Even if you imagined the heart attack had a psychological origin, once the cardiac muscle was damaged it needed to be treated as a physical injury. Thus the medical care we were giving was appropriate.

I wasn't so sure about this. Because, if you imagined that the   45 mental process had injured the heart, then couldn't the mental process also heal the heart? Shouldn't we be encouraging people to invoke their inner resources to deal with the injury? We certainly weren't doing that. We were doing the opposite: we were constantly telling people to lie down, to take it easy, to give over their treatment to us. We were reinforcing the idea that they were helpless and weak, that there was nothing they could do, and they'd better be careful even going to the bathroom because the least strain and—poof!—you were dead. That was how weak you were.

This didn't seem like a good instruction from an authority figure   46 to a patient's unconscious mental process. It seemed as if we might actually be delaying the cure by our behavior. But, on the other hand, some patients who refused to listen to their doctors, who jumped out of bed, would die suddenly while having a bowel movement. And who wanted to take responsibility for that?

Many years passed, and I had long since left medicine, before I   47 arrived at a view of disease that seemed to make sense to me. The view is this:

We cause our diseases. We are directly responsible for an illness   48 that happens to us.

In some cases, we understand this perfectly well. We knew we should not have gotten run-down and caught a cold. In the case of more catastrophic illnesses, the mechanism is not so clear to us. But whether we can see a mechanism or not—whether there is a mechanism or not—it is healthier to assume responsibility for our lives and for everything that happens to us. 49

Of course it isn't helpful to blame ourselves for an illness. That much is clear. (It's rarely helpful to blame anybody for anything.) But that doesn't mean we should abdicate all responsibility as well. To give up responsibility for our lives is not healthy. 50

In other words, given a choice of saying to ourselves, "I am sick but it has nothing to do with me," or saying, "I am sick because I caused the sickness," we are better off behaving as if we did it to ourselves. I believe we are more likely to recover if we take that responsibility. 51

For one thing, when we take responsibility for a situation, we also take control of it. We are less frightened and more practical. We are better able to focus on what we can do now to ameliorate the illness, and to assist healing. 52

We also keep the true role of the doctor in better perspective. The doctor is not a miracle worker who can magically save us but, rather, an expert adviser who can assist us in our own recovery. We are better off when we keep that distinction clear. 53

When I get sick, I go to my doctor like everyone else. A doctor has powerful tools that may help me. Or those tools may hurt me, make me worse. I have to decide. It's my life. It's my responsibility. 54

READING QUESTIONS FOR "Heart Attack!"

Main Idea

1. State the essay's main idea in your own words. Compare it to your prediction of the main idea. (*Note:* The main idea should sum up the smaller ideas of the essay.)

   a. According to Crichton, what is the relationship between our mental state and our physical health?

   b. According to Crichton, how much responsibility are we supposed to take for our physical health?

Organization

2. a. Where in the essay is the main idea found?

   b. Why has the author placed the main idea there?

3. In what order are the paragraphs arranged? (Underline one.) Time/ Least to most important/Most to least important/Simple listing/ Logic: cause and effect/Other logic/Other

Style

4. How formal is the essay? (Circle your choice.)

[Informal—1—2—3—4—5—6—7—8—9—10—Formal]

What indicators convinced you? (For a list of possible indicators and two benchmark essays, see Appendix F, The Formality Spectrum, on page 298.)

5. Where do you see the following features of style? List one or two examples of each with their paragraph numbers.

Features (For definitions, see Appendix B, page 288.)

   a. jargon

   b. metaphor

   c. overstatement

   d. simile

Content

6. Does the author propose any change? If so, what do you think would be the result of such change?

7. Do you agree with the author's main idea? Why or why not?

If you have not already read the essay and answered the Reading Questions, be sure to do so before you proceed.

COMPOSITION QUESTIONS

Listed below are the writing questions. Choose one and write an essay that answers it. (If your instructor is willing, try adapting one of these questions or even writing your own. Be sure to get your instructor's approval—and possibly suggestions for change—before answering your question.)

    Whichever question you choose, think of the person who will read your answer. The question may tell who your audience is. If not, think of a person you know and respect—preferably your instructor or a fellow student who will read your essay. Try to convince that person to believe you.

Bring in useful details from the selection(s) you have read and perhaps other incidents you know of. For ideas, review your answers to questions in the Preview and Reading Steps. When you first refer to a reading, give its title (in quotation marks) and the author's full name. Also, give the full name of anyone featured in the article the first time you mention that person. In making any later references, use only the person's last name.

Note: If you are assigned to write one paragraph, think of your answer to the question and list several key points you could make to support your answer. Then choose just one of the points and explain it in detail.

1. Kushner points out that believing every event has a cause is different from believing that we ourselves are the cause of every disaster (paragraph 5). Kushner's final paragraph lists many causes of misfortune besides one person's making "a wrong decision in a crucial moment." How can Kushner's distinction help us take the right amount of responsibility for our lives? Would it make sense to take part of the responsibility for an illness or accident without following Crichton's suggestion to take it all (paragraph 51)? Consider an illness or accident and analyze the possible variables, including mental state and physical causes, that could have contributed to it.

2. Crichton says that, rather than feeling we have no control, "it is healthier to assume responsibility for our lives" (paragraph 49). Yet he also admits that "it isn't helpful to blame ourselves for an illness" (paragraph 50). Kushner, too, says people "make a bad situation worse by blaming themselves" (paragraphs 1 through 3). Research has shown that women are especially prone to blame themselves. Does it make sense to take responsibility without taking blame?

3. Kushner says in paragraph 4 that we "need to believe that the world makes sense, that there is a cause" for our misfortunes. He suggests that this need leads us to superstitious behavior, as in Crichton's "arthritis patient who blamed his mother-in-law" and the cancer patient who blamed her "fondness for Boston cream pie" in paragraph 22. How can we look for cause and effect in our lives without creating superstitions?

4. When doctors ask people why they had a skiing accident (Crichton, paragraph 6) or a heart attack (paragraph 21), they almost always say

the cause was their mental state. Kushner says people may even go so far as to believe their "wishes cause things to happen," seeing themselves as omnipotent (paragraph 5). To what extent is it reasonable to attribute misfortunes to our mental state?

5. According to Crichton, we feel better when we "assume responsibility for our lives" (paragraph 49). Yet Kushner's final paragraph suggests that overdoing this attitude makes us feel worse. Does it help to assume responsibility if we are looking backward at the causes of a problem or only if we are looking forward to possible solutions?

6. Some systems of healing, including Christian Science and laughter therapy, suggest that our attitudes can lead to cures even without medical treatment. Choose one of the two systems and show how it relates to Crichton's proposal that we take more responsibility for our fate. To what extent do you agree with this system's attitude toward responsibility?

7. In "Heart Attack!" Michael Crichton suggests taking responsibility for our own misfortunes. Would this view apply to rape victims? To victims of a "hate crime"? Or would it be a way for the criminal and others to avoid facing their own responsibility?

8. Teachers, counselors, and medical personnel sometimes tell a crime victim, "There are steps you can take to prevent future problems." Does this advice help a victim develop a sense of control over the future? Or does the advice cause guilt about being a victim of the original crime?

9. In "Heart Attack!" Crichton says, "A doctor has powerful tools that may help me. Or these tools may hurt me. . . . I have to decide" (paragraph 54). How much responsibility should the patient take when dealing with an expert? Is a customer at a repair shop in the same position as a patient?

REVISION QUESTIONS

Once you have finished writing your essay, ask yourself the following questions.

1. Is there any statement the reader might not understand?
2. Is there any statement that might offend the reader?

3. Is there anything that's not very convincing?
4. Have I changed the subject and then changed it back again?
5. Have I said the same thing twice?
6. Do I want to try using any feature of style I've seen in the reading selection?

EDITING QUESTIONS

Once you've made changes, ask someone else to read your essay. Change it again as needed. Then read your essay out loud and answer the following questions.

1. Does every sentence make sense?
2. Does every sentence use the kind of language that most people consider "good English" these days? (*Hint:* Imagine a TV announcer reading it.)
3. Do the periods, commas, and other punctuation show the reader how to interpret what I am writing? Does the use of each punctuation mark conform to the rules that readers expect me to follow?
4. Are the words spelled right?

Note that good grammar, punctuation, and spelling usually make your writing clearer—and always improve your image as a competent, educated writer.

If you make changes in your paper, proofread it again!

UNIT

N I N E

Rap as a Cultural Force

PREVIEW STEPS FOR UNIT NINE

In response to questions 1 and 2, try these steps: Write your answers, talk them over with three or four classmates, and then discuss them with the whole class.

1. a. This is private writing (the topic may have personal meaning to other students in your class), so you might want to use scrap paper. Jot down four or five words that come to your mind when you hear the words "rap music."

   b. To the left of each word, put a plus sign if the word sounds positive to you; write a minus sign if the word sounds negative. Do you have more positive words than negative ones or the reverse?

2. Does it help you or make you feel worse if you talk about negative things such as personal problems or bad situations at school? Do you think it helps people if they rap or sing about negative things?

3. a. Read the title of the first essay (page 128). Name the topic. Who or what is this essay about?

   b. Now predict the main idea. (What is the main point the author wants to make about this topic?)

    c. Read the first and last paragraphs. Revise your prediction if necessary. (*Note:* The main idea should sum up the smaller ideas of the essay.)

4. Some words from the essay are listed below, accompanied by quotations. Mark any words you do not know and make an educated guess about their meanings using the context supplied by the quotations—and possibly Appendix A, Word Parts, on page 285. You may want to work with a small group of classmates.

façade "We see them slouched against walls, hats pulled low, hands shoved into pockets. . . . Searching for the elusive *façade* of perfect cool"

immersion "In the midst of all this 'Africanness' and cultural *immersion,* I was hardly prepared for a run-in with . . . Dr. Dre . . . blasting from the speakers of a neighborhood hangout."

intricacies "Many of hip-hop's most devoted followers in Dakar don't understand standard English, much less the *intricacies* of Black American slang."

condone "Even if we don't *condone* these things, our initial indignation eventually subsides and then disappears altogether as we slide into the familiar seduction of pop-culture marketing at its best."

Pan- "If young Black America is going to be a cultural trendsetter on a global scale, why not use this to our advantage. . . . to inspire a new wave in *Pan*-African thinking?"

5. Now read the following essay. As you read, jot down any questions that occur to you.

(*Note:* Question 6 appears after the essay.)

If Hip-Hop Ruled the World

Aisha K. Finch

You know them well. You can pick them out anywhere. They are the   1
homeboys. The B-boys. The hip-hop kids. We see them slouched
against walls, hats pulled low, hands shoved into pockets. They nod
a silent greeting to a member of the crew who passes, mumble a
crude appreciation for the "honeys." Searching for the elusive
façade of perfect cool, while gingerly holding up the walls on street
corners everywhere. Atlanta. New York. Los Angeles. Even Dakar,
Senegal.

I spent my first few days in Senegal trying to adjust to many   2
things: the sometimes-on-but-never-warm tap water, strangers who
greeted me as if I were family, women who created five-course meals
out of fish and rice. In the midst of all this "Africanness" and cultural
immersion, I was hardly prepared for a chance run-in with the former
president of Death Row Records: Dr. Dre himself was blasting from
the speakers of a neighborhood hangout. He was followed in turn by
Warren G, Snoop Doggy Dogg and Tupac Shakur. I had come to the
Motherland in search of ancestral roots and cultural understanding,
and here I was, in the French-speaking nation of Senegal, face-to-face
with a spread from *Rap Pages.*

My first reaction was to smile and shake my head. I was in a   3
foreign land with so little familiar to me, so the rhythms of Black
America fell on my ears like the voice of an old friend. It is no secret
that hip-hop as both a musical genre and a defined lifestyle has gained
recognition and popularity around the globe. Acknowledging this on
a cerebral level, however, and confronting it in person are two entirely
different things.

Just as in the United States, the hard-core players of hip-hop   4
seem to have the most influence with the young people of Dakar. But
what kind of message is being sent out to Black people around the
world when the main ambassadors of hip-hop are people like the
Notorious B.I.G. and Lil' Kim? Yes, it's true that many of hip-hop's
most devoted followers in Dakar don't understand standard English,
much less the intricacies of Black American slang. But just because

they cannot dissect the individual words doesn't mean they don't grasp the message. Besides, the videos that follow closely behind leave little room for confusion as to underlying meanings.

We as African-Americans seriously need to stop and think about   5
what our music, and our popular culture in general, is saying about us. Certainly we have all heard songs whose lyrics we neither endorse nor act upon. Yet the extensive air time allotted to songs with destructive lyrics, coupled with the visual counterpart, does take its toll. The repeated exposure to these sounds and images slowly desensitizes us to the violence, anger and exploitative sexual images that have become staples in much of hip-hop music. Even if we don't condone these things, our initial indignation eventually subsides and then disappears altogether as we slide into the familiar seduction of pop-culture marketing at its best. I may realize that the by-now-trite image of the gun-toting gangbanger is hardly representative of Black youth culture in the United States. But we would do well to remember that foreign listeners who have had little or no interaction with African-Americans have no reason *not* to take the face on the screen or behind the album as a representative of contemporary Black American morals, values and lifestyles.

Say what you like in defense of gangsta lyrics, but there is no way   6
to rewrite the following party scene to make it any less disturbing: A group of teenage partygoers keeps right on groovin' as the sound of recorded gunshots rips through a heavy bass line. This is something I've witnessed a number of times on the home turf, and yet I had to travel four thousand miles to feel the full impact of those bullets. Maybe we've all become a little too indifferent to that sound. Or maybe those Senegalese teenagers in their baggy clothes don't quite understand that if you listen long enough, that hollow pelting can start to sound like the 3,862 Black American males who were murdered in 1995 before the age of 25.

The fact is, from Senegal to South Africa, from England to   7
Japan, the export of hip-hop around the globe is more than just a pop phenomenon. So consider this: If young Black America is going to be a cultural trendsetter on a global scale, why not use this to our advantage? Can you imagine what our influence could be if more groups like The Fugees or Tribe Called Quest created music and lyrics to inspire a new wave in Pan-African thinking? If hip-hop is destined to rule youth culture around the world, wouldn't you rather it be a reign that will unite and empower Black people everywhere?

6. State the essay's main idea in your own words. Compare it to your prediction of the main idea. (*Note:* The main idea should sum up the smaller ideas of the essay.)

PREVIEW STEPS FOR "Organizing the Hip-Hop Generation"

1. a. Read the title of the second essay (page 132). Name the topic. (Who or what is this essay about?)

   b. Now predict the main idea. (What is the main point the author wants to make about this topic?)

   c. Read the first and last paragraphs of the essay. Revise your prediction if necessary. (*Note:* The main idea should sum up the smaller ideas of the essay.)

2. What in the author's background may have led her to the main idea? (See author's background, below title.)

3. Some words from the essay are listed below, accompanied by quotations. Mark any words you do not know and make an educated guess about their meanings using the context supplied by the quotations— and possibly Appendix A, Word Parts, on page 285. You may want to work with a small group of classmates.

radical "but once the institutions that supported *radical* movements collapsed or turned their attention elsewhere"

germinate "The seeds of hip-hop were left to *germinate* in American society at large—fed by . . . *misogyny* and a new, more *insidious* kind of state violence."

misogyny See above quotation.

insidious See above quotation.

blight "The South Bronx . . . came to symbolize urban *blight*."

epitomized "Bull Connor's Birmingham *epitomized* American racism."

alienated "lyrics reflecting their *alienated* reality"

credibility "Many of the lyrics were recycled from artists with more street *credibility*."

risqué "*risqué* 'hotel-motel' rhymes"

devastation "The creation of hip-hop amid social *devastation* is in itself a political act."

concerted "*Concerted* political action will not necessarily follow from such a restoration of confidence . . . but . . . radical movements never develop out of despair."

improvise "'cipher workshops,' in which circles of artists *improvise* raps"

tenet "No battling . . . defies a key *tenet* of hip-hop."

4. At the end of the Preview, you may want to go over any new features of style that occur in the following reading selection. You will need to know the terms *allusion* and *metaphor*. For help, see Appendix B, Guide to Literary Terms (page 288), with accompanying exercises on individual features.

5. Before reading "Organizing the Hip-Hop Generation," turn to pages 135–136 and skim the Reading Questions. Then read the essay to find answers to these questions. As you read, jot down any questions that occur to you.

Organizing the Hip-Hop Generation

Angela Ards

Angela Ards (1969–) does research and writing at The Nation Institute in New York. A regular contributor to The Nation *magazine, Ards has also published in* The Village Voice *and* VIBE *magazines. She has written a book on a public/private housing plan to combat homelessness in New York City and has contributed to* Still Lifting, Still Climbing: Contemporary African American Women's Activism *(1999). She has coordinated a career development program for adolescent mothers and taught at the Center for Afro-American Studies at the University of California. A special interest for her is the effect of the criminal justice system on African-American youth. This article is part of the Haywood Burns Community Activist Journalism series.*

Hip-hop was created in the mid-seventies as black social movements   1
quieted down, replaced by electoral politics. It has deep sixties cultural and political roots; Gil Scott-Heron and The Last Poets are considered the forebears of rap. But once the institutions that supported radical movements collapsed or turned their attention elsewhere, the seeds of hip-hop were left to germinate in American society at large—fed by its materialism, misogyny and a new, more insidious kind of state violence.

Under the watch of a new establishment of black and Latino   2
elected officials, funding for youth services, arts programs and community centers was cut while juvenile detention centers and prisons

---

Reprinted with permission from the July 26, 1999 issue of *The Nation*. For subscription information, call 1-800-333-8536. Portions of each week's Nation magazine can be accessed at http://www.thenation.com.

grew. Public schools became way stations warehousing youth until they were of prison age. Drugs and the violence they attract seeped into the vacuum that joblessness left. Nowhere was this decay more evident than in the South Bronx, which came to symbolize urban blight the way Bull Connor's Birmingham epitomized American racism—and black and Latino youth in the Boogie Down made it difficult for society to pretend that it didn't see them.

In the tradition of defiance, of creating "somethin' outta nothin'," they developed artistic expressions that came to be known as hip-hop. Rapping, or MC-ing, is now the most well-known, but there are three other defining elements: DJ-ing, break dancing and graffiti writing. For most of the seventies hip-hop was an underground phenomenon of basement parties, high school gyms and clubs, where DJs and MCs "took two turntables and a microphone," as the story has come to be told, creating music from the borrowed beats of soul, funk, disco, reggae and salsa, overlaid with lyrics reflecting their alienated reality. On city streets and in parks, hip-hop crews—the peaceful alternative to gangs—sought to settle disputes through lyrical battles and break-dancing competitions rather than violence. On crumbling walls and subways, graffiti writers left their tags as proof that they'd passed that way or that some friend had passed on. Eventually, all of these mediums shaped in New York morphed into regional styles defined by the cities in which they arose— Los Angeles, Oakland, Chicago, Philadelphia, Atlanta.

Underground tapes showcasing a DJ's skills or an MC's rhymes were all the outside world knew of rap music until 1979, when the Sugar Hill Gang released "Rapper's Delight" on a small independent black label. It wasn't the first rap album; many of the lyrics were recycled from artists with more street credibility. But it was a novelty to the mainstream. The record reached No. 36 on U.S. charts and was a huge international hit, purchased largely by young white males, whose tastes have dictated the way rap music has been marketed and promoted ever since. From those classic "a hip hippin to the hip hip hop" lyrics and risqué "hotel-motel" rhymes, rap music has gone through various phases—early eighties message raps, late-eighties Afrocentricity, early nineties gangsta rap, today's rank materialism—and shows no signs of stopping. . . .

If nothing else, rapping about revolution did raise consciousness. Public Enemy inspired a generation to exchange huge gold rope chains, which the group likened to slave shackles, for Malcolm X medallions. From PE and others like KRS-ONE, X-Clan and the Poor Righteous Teachers, urban youth were introduced to sixties figures like Assata Shakur and the Black Panther Party, then began to contemplate issues like the death penalty, police brutality, nationalism and the meaning of American citizenship. . . .

For many activists, the creation of hip-hop amid social devasta-   6
tion is in itself a political act. "To—in front of the world—get up on a turntable, a microphone, a wall, out on a dance floor, to proclaim your self-worth when the world says you are nobody, that's a huge, courageous, powerful, exhilarating step," says Jakada Imani, a civil servant in Oakland by day and a co-founder of the Oakland-based production company Underground Railroad. Concerted political action will not necessarily follow from such a restoration of confidence and self-expression, but it is impossible without it. Radical movements never develop out of despair. . . .

At the Freestyle Union (FSU) in Washington, DC, artist devel-   7
opment isn't complete without community involvement. That philosophy grew out of weekly "cipher workshops," in which circles of artists improvise raps under a set of rules: no hogging the floor, no misogyny, no battling. The last of those, which defies a key tenet of hip-hop, has outraged traditionalists, who see it feminizing the culture. What this transformation has created is a cadre of trained poet-activists, the Performance Corps, who run workshops and panels with DC-based universities, national educational conferences, the Smithsonian Institution and the AIDS Project, on issues ranging from domestic violence to substance abuse and AIDS prevention. This summer FSU and the Empower Program are holding a twelve-week Girls Hip-Hop Project, which tackles violence against women.

Obviously, as Tricia Rose points out, this stretching of the cul-   8
ture, even if it does raise political consciousness, "is not the equivalent of protesting police brutality, voting, grassroots activism against toxic waste dumping, fighting for more educational resources, protecting young women from sexual violence." Toni Blackman, the founder of FSU, admits as much. "As artists," she says, "we're not necessarily interested in being politicians. We are interested in making political statements on issues that we care about. But how do you give young people the tools to decide how to spend their energy to make their lives and the world better?"

READING QUESTIONS FOR "Organizing the Hip-Hop Generation"

Main Idea

1. State the essay's main idea in your own words. Compare it to your prediction of the main idea. (*Note:* The main idea should sum up the smaller ideas of the essay.)

Organization

2. a. Where in the essay is the main idea found?

   b. Why has the author placed the main idea there?

3. In what order are the paragraphs arranged? (Underline one.) Time/ Least to most important/Most to least important/Simple listing/ Logic: cause and effect/Other logic/Other

Style

4. How formal is the essay? (Circle your choice.)

   [Informal—1—2—3—4—5—6—7—8—9—10—Formal]

   What indicators convinced you? (For a list of possible indicators and two benchmark essays, see Appendix F, The Formality Spectrum, on page 298.)

5. Where do you see the following features of style? List one or two examples of each with their paragraph numbers.

   Features (For definitions, see Appendix B, page 288.)

a. allusion

b. metaphor

Content

6. What faults does Ards see in American society?

7. According to Ards, who is to blame for drugs and violence?

8. Does the author propose any change? If so, what do you think would be the result of such change?

9. Do you agree with the author's main idea? Why or why not?

If you have not already read the essay and answered the Reading Questions, be sure to do so before you proceed.

COMPOSITION QUESTIONS

Listed below are the writing questions. Choose one and write an essay that answers it. (If your instructor is willing, try adapting one of these questions or even writing your own. Be sure to get your instructor's approval—and possibly suggestions for change—before answering your question.)

Whichever question you choose, think of the person who will read your answer. The question may tell who your audience is. If not, think of a person you know and respect—preferably your instructor or a fellow student who will read your essay. Try to convince that person to believe you.

Bring in useful details from the selection(s) you have read and perhaps other incidents you know of. For ideas, review your answers to questions in the Preview and Reading Steps. When you first refer to a reading, give its title (in quotation marks) and the author's full name. Also, give the full name of anyone featured in the article the first time you mention that person. In making any later references, use only the person's last name.

Note: If you are assigned to write one paragraph, think of your answer to the question and list several key points you could make to support your answer. Then choose just one of the points and explain it in detail.

1. Both Finch and Ards say that rap is a cultural force and agree that it can be a force for good. To what extent can music (especially the lyrics) influence people's beliefs, attitudes, and behavior? Do other types of music have the same amount of influence as rap does?

2. Both Finch and Ards say that rap can be a force for positive social change. Yet Finch calls attention to lyrics filled with violence, anger, and misogyny. On balance, is rap's influence more positive than negative or the reverse?

3. Ards says that rap is legitimate protest against the evils of American society. If so, why does Finch find that rap is popular in the West African country of Senegal?

4. Ards notes in paragraph 4 that young white males are big buyers of rap. If rap is protesting discrimination against African Americans, what is its appeal to white males?

5. Ards reports that groups of artists are using rap music to inspire political reform. Should artists act as public spokespersons for their political views? Or do their looks and talent give them unfair advantage over nonartists? That is, does their status as celebrities give undeserved weight to their views, considering that they are not experts on politics?

6. When the Freestyle Union banished battling, was it "feminizing the culture"? Is that a bad thing to do? (Consider that paragraph 3 refers to battling that uses song lyrics and contests.)

REVISION QUESTIONS

Once you have finished writing your essay, ask yourself the following questions.

1. Is there any statement the reader might not understand?
2. Is there any statement that might offend the reader?
3. Is there anything that's not very convincing?
4. Have I changed the subject and then changed back again?
5. Have I said the same thing twice?
6. Do I want to try any feature of style I've seen in the reading selection?

EDITING QUESTIONS

Once you've made changes, ask someone else to read your essay. Change it again as needed. Then read your essay out loud and answer the following questions.

1. Does the sentence make sense?
2. Does every sentence use the kind of language that most people consider "good English" these days? (*Hint:* Imagine a TV announcer reading it.)
3. Do the periods, commas, and other punctuation show the reader how to interpret what I am writing? Does the use of each punctuation mark conform to the rules that readers expect me to follow?
4. Are the words spelled right?

Note that good grammar, punctuation, and spelling usually make your writing clearer—and always improve your image as a competent, educated writer.

If you make changes in your paper, proofread it again!

UNIT
T E N

---◈---

Welfare Versus Workfare

PREVIEW STEPS FOR UNIT TEN

In response to questions 1 and 2, try these steps: Write your answers, talk them over with three or four classmates, and then discuss them with the whole class.

1. a. This is private writing (the topic may have personal meaning to other students in your class), so you might want to use scrap paper. Jot down five or six words that come to mind when you hear the words "welfare mother."

   b. To the left of each word, put a plus sign if the word sounds positive to you; put a minus sign if the word sounds negative. Do you have more positive words than negative ones or the reverse?

2. Imagine that your neighbor has just lost a job as a secretary. She has been offered a job right now cleaning restrooms. She can take the job or she can spend time searching for a secretarial position. Which should she do? Would your answer change if she asked you for a loan to cover expenses while she looked for work?

3. a. Read the title of the first essay (page 142). Name the topic. Who or what is this essay about?

   b. Now predict the main idea. (What is the main point the author wants to make about this topic?)

    c. Read the first and last paragraphs. Revise your prediction if necessary. (*Note:*The main idea should sum up the smaller ideas of the essay.)

4. Some words from the essay are listed below, accompanied by quotations. Mark any words you do not know and make an educated guess about their meanings using the context supplied by the quotations—and possibly Appendix A, Word Parts, on page 285. You may want to work with a small group of classmates.

    bipartisan "The success of earlier reforms . . . led to a *bipartisan* effort by a Republican Congress and [a Democratic President] to 'end welfare as we know it' by forcing *recipients* in all states to look for work."

    recipients See above quotation.

    destitute "They argued that most women forced off welfare would become homeless or *destitute.*"

    buoyant "The authors' research attributes more than one-third of the decline in that state's welfare rolls since 1995 to the reforms and not simply to its *buoyant* economy."

    inducing "Welfare reform has been a resounding success in *inducing* unmarried mothers to find jobs."

    incentives "The vast majority of families do much better when treated as responsible adults and offered effective *incentives* to help themselves."

5. Now read the following essay. As you read, jot down any questions that occur to you.

(*Note:* Question 6 appears after the essay.)

Guess What? Welfare Reform Works

Gary S. Becker

The welfare reform act of 1996 is one of the most revolutionary pieces   1
of legislation since the welfare state began half a century ago. Contrary
to the predictions of many skeptics, this law has been remarkably
successful—helped, to be sure, by the strong economy of the past
several years.

The success of earlier reforms by a few states led to a bipartisan   2
effort by a Republican Congress and [a Democratic President] to
"end welfare as we know it" by forcing recipients in all states to look
for work. The 1996 law limits families to two years of welfare income
during any one spell and caps the total time on welfare over a mother's
lifetime at five years.

The number of recipients rose sharply from the early 1960s to a   3
peak in 1993, when over 4 million American families were on welfare.
In that year, an incredible 1 million residents of New York City alone
were receiving welfare, up from 250,000 in 1960.

Wisconsin, Massachusetts, New Jersey, and a few other states   4
decided in the late 1980s that this upward trend in welfare was unac-
ceptable and could be reversed. They introduced reforms that
discouraged women from having children while on welfare. More important, they dropped the assumption that most women on welfare
are not capable of getting and holding jobs, and put pressure on them
to find employment to help support their families.

Pioneers.   These states managed to cut their welfare popula-   5
tions while at the same time improving the economic situation of
single-parent families. Recently, a careful evaluation of the Massachusetts reforms by economists M. Anne Hill and Thomas J. Main of the
City University of New York concluded that they not only greatly reduced that state's welfare caseload but also encouraged more young
women to finish high school and sharpen their economic skills.

What worked in Massachusetts and other pioneering states was   6
applicable throughout the nation, but the reassessment of federal welfare policy was opposed by many intellectuals. Some members of [the

Guess What? Welfare Reform Works, by Gary S. Becker, in *Business Week,* May 24, 1999.
Used by permission.

President's] team quit after the 1996 federal law, over what they considered a betrayal of the welfare state. They argued that most women forced off welfare would become homeless or destitute, since they supposedly are too mentally or physically handicapped or lacking in requisite skills to obtain and hold jobs.

However, this law has been highly successful in reversing the large growth in the number of welfare recipients in the U.S. Most mothers forced off welfare found work and provide financial support for their children. 7

Certainly, the huge decline—by over 40%—in the number of single mothers on welfare from the 1993 peak is partly due to the booming economy of the past seven years. However, most of this decline took place in the two years after passage of the 1996 act. The study of Massachusetts' experience cited earlier confirms the importance of the new approach to welfare, since the authors' research attributes more than one-third of the decline in that state's welfare rolls since 1995 to the reforms and not simply to its buoyant economy. 8

Good Times. The federal law recognizes that the number of families in need of assistance always rises sharply during bad economic times. This is why each welfare spell is allowed to last up to two years, and mothers with dependent children can have multiple spells, up to a total of five years over their lifetimes. It further acknowledges that some women are handicapped and unable to work. What it aims to discourage is the attraction of welfare to able-bodied women during good times when jobs are available. 9

The act also recognizes that many poor working mothers will not earn enough to provide a decent standard of living for their families. Children of unmarried working mothers continue to be eligible for Medicaid and food stamps, and they benefit from the earned-income tax credit that is available only to poorer working parents with children. 10

One of the most important, if hardest to document, gains from taking families off welfare is their greater self-respect when they provide for themselves. Mothers on welfare convey the impression to their children that it is normal to live off government handouts. In such an environment, it is difficult for children to place a high value on doing well at school and preparing for work by seeking out training on jobs and in schools. 11

Welfare reform has been a resounding success in inducing unmarried mothers to find jobs. This revolutionary approach to welfare is based on the appreciation that the vast majority of families do much 12 better when treated as responsible adults and offered effective incentives to help themselves.

6. State the essay's main idea in your own words. Compare it to your prediction of the main idea. (*Note:* The main idea should sum up the smaller ideas of the essay.)

PREVIEW STEPS FOR "A Step Back to the Workhouse?"

1. a. Read the title of the second essay (page 147). Name the topic. (Who or what is this essay about?)

   b. Now predict the main idea. (What is the main point the author wants to make about this topic?)

   c. Read the first and last paragraphs of the essay. Revise your prediction if necessary. (*Note:* The main idea should sum up the smaller ideas of the essay.)

2. What in the author's background may have led her to the main idea? (See author's background, below title.)

3. Some words from the essay are listed below, accompanied by quotations. Mark any words you do not know and make an educated guess about their meanings using the context supplied by the quotations— and possibly Appendix A, Word Parts, on page 285. You may want to work with a small group of classmates.

   consensus "The commentators are calling it a 'remarkable *consensus*.'. . . No political candidate dares step outdoors without some plan for . . . putting . . . *hapless* victims to work."

   hapless See above quotation.

abhorred "Workfare . . . was once *abhorred* by liberals as a step back toward the 17th-century *workhouse* or—worse—slavery."

workhouse See above quotation.

aspire "It is as if the men who . . . *aspire* to run things . . . had . . . *caucused* . . . and decided on the one *constituency* that could be safely sacrificed in the name of political *expediency* and 'new ideas,' and that constituency is poor women."

caucused See above quotation.

constituency See above quotation.

expediency See above quotation.

dissolute "stereotypes . . . that . . . the poor are poor because they are lazy and *dissolute*"

slovenly "the image that haunts the workfare advocates: a *slovenly*, overweight, black woman who produces a baby a year in order to *augment* her welfare checks"

augment See above quotation.

proponents "Many of the *proponents* of workfare . . . have mounted the bandwagon with the best of intentions."

depravity "'Dependency'—with all its implications of laziness and *depravity*—is not the problem."

rhetoric "Real people, as opposed to imaginative stereotypes, never seem to make an appearance in the current *rhetoric* on welfare."

intergenerational "She is not herself the daughter of a welfare recipient, and hence not part of anything that could be called an '*intergenerational* cycle of dependency.'"

psychic "She resents the bureaucratic hassles that are the *psychic* price of welfare."

estranged "scared about whether she could survive on her own and scared of her *estranged* husband"

foibles "In fact, most of the time we spent together was probably spent laughing—over the *foibles* of the neighbors."

menial "Suppose she had . . . been told she would have to 'work off' her benefits in some *menial* government job."

sector "she had been told she would have to take the first available private *sector* job."

vociferous "In fact, even some of the most *vociferous* advocates of . . . workfare admit that . . . only about 15 percent of welfare recipients fit the stereotype associated with 'welfare dependency': *demoralization, long-term welfare use, lack of drive, and so on."*

demoralization See above quotation.

juggernaut "Some of my feminist activist friends argue that it is too late to stop the workfare *juggernaut.*"

pernicious "The best we can do, they say, is to try to defeat the more *pernicious* proposals: those that are *over-coercive,* that do not offer funds for child care, or that would *relegate* work clients to a 'subemployee' status."

over-coercive See above quotation.

relegate See above quotation.

pragmatists "Our goal, the *pragmatists* argue, should be to harness the current enthusiasm for workfare to push for services welfare recipients genuinely need."

trauma "as an emergency measure in a time of personal *trauma* and dire need"

nurture "And those who labor to raise their children in poverty—to feed and clothe them on meager budgets and to *nurture* them in an uncaring world—are working the hardest."

4. At the end of the Preview, you may want to go over any new features of style that occur in the following reading selection. You will need to know the term *metaphor*. For help, see Appendix B, Guide to Literary Terms (page 288), with accompanying exercises on individual features.

5. Before reading "A Step Back to the Workhouse?" turn to pages 152–153 and skim the Reading Questions. Then read the essay to find answers to these questions. As you read, jot down any questions that occur to you.

A Step Back to the Workhouse?

Barbara Ehrenreich

Barbara Ehrenreich (1941–), a feminist and socialist, has contributed to several magazines, including Vogue, Harper's, The New Republic, *and* Time. *Her books include* The Snarling Citizen *and* The Worst Years of Our Lives. *Ehrenreich has won many awards, among others a National Magazine Award for Excellence in Reporting. Her TV appearances include* Today, Good Morning America, *and* Nightline. *She earned her bachelor's degree from Reed College and her doctorate from Rockefeller University.*

The commentators are calling it a "remarkable consensus." Workfare, 1 as programs to force welfare recipients to work are known, was once abhorred by liberals as a step back toward the 17th-century workhouse or—worse—slavery. But today no political candidate dares step outdoors without some plan for curing "welfare dependency" by putting its hapless victims to work—if necessary, at the nearest Burger King. It is as if the men who run things, or who aspire to run things (and we are, unfortunately, talking mostly about men when we talk about candidates), had gone off and caucused for a while and decided on the one constituency that could be safely sacrificed in the name of political expediency and "new ideas," and that constituency is poor women.

Most of the arguments for workfare are simply the same inde-   2
structible stereotypes that have been around, in one form or another,
since the first public relief program in England 400 years ago: that the
poor are poor because they are lazy and dissolute, and that they are
lazy and dissolute because they are suffering from "welfare dependency." Add a touch of modern race and gender stereotypes and you
have the image that haunts the workfare advocates: a slovenly, overweight, black woman who produces a baby a year in order to augment
her welfare checks.

But there is a new twist to this season's spurt of welfare-bashing: 3
Workfare is being presented as a kind of *feminist* alternative to welfare. As Senator Daniel Patrick Moynihan (D.–N.Y.) has put it, "A
program that was designed to pay mothers to stay at home with their
children [i.e., welfare, or Aid to Families with Dependent Children]
cannot succeed when we now observe most mothers going out to
work." Never mind the startling illogic of this argument, which is on
a par with saying that no woman should stay home with her children
because other women do not, or that a laid-off male worker should
not receive unemployment compensation because most men have
been observed holding jobs. We are being asked to believe that push-
ing destitute mothers into the work force (in some versions of workfare, for no other compensation than the welfare payments they would
have received anyway) is consistent with women's strivings toward
self-determination.

Now I will acknowledge that most women on welfare—like most   4
unemployed women in general—would rather have jobs. And I will
further acknowledge that many of the proponents of workfare, possibly including Senator Moynihan and the Democratic Presidential candidates, have mounted the bandwagon with the best of intentions.
Welfare surely needs reform. But workfare is not the solution, because
"dependency"—with all its implications of laziness and depravity—is
not the problem. The problem is poverty, which most women enter in
a uniquely devastating way—with their children in tow.

Let me introduce a real person, if only because real people, as   5
opposed to imaginative stereotypes, never seem to make an appearance in the current rhetoric on welfare. "Lynn," as I will call her, is a
friend and onetime neighbor who has been on welfare for two years.
She is also about as unlike the stereotypical "welfare mother" as one
can get—which is to say that she is a fairly typical welfare recipient.
She has only one child, which puts her among the 74 percent of

welfare recipients who have only one or two children. She is white (not that that should matter), as are almost half of welfare recipients. Like most welfare recipients, she is not herself the daughter of a welfare recipient, and hence not part of anything that could be called an "intergenerational cycle of dependency." And like every woman on welfare I have ever talked to, she resents the bureaucratic hassles that are the psychic price of welfare. But, for now, there are no alternatives.

When I first met Lynn, she seemed withdrawn and disoriented. She had just taken the biggest step of her 25 years; she had left an abusive husband and she was scared: scared about whether she could survive on her own and scared of her estranged husband. He owned a small restaurant; she was a high school dropout who had been a waitress when she met him. During their three years of marriage he had beaten her repeatedly. Only after he threw her down a flight of stairs had she realized that her life was in danger and moved out. I don't think I fully grasped the terror she had lived in until one summer day when he chased Lynn to the door of my house with a drawn gun.

Gradually Lynn began to put her life together. She got a divorce and went on welfare; she found a pediatrician who would accept Medicaid and a supermarket that would take food stamps. She fixed up her apartment with second-hand furniture and flea market curtains. She was, by my admittedly low standards, a compulsive housekeeper and an overprotective mother; and when she wasn't waxing her floors or ironing her two-year-old's playsuits, she was studying the help-wanted ads. She spent a lot of her time struggling with details that most of us barely notice—the price of cigarettes, mittens, or a bus ticket to the welfare office—yet, somehow, she regained her sense of humor. In fact, most of time we spent together was probably spent laughing—over the foibles of the neighbors, the conceits of men, and the snares of welfare and the rest of "the system."

Yet for all its inadequacies, Lynn was grateful for welfare. Maybe if she had been more intellectually inclined she would have found out that she was suffering from "welfare dependency," a condition that is supposed to sap the will and demolish the work ethic. But "dependency" is not an issue when it is a choice between an abusive husband and an impersonal government. Welfare had given Lynn a brief shelter in a hostile world, and as far as she was concerned, it was her ticket to *independence*.

Suppose there had been no welfare at the time when Lynn finally   9
summoned the courage to leave her husband. Suppose she had gone
for help and been told she would have to "work off" her benefits in
some menial government job (restocking the toilet paper in restrooms
is one such "job" assigned to New York women in a current workfare
program). Or suppose, as in some versions of workfare, she had been
told she would have to take the first available private sector job, which
(for a non–high school graduate like Lynn) would have paid near the
minimum wage, or $3.35 an hour. How would she have been able to
afford child care? What would she have done for health insurance (as
a welfare recipient she had Medicaid, but most low-paying jobs offer
little or no coverage)? Would she have ever made the decision to leave
her husband in the first place?

As Ruth Sidel points out in *Women and Children Last* (Viking),   10
most women who are or have been on welfare have stories like Lynn's.
They go onto welfare in response to a crisis—divorce, illness, loss of a
job, the birth of an additional child to feed—and they remain on
welfare for two years or less. They are not victims of any "welfare
culture," but of a society that increasingly expects women to both
raise and support children—and often on wages that would barely
support a woman alone. In fact, even some of the most vociferous advocates of replacing welfare with workfare admit that, in their own es-
timation, only about 15 percent of welfare recipients fit the stereotype
associated with "welfare dependency": demoralization, long-term
welfare use, lack of drive, and so on.

But workfare will not help anyone, not even the presumed   11
15 percent of "bad apples" for whose sake the majority will be penal-
ized. First, it will not help because it does not solve the problem that
drives most women into poverty in the first place: how to hold a job
and care for children. Child care in a licensed, professionally run center can easily cost as much as $100 a week per child—more than most
states now pay in welfare benefits (for two children) and more than
most welfare recipients could expect to earn in the work force. Any
serious effort to get welfare recipients into the work force would require child care provisions at a price that would probably end up
higher than the current budget for AFDC. But none of the workfare
advocates are proposing that sort of massive public commitment to
child care.

Then there is the problem of jobs. So far, studies show that   12
existing state workfare programs have had virtually no success in

improving their participants' incomes or employment rates. Small wonder: Nearly half the new jobs generated in recent years pay poverty-level wages; and most welfare recipients will enter jobs that pay near the minimum wage, which is $6,900 a year—26 percent less than the poverty level for a family of three. A menial, low-wage job may be character-building (from a middle-class vantage point), but it will not lift anyone out of poverty.

Some of my feminist activist friends argue that it is too late to stop the workfare juggernaut. The best we can do, they say, is to try to defeat the more pernicious proposals: those that are over-coercive, that do not offer funds for child care, or that would relegate work clients to a "subemployee" status unprotected by federal labor and civil rights legislation. Our goal, the pragmatists argue, should be to harness the current enthusiasm for workfare to push for services welfare recipients genuinely need, such as child care and job training and counseling.   13

I wish the pragmatists well, but for me, it would be a betrayal of women like Lynn to encourage the workfare bandwagon in any way. Most women, like Lynn, do not take up welfare as a career, but as an emergency measure in a time of personal trauma and dire need. At such times, the last thing they need is to be hustled into a low-wage job, and left to piece together child care, health insurance, transportation, and all the other ingredients of survival. In fact, the main effect of workfare may be to discourage needy women from seeking any help at all—a disastrous result in a nation already suffering from a child poverty rate of nearly 25 percent. Public policy should be aimed at giving impoverished mothers (and, I would add, fathers) the help they so urgently need—not only in the form of job opportunities but sufficient income support to live on until a job worth taking comes along.   14

Besides, there is an ancient feminist principle at stake. The premise of all the workfare proposals—the more humane as well as the nasty—is that single mothers on welfare are not *working*. But, to quote the old feminist bumper sticker: EVERY MOTHER IS A WORKING MOTHER. And those who labor to raise their children in poverty—to feed and clothe them on meager budgets and to nurture them in an uncaring world—are working the hardest. The feminist position has never been that all women must pack off their children and enter the work force, but that all women's work—in the home or on the job—should be valued and respected.   15

READING QUESTIONS FOR "A Step Back to the Workhouse?"

Main Idea

1. State the essay's main idea in your own words. Compare it to your prediction of the main idea. (*Note:* The main idea should sum up the smaller ideas of the essay.)

Organization

2. a. Where in the essay is the main idea found?

   b. Why has the author placed the main idea there?

3. In what order are the paragraphs arranged? (Underline one.) Time/ Least to most important/Most to least important/Simple listing/ Logic: cause and effect/Other logic/Other

Style

4. How formal is the essay? (Circle your choice.)

   [Informal—1—2—3—4—5—6—7—8—9—10—Formal]

   What indicators convinced you? (For a list of possible indicators and two benchmark essays, see Appendix F, The Formality Spectrum, on page 298.)

5. Where do you see the following feature of style? List one or two examples with their paragraph numbers.

Feature (For a definition, see Appendix B, page 288.)

metaphor

Content

6. According to Becker (paragraph 10), what benefits does workfare give to poor mothers and their children? What is missing, according to Ehrenreich (paragraph 9)?

7. What does Ehrenreich mean by "a job worth taking" (paragraph 14)— a personally satisfying job or a job that pays enough to cover day care, health insurance, and so forth?

8. According to Ehrenreich, what is a major unsolved problem with women going out to work?

9. Does the author propose any change? If so, what do you think would be the result of such change?

10. Do you agree with the author's main idea? Why or why not?

If you have not already read the essay and answered the Reading Questions, be sure to do so before you proceed.

COMPOSITION QUESTIONS

Listed below are the writing questions. Choose one and write an essay that answers it. (If your instructor is willing, try adapting one of these questions or even writing your own. Be sure to get your instructor's approval—and possibly suggestions for change—before answering your question.)

Whichever question you choose, think of the person who will read your answer. The question may tell who your audience is. If not, think of a person you know and respect—preferably your instructor or a fellow student who will read your essay. Try to convince that person to believe you.

Bring in useful details from the selection(s) you have read and perhaps other incidents you know of. For ideas, review your answers to questions in the Preview and Reading Steps. When you first refer to a reading, give its title (in quotation marks) and the author's full name. Also, give the full name of anyone featured in the article the first time you mention that person. In making any later references, use only the person's last name.

Note: If you are assigned to write one paragraph, think of your answer to the question, and list several key points you could make to support your answer. Then choose just one of the points and explain it in detail.

1. Workfare forces women to work, according to both Becker (paragraph 2) and Ehrenreich (paragraph 1). Becker shows that workfare is a success from the taxpayer's point of view because women are getting jobs and going off welfare (paragraph 7). However, Ehrenreich says women who go off welfare—and their children—still don't have enough to live on and often get no health benefits (paragraph 14). On balance, is workfare a success?

2. Becker says that workfare raises the educational goals of young women and possibly their children (paragraphs 5 and 11). Ehrenreich, however, says that workfare forces women to take the first available job rather than work up to their current level of education (paragraph 9). Such work might also interfere with their getting further education. What is the overall effect of workfare on educational levels?

3. Should welfare reform be designed to affect the 15% who suffer from "welfare dependency," in which a tradition of joblessness is passed on from one generation to the next (Ehrenreich, paragraph 10)? Should

reform be designed to fit the other 85%, who use welfare "as an emergency measure in a time of personal trauma and dire need" (Ehrenreich, paragraph 14)? Or can you think of reforms that would fit both groups?

4. Becker says workfare has caused women to get jobs (paragraphs 2 and 7). Ehrenreich says that many times these jobs are menial, low paying, dead end, and lacking in health benefits (paragraph 9). Should someone who has, say, a college degree in business have to take the first job that comes along—for example, cleaning rest rooms—instead of taking time to search for a job that uses the college degree? Consider the viewpoint of the person involved, as well as that of a taxpayer who is paying for welfare.

5. Becker and Ehrenreich both imply that supporting children is the mother's responsibility. Ehrenreich also says workfare would work only if paired with good day care, and she says such day care would be costlier than welfare (paragraph 11). What solutions would provide decent care for children? Consider possible changes or additions to workfare; consider other possible solutions that could be used along with workfare.

6. Ehrenreich mentions child poverty and domestic abuse as two major problems that already exist (paragraphs 9 and 14). She also says that workfare is so bad that women with children won't apply. Predict the effects of workfare, as it is currently written, on child poverty and domestic abuse. What changes might solve these problems? (Consider possible changes or additions to workfare; consider other laws that could be used along with workfare.)

REVISION QUESTIONS

Once you have finished writing your essay, ask yourself the following questions.

1. Is there any statement the reader might not understand?
2. Is there any statement that might offend the reader?
3. Is there anything that's not very convincing?

4. Have I changed the subject and then changed back again?
5. Have I said the same thing twice?
6. Do I want to try any feature of style I've seen in the reading selection?

EDITING QUESTIONS

Once you've made changes, ask someone else to read your essay. Change it again as needed. Then read your essay out loud and answer the following questions.

1. Does the sentence make sense?
2. Does every sentence use the kind of language that most people consider "good English" these days? (*Hint:* Imagine a TV announcer reading it.)
3. Do the periods, commas, and other punctuation show the reader how to interpret what I am writing? Does the use of each punctuation mark conform to the rules that readers expect me to follow?
4. Are the words spelled right?

Note that good grammar, punctuation, and spelling usually make your writing clearer—and always improve your image as a competent, educated writer.

If you make changes in your paper, proofread it again!

Human Cloning and Human Rights

PREVIEW STEPS FOR UNIT ELEVEN

In response to questions 1 and 2, try these steps: Write your answers, talk them over with three or four classmates, and then discuss them with the whole class.

1. a. What is cloning? (If you've seen *Jurassic Park,* that should help.)

   b. Imagine that human cloning is possible and that even dead people can be cloned using *Jurassic Park* technology. What person in the past would you like to see cloned? Why?

   c. Would this clone have the same knowledge and mind-set as the original genetic person? The same values? The same soul? Why or why not?

2. If you were cloned, this person would be like an identical twin to you but would be much younger than you. How do you think you would react to such a person?

3. a. Read the title of the first essay (page 160). Name the topic. (Who or what is this essay about?)

   b. Now predict the main idea. (What is the main point the author wants to make about this topic?)

    c. Read the first and last paragraphs. Revise your prediction if necessary. (*Note:* The main idea should sum up the smaller ideas of the essay.)

4. Some words from the essay are listed below, accompanied by quotations. Mark any words you do not know and make an educated guess about their meanings using the context supplied by the quotations—and possibly Appendix A, Word Parts, on page 285. You may want to work with a small group of classmates.

commodities "The manufacture of a person made to order undermines human dignity and individuality, and encourages us to treat children like *commodities.*"

in vitro fertilization "*In vitro fertilization* is no *precedent* for cloning; the child is still conceived by the union of the egg and sperm from two separate persons."

precedent See above quotation.

replication "Cloning is *replication,* not *reproduction,* and represents a difference . . . in the way humans continue the species."

reproduction See above quotation.

hypotheticals "Rather than look deeply into ethics and world literature, supporters of human cloning have tried to come up with extreme and improbable *hypotheticals* to sell this technique to the American public."

dehumanization "But these hypotheticals only demonstrate that the risks of *dehumanization* and *commodification* are real."

commodification See above quotation.

feasible "We could only discover whether cloning is even *feasible* in humans by unethically subjecting the planned child to the risk of serious genetic and physical injury."

5. Now read the following essay. As you read, jot down any questions that occur to you.

(*Note* Question 6 appears after the essay.)

Should the United States Ban Human Cloning? Yes: Individual Dignity Demands Nothing Less

George J. Annas

Human cloning should be banned because it would radically alter our   1
very definition of ourselves by producing the world's first human with
a single genetic parent. This manufacture of a person made to order
undermines human dignity and individuality, and encourages us to
treat children like commodities. . . .

In vitro fertilization is no precedent for cloning; the child is still   2
conceived by the union of the egg and sperm from two separate persons, and the child is genetically unique. Cloning is replication, not
reproduction, and represents a difference in kind, not in degree, in
the way humans continue the species. . . .

Rather than look deeply into ethics and world literature, sup-   3
porters of human cloning have tried to come up with extreme and improbable hypotheticals to sell this technique to the American public.
But these hypotheticals only demonstrate that the risks of dehumanization and commodification are real. . . .

The most popular suggestion is that parents of a dying child   4
should be able to clone the child for a replacement. But when a child
is cloned, it is not the parents who are replicated, but the child. No
one should have such dominion over a child as to be allowed to use its
genes to create the child's child.

Ethical human reproduction requires the voluntary participa-   5
tion of the genetic parents, and this is impossible for the young child.
Nor, of course, should one have an "extra" child for organs or other
spare parts. . . .

Reprinted by permission of the author.

Humans have a basic right not to reproduce, and human dignity   6
requires that human reproduction not be equated with that of farm
animals or even pets. We could only discover whether cloning is even
feasible in humans by unethically subjecting the planned child to the
risk of serious genetic and physical injury. Congress and states should
take a stand at this boundary.

6. State the essay's main idea in your own words. Compare it to your
prediction of the main idea. (*Note:* The main idea should sum up the
smaller ideas of the essay.)

PREVIEW STEPS FOR "Human Cloning? Don't Just Say No"

1. a. Read the title of the second essay (page 163). Name the topic.
(Who or what is this essay about?)

b. Now predict the main idea. (What is the main point the author
wants to make about this topic?)

c. Read the first and last paragraphs of the essay. Revise your prediction if necessary. (*Note:* The main idea should sum up the smaller
ideas of the essay.)

2. What in the author's background may have led her to the main idea?
(See author's background, below title.)

3. Some words from the essay are listed below, accompanied by quotations. Mark any words you do not know and make an educated
guess about their meanings using the context supplied by the

quotations—and possibly Appendix A, Word Parts, on page 285. You may want to work with a small group of classmates.

ethicists "[The 'yuk factor'] makes it hard for even trained scientists and *ethicists* to see the matter clearly."

theologians "*Theologians* contend that to clone a human would violate human dignity."

stature "if a cloned individual were treated as a lesser being, with fewer rights or lower *stature*"

scenarios "Many of the science-fiction *scenarios* prompted by the prospect of human cloning turn out, upon reflection, to be absurdly improbable."

perpetrated "Such ideas are repulsive . . . because of the horrors *perpetrated* by the Nazis in the name of *eugenics*."

eugenics See above quotation.

totalitarian "But there's a vast difference between 'selective breeding' as practiced by *totalitarian* regimes (where the urge to *propagate* certain types of people leads to efforts to *eradicate* other types) and the immeasurably more *benign* forms already practiced in democratic societies."

propagate See above quotation.

eradicate See above quotation.

benign See above quotation.

impregnate "They haven't created a master race because only a tiny number of women have wanted to *impregnate* themselves this way."

dubious "A grieving couple . . . might seem psychologically twisted. But a cloned child born to such *dubious* parents. . . ."

moratorium "a *moratorium* on further research . . . . in order to consider . . . the grave questions it raises"

4. At the end of the Preview, you may want to go over any new features of style that occur in the following reading selection. You will need to know the term *metaphor.* For help, see Appendix B, Guide to Literary Terms (page 288), with accompanying exercises on individual features.

5. Before reading "Human Cloning? Don't Just Say No," turn to pages 165–167 and skim the Reading Questions. Then read the essay to find answers to these questions. As you read, jot down any questions that occur to you.

Human Cloning? Don't Just Say No

Ruth Macklin

Ruth Macklin is Professor of Bioethics at Albert Einstein College of Medicine at Yeshiva University in the Bronx, New York. She is the author or editor of 10 books, including Mortal Choices *(1988),* Enemies of Patients *(1993),* Surrogates and Other Mothers *(1994), and* Against Relativism *(1999). Her publications include over 170 articles on topics covering research with human subjects, AIDS, human reproduction, human cloning, and health policy. Dr. Macklin is an elected member of the Institute of Medicine and of the National Academy of Sciences. She is co-chair of the National Advisory Board on Ethics in Reproduction, a member of the Executive Board of the American Association of Bioethics, and a member of the Board of Directors of the International Association of Bioethics. She also serves on the scientific and ethical review group of the Human Reproduction Program of the World Health Organization.*

Last week's news that scientists had cloned a sheep sent academics   1
and the public into a panic at the prospect that humans might be next. That's an understandable reaction. Cloning is a radical challenge to

the most fundamental laws of biology, so it's not unreasonable to be concerned that it might threaten human society and dignity. Yet much of the ethical opposition seems also to grow out of an unthinking disgust—a sort of "yuk factor." And that makes it hard for even trained scientists and ethicists to see the matter clearly. While human cloning might not offer great benefits to humanity, no one has yet made a persuasive case that it would do any real harm, either.

Theologians contend that to clone a human would violate   2
human dignity. That would surely be true if a cloned individual were treated as a lesser being, with fewer rights or lower stature. But why suppose that cloned persons wouldn't share the same rights and dignity as the rest of us? A leading lawyer-ethicist has suggested that cloning would violate the "right to genetic identity." Where did he come up with such a right? It makes perfect sense to say that adult persons have a right not to be cloned without their voluntary, informed consent. But if such consent is given, whose "right" to genetic identity would be violated?

Many of the science-fiction scenarios prompted by the prospect   3
of human cloning turn out, upon reflection, to be absurdly improbable. There's the fear, for instance, that parents might clone a child to have "spare parts" in case the original child needs an organ transplant. But parents of identical twins don't view one child as an organ farm for the other. Why should cloned children's parents be any different?

Vast difference. Another disturbing thought is that cloning will   4
lead to efforts to breed individuals with genetic qualities perceived as exceptional (math geniuses, basketball players). Such ideas are repulsive, not only because of the "yuk factor" but also because of the horrors perpetrated by the Nazis in the name of eugenics. But there's vast difference between "selective breeding" as practiced by totalitarian regimes (where the urge to propagate certain types of people leads to efforts to eradicate other types) and the immeasurably more benign forms already practiced in democratic societies (where, say, lawyers freely choose to marry other lawyers). Banks stocked with the frozen sperm of geniuses already exist. They haven't created a master race because only a tiny number of women have wanted to impregnate themselves this way. Why think it will be different if human cloning becomes available?

So who will likely take advantage of cloning? Perhaps a grieving couple whose child is dying. This might seem psychologically twisted. But a cloned child born to such dubious parents stands no greater or lesser chance of being loved, or rejected, or warped than a child normally conceived. Infertile couples are also likely to seek out cloning. That such couples have other options (in vitro fertilization or adoption) is not an argument for denying them the right to clone. Or consider an example raised by Judge Richard Posner: a couple in which the husband has some tragic genetic defect. Currently, if this couple wants a genetically related child, they have four not altogether pleasant options. They can reproduce naturally and risk passing on the disease to the child. They can go to a sperm bank and take a chance on unknown genes. They can try in vitro fertilization and dispose of any afflicted embryo—though that might be objectionable, too. Or they can get a male relative of the father to donate sperm, if such a relative exists. This is one case where even people unnerved by cloning might see it as not the worst option.

Even if human cloning offers no obvious benefits to humanity, why ban it? In a democratic society we don't usually pass laws outlawing something before there is actual or probable evidence of harm. A moratorium on further research into human cloning might make sense, in order to consider calmly the grave questions it raises. If the moratorium is then lifted, human cloning should remain a research activity for an extended period. And if it is ever attempted, it should—and no doubt will—take place only with careful scrutiny and layers of legal oversight. Most important, human cloning should be governed by the same laws that now protect human rights. A world not safe for cloned humans would be a world not safe for the rest of us.

READING QUESTIONS FOR "Human Cloning? Don't Just Say No"

Main Idea

1. State the essay's main idea in your own words. Compare it to your prediction of the main idea. (*Note:* The main idea should sum up the smaller ideas of the essay.)

Organization

2. a. Where in the essay is the main idea found?

b. Why has the author placed the main idea there?

3. In what order are the paragraphs arranged? (Underline one.) Time/
Least to most important/Most to least important/Simple listing/
Logic: cause and effect/Other logic/Other

Style

4. How formal is the essay? (Circle your choice.)

[Informal—1—2—3—4—5—6—7—8—9—10—Formal]

What indicators convinced you? (For a list of possible indicators and
two benchmark essays, see Appendix F, The Formality Spectrum, on
page 298.)

5. Where do you see the following feature of style? List one or two
examples with their paragraph numbers.

Feature (For a definition, see Appendix B, page 288.)

metaphors

Content

6. a. To come across as open-minded, the author concedes a point in the
first paragraph. What is it?

    b. In the conclusion, she offers what she feels will be a temporary compromise. What is it?

7. Does the author propose any change? If so, what do you think would be the result of such change?

8. Do you agree with the author's main idea? Why or why not?

If you have not already read the essay and answered the Reading Questions, be sure to do so before you proceed.

COMPOSITION QUESTIONS

Listed below are the writing questions. Choose one and write an essay that answers it. (If your instructor is willing, try adapting one of these questions or even writing your own. Be sure to get your instructor's approval—and possibly suggestions for change—before answering your question.)

    Whichever question you answer, think of the person who will read your answer. The question may tell who your audience is. If not, think of a person you know and respect—preferably your instructor or a fellow student who will read your essay. Try to convince that person to believe you.

    Bring in useful details from the selection(s) you have read and perhaps other incidents you know of. For ideas, review your answers to questions in the Preview and Reading Steps. When you first refer to a reading, give its title (in quotation marks) and the author's full name. Also, give the full name of anyone featured in the article the first time you mention that person. In making any later references, use only the person's last name.

Note: If you are assigned to write one paragraph, think of your answer to the question and list several key points you could make to support your answer. Then choose just one of the points and explain it in detail.

1. According to Macklin, what are the advantages of human cloning? Do you agree or disagree? Why?

2. A few years ago, news articles reported the story of a teenage girl who needed a kidney transplant because she was slowly dying from an infection. Neither of her parents was a compatible donor. Although they had originally decided to limit themselves to one child, they decided to have a second child in hopes of creating a compatible donor. The baby was compatible. By the time the older daughter was in her early twenties, she was bedridden and attached to a machine. The younger daughter then gave her big sister a kidney, and both daughters did fine. Were the parents' actions morally right? Unlike having a child by ordinary reproduction, as these parents did, cloning a child guarantees donor compatibility. If human cloning is perfected, would cloning for spare parts become more common? Would it be right?

3. People are divided over whether human cloning is right morally. Discuss the reasoning and feelings of both sides, and explain why you agree with the side you do.

4. Annas and Macklin differ on "the right to genetic identity." Is it a right? What are the issues? Which side do you agree with? Why?

5. Annas says, "Human cloning should be banned because it would radically alter our very definition of ourselves by producing the world's first human with a single genetic parent." Would human cloning redefine humanity? If so, is this an issue we should be concerned with? Consider that sexual relationships would not be necessary in order to have a child, that a child could have a child, and that the original and the copy would be exactly alike genetically.

6. Annas says, "No one should have such dominion over a child as to be allowed to use its genes to create the child's child." Would this second child be the child's child, or, since its genes would be a combination of those of the two adults who had the first child, would this second child be the two adults' child? How important is this issue in our society?

7. Macklin discusses what she calls the "yuk factor" about human cloning. What is the "yuk factor"? How important is it in considering whether or not human cloning should be banned?

8. Annas says that human cloning would equate human reproduction with that of farm animals. Do you agree? Why or why not?

9. How would you feel about being a clone? In what ways might your life be different—and in what ways might it be the same? Would it matter whether you were the original or the copy?

REVISION QUESTIONS

Once you have finished writing your essay, ask yourself the following questions.

1. Is there any statement the reader might not understand?
2. Is there any statement that might offend the reader?
3. Is there anything that's not very convincing?
4. Have I changed the subject and then changed back again?
5. Have I said the same thing twice?
6. Do I want to try any feature of style I've seen in the reading selection?

EDITING QUESTIONS

Once you've made changes, ask someone else to read your essay. Change it again as needed. Then read your essay out loud and answer the following questions.

1. Does the sentence make sense?
2. Does every sentence use the kind of language that most people consider "good English" these days? (*Hint:* Imagine a TV announcer reading it.)
3. Do the periods, commas, and other punctuation show the reader how to interpret what I am writing? Does the use of each punctuation mark conform to the rules that readers expect me to follow?
4. Are the words spelled right?

Note that good grammar, punctuation, and spelling usually make your writing clearer—and always improve your image as a competent, educated writer.

If you make changes in your paper, proofread it again!

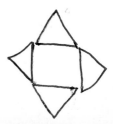

UNIT
TWELVE

The Right to Bear Arms

PREVIEW STEPS FOR UNIT TWELVE

In response to questions 1 and 2, try these steps: Write your answers, talk them over with three or four classmates, and then discuss them with the whole class.

1. a. This is private writing (the topic may have personal meaning to other students in your class), so you might want to use scrap paper. Jot down five words that come to mind when you hear the word "gun."

   b. Reread your ideas and put a plus sign by any word or phrase that sounds good or appealing about guns. Put a minus sign by anything that sounds negative.

   c. Judging from your own reactions, what do you think most people like about guns?

   What do they dislike?

2. Under what circumstances would you carry a firearm? Check any that apply.
   - ☐ to safeguard your family
   - ☐ for hunting
   - ☐ live/work in a dangerous area
   - ☐ have a dangerous occupation such as police work
   - ☐ live under a dictatorship
   - ☐ in war (*Note:* "Conscientious objectors" can opt out of fighting.)
   - ☐ never (would rather die than take a life)
   - ☐ other: _____

3. a. Read the title of the first essay (page 174). Name the topic. (Who or what is this essay about?)

   b. Now predict the main idea. (What is the main point the author wants to make about this topic?)

   c. Read the first and last paragraphs. Revise your prediction if necessary. (*Note:* The main idea should sum up the smaller ideas of the essay.)

4. Some words from the essay are listed below, accompanied by quotations. Mark any words you do not know and make an educated guess about their meanings using the context supplied by the quotations—and possibly Appendix A, Word Parts, on page 285. You may want to work with a small group of classmates.

militia "*Militias,* such as the Minutemen, were composed of private citizens who supplied their own weapons."

construed "The Constitution shall never be *construed* to prevent the people from keeping arms."

infringed "A well-regulated militia, being necessary to preserve the security of the Free State, the right of the people to bear arms shall not be *infringed.*"

ordnance (not ordinance) "Many antigun activists believe that . . . the rights of private citizens to maintain their own *ordnance* does not exist."

tyranny "Our founding fathers used their own privately-held military weapons . . . to overthrow *tyranny* in government."

revocation "We, the people, retain the right to . . . protect ourselves from illegal *revocation* of our constitutional rights."

usurped "If any of these rights is ever *usurped,* it is the duty of the armed citizen to . . . defend the Constitution—by force."

concur "The Bureau of Alcohol, Tobacco, and Firearms now says only 'sporting purpose' firearms are legal. Congress, the President, and the Supreme Court *concur.*"

viable "Even after the Civil War, militarily *viable* weapons have remained in citizens' hands."

5. Now read the following essay. As you read, jot down any questions that occur to you.

(*Note:* Question 6 appears after the essay.)

American Revolutionary

Matthew Edwards

"Firearms stand next in importance to the Constitution itself.   1
They are the American people's liberty, teeth, and keystone
under independence. The rifle and pistol are equally indispens-
able and they deserve a place of honor with all that's good. When
firearms go, all goes. We need them every hour."
                                                —George Washington

The Constitution preserves "the advantage of being armed,   2
which Americans possess over the people of almost every other
nation . . . [where] the governments are afraid to trust the people with arms."
                        —James Madison, *The Federalist Papers,* #46

"I ask, sir, what is the militia? It is the whole people. . . . To dis-   3
arm the people is the best and most effectual way to enslave
them."
                                                —George Mason

---

Reprinted by permission.

"The Constitution shall never be construed to prevent the peo-   4
ple from keeping arms."

—Samuel Adams

The Second Amendment of the U.S. Constitution reads, "A   5
well-regulated militia, being necessary to preserve the security of the
Free State, the right of the people to bear arms shall not be infringed."
Many antigun activists believe that the Second Amendment allows
only state police and national guard units to own guns. In their view,
the rights of private citizens to maintain their own ordnance does not
exist. History shows this view to be false.

Militias, such as the Minutemen, were composed of private citi-   6
zens who supplied their own weapons and kept them in their own
homes. The British marched on Lexington and Concord to seize private arms stockpiles from the citizens of those towns. That march was
the spark that brought on a Revolutionary War. Our founding fathers
used their own privately-held military weapons to overthrow tyranny
in government, and out of this came a new nation. The Second
Amendment was written to ensure the people the means to throw off
government again should it become necessary.

The Second Amendment recognized the rights of citizens to   7
defend their rights, lives, and property from anyone who threatened
them, including their own government. The Federal Government has
no authority to revoke citizen militia privileges unless the people
amend the Constitution so as to grant the government this power.
We, the people, retain the right to bear arms in order to protect ourselves from illegal revocation of our constitutional rights, including
the Second Amendment. If any of these rights is ever usurped, it is
the duty of the armed citizen to preserve, protect, and defend the
Constitution—by force, as a means of last resort.

In fact, the Second Amendment has been illegally usurped by   8
government. The 1968 Gun Control Act, a direct translation of
Hitler's own gun-control legislation, declares that only sporting-
purpose arms may be lawfully owned by civilians. But the Second
Amendment is not about duck-hunting: The Second Amendment was
created to afford citizens the protection of ordnance for military
purpose. Changing our Constitution requires an amendment in itself,
not just a law. The Bureau of Alcohol, Tobacco, and Firearms now says
only "sporting purpose" firearms are legal. Congress, the President,
and the Supreme Court concur. Thus, the Second Amendment has
been unconstitutionally abridged.

Some say that street crime justifies our government's illegal ban   9
on semi-automatic "assault rifles." First of all, even if street crime is
considered just cause to change our Constitution, we must uphold
the Constitution until it is changed. Second, assault rifles are rarely
used in crime. Pistols and shotguns are much more effective at the
close ranges at which crimes generally occur. Criminals realize this:
Fewer than 1% of all firearms crimes involve assault rifles, according
to the Bureau of Alcohol, Tobacco, and Firearms. A third point: Even
after the Civil War, militarily viable weapons have remained in citizens' hands. Street crime is, by comparison, a small problem—a small
excuse for taking away the freedom of law-abiding citizens to arm
themselves.

The government has illegally done away with an important con-   10
stitutional liberty. It is your duty as a citizen to defend the Constitution of the United States against all enemies, foreign and domestic.
Prepare now to defend liberty.

"The strongest reason for the people to retain the right to keep   11
and bear arms is, as a last resort, to protect themselves against
tyranny in government."

—Thomas Jefferson

6. State the essay's main idea in your own words. Compare it to your
prediction of the main idea. (*Note:* the main idea should sum up the
smaller ideas of the essay.)

PREVIEW STEPS FOR "The Hydrogen Bomb Lobby"

1. a. Read the title of the second essay (page 178). Name the topic.
(Who or what is this essay about?)

b. Now predict the main idea. (What is the main point the author
wants to make about this topic?)

   c. Read the first and last paragraphs of the essay. Revise your prediction if necessary. (*Note:* The main idea should sum up the smaller ideas of the essay.)

2. What in the author's background may have led him to the main idea? (See author's background, below title.)

3. Some words from the essay are listed below, accompanied by quotations. Mark any words you do not know and make an educated guess about their meanings using the context supplied by the quotations— and possibly Appendix A, Word Parts, on page 285. You may want to work with a small group of classmates.

zealot "A group of firearm *zealots* formed the National Hydrogen Bomb Assn."

deterrent "The bomb . . . has a *deterrent* effect. If somebody knows you have a nuclear weapon in your house, they're going to think twice about breaking in."

4. At the end of the Preview, you may want to go over any new features of style that occur in the following reading selection. You will need to know the terms *cliché, irony of wording,* and *understatement.* For help, see Appendix B, Guide to Literary Terms (page 288), with accompanying exercises on individual features.

5. What is the topic of this chapter?

6. So far, each chapter in this book has presented two opposing views on a topic. What is the stand that the first essay takes on this topic?

7. What stand do you expect to see in the second essay?

8. Art Buchwald worked for a humor magazine in college and went on to write humorous columns on American life. If he wants to attack Edwards's ideas, how is he apt to do it?

9. An actual hydrogen bomb would sicken or kill people for hundreds of square miles. Would a lobbying group really demand private ownership of hydrogen bombs? If not, why does Buchwald say a group is doing this?

10. Buchwald presents an imaginary conversation between a man who wants "bomb control" and a spokesman for the Hydrogen Bomb Association. Label each paragraph to show who is speaking—either **C** for control or **R** for rights. *Hint:* The first speaker (paragraph 2) is an **R**.

Turn to pages 180–182 and skim the Reading Questions, particularly question 8, which shows some progun arguments. Try filling in the chart in pencil, using your own ideas.

Now read the essay to find answers to these questions. Two people could even read the parts (labeled **C** and **R**) out loud—as a short play.

The Hydrogen Bomb Lobby

Art Buchwald

Art Buchwald (1925–) joined the Marines at 17 and spent over three years in the Pacific during World War II. After college, where he edited the campus humor magazine, Buchwald began writing newspaper columns, first in Paris and, since 1952, in

Washington, DC. In 1982, he won a Pulitzer Prize for outstanding commentary. He has also written a Broadway play and 30 books, including two memoirs.

Note: **Like Edwards, the National Rifle Association (NRA) says that individuals have the right to own guns. In this essay, Buchwald ridicules NRA arguments by applying their logic to bombs.**

As soon as it was revealed that a reporter for *Progressive* magazine had discovered how to make a hydrogen bomb, a group of firearm zealots formed the National Hydrogen Bomb Assn., and they are now lobbying against any legislation to stop Americans from owning one. 1

"The Constitution," said the association's spokesman, "gives everyone the right to own and bear arms. It doesn't spell out what kind of arms. But since anyone can now make a hydrogen bomb, the public should be able to buy it to protect themselves." 2

"Don't you think it's dangerous to have one in the house, particularly where there are children around?" 3

"The National Hydrogen Bomb Assn. hopes to spend a good portion of its dues on educating people in the safe handling of this type of weapon. We are instructing owners to keep the bomb in a locked closet and the fuse separately in a drawer. We also will hold classes in how to fire the bomb. We believe that if a person knows how to take care of his bomb there is no danger to himself or his family." 4

"Some people consider the hydrogen bomb a very lethal weapon which could kill somebody." 5

The spokesman said, "Hydrogen bombs don't kill people—people kill people. The bomb is for self-protection and it also has a deterrent effect. If somebody knows you have a nuclear weapon in your house, they're going to think twice about breaking in." 6

"But those who want to ban the bomb for American citizens claim that if you have one locked in the closet, with the fuse in a drawer, you would never be able to assemble it in time to repulse an intruder." 7

"That's garbage put out by the anti-nuclear weapon people. We are only advocating ownership of hydrogen weapons by law-abiding citizens. If someone commits a crime with one, he should get a stiff jail sentence." 8

"Another argument against allowing people to own a bomb is that at the moment it is very expensive to build one. So what your association is backing is a program which would allow the middle and upper classes to acquire a bomb while poor people will be left defenseless with just handguns." 9

"That's pure propaganda put out by the bleeding hearts. In a   10
year or two there will be Saturday Night Hydrogen Bomb Specials
costing less than a hundred dollars. It's worth that to protect your
family."

"Would your association be willing to permit the registration of   11
bombs by their owners?"

"Absolutely not. If we ever go to war the Communists will have   12
a list of everybody in this country who owns the bomb. They could
disarm us overnight. The strength of this nation is still in a citizens'
army, and our members are pledged to fight to the last man."

"Do you plan to use the bomb for hunting?"   13

"Only for big game. We're not going to use it on a rabbit or a   14
duck because that would be overkill. But it's a perfect weapon for
knocking down an elk or a bear."

"A recent Gallup survey has indicated that 78 percent of the   15
people polled said they were in favor of banning the hydrogen bomb
in private hands. What is your response to that?"

"Our recent survey indicates just the opposite," he replied.   16
"People favor keeping the bomb out of the hands of criminal elements, and believe that if you carry one around in your pocket you
should have a license. But it's nobody's damn business what you do
with one at home."

READING QUESTIONS FOR "The Hydrogen Bomb Lobby"

Main Idea

1. State the essay's main idea in your own words. Compare it to your prediction of the main idea. (*Note:* The main idea should sum up the
   smaller ideas of the essay.)

Organization

2. a. Where in the essay is the main idea found?

b. Why has the author placed the main idea there?

3. In what order are the paragraphs arranged? (Underline one.) Time/ Least to most important/Most to least important/Simple listing/ Logic: cause and effect/Other logic/Other

Style

4. How formal is the essay? (Circle your choice.)

[Informal—1—2—3—4—5—6—7—8—9—10—Formal]

What indicators convinced you? (For a list of possible indicators and two benchmark essays, see Appendix F, The Formality Spectrum, on page 298.)

5. Where do you see the following features of style? List one or two examples of each with their paragraph numbers.

Features (For definitions, see Appendix B, page 288.)

a. cliché

b. irony of wording

c. understatement

Content

6. Does the author propose any change? If so, what do you think would be the result of such change?

7. Do you agree with the author's main idea? Why or why not?

8. Complete the following chart of progun and antigun arguments. Fill in as many antigun arguments as you can, using inference or your own logic. The first antigun argument is completed for you.

    Remember that in place of the word *gun,* Buchwald substitutes *bomb* for the purpose of satire (ridicule).

Progun Arguments (Edwards/Buchwald)	Antigun Arguments (Supply your own)
a. The Constitution gives the "right to bear arms" (Edwards, par. 5) and doesn't say what kind (Buchwald, par. 2).	Our forefathers could not foresee hydrogen bombs or even semi-automatic (rapid-fire) guns.
b. Without guns, we can be controlled by tyrants (Edwards, par. 6, 7).	
c. To change the Constitution legally, we must use the process of constitutional amendment [approval by convention or by legislatures of 3/4 of the states] (Edwards, par. 8).	
d. Guns are safe if people learn to use them safely (Buchwald, par. 4).	
e. Guns don't kill people—people kill people (Buchwald, par. 6).	
f. Guns deter crime (Buchwald, par. 6).	
g. Anyone can afford an inexpensive gun (Buchwald, par. 10).	
h. Guns are useful for hunting (Buchwald, par. 14).	

If you have not already read the essay and answered the Reading Questions, be sure to do so before you proceed.

COMPOSITION QUESTIONS

Listed below are the writing questions. Choose one and write an essay that answers it. (If your instructor is willing, try adapting one of these questions or even writing your own. Be sure to get your instructor's approval—and possibly suggestions for change—before answering your question.)

Whichever question you choose, think of the person who will read your answer. The question may tell who your audience is. If not, think of a person you know and respect—preferably your instructor or a fellow student who will read your essay. Try to convince that person to believe you.

Bring in useful details from the selection(s) you have read and perhaps other incidents you know of. For ideas, review your answers to questions in the Preview and Reading Steps. When you first refer to a reading, give its title (in quotation marks) and the author's full name. Also, give the full name of anyone featured in the article the first time you mention that person. In making any later references, use only the person's last name.

Note: If you are assigned to write one paragraph, think of your answer to the question, and list several key points you could make to support your answer. Then choose just one of the points and explain it in detail.

1. The Second Amendment gives people the right to bear arms but does not say what kind—so Buchwald's fictional "Bomb Lobby" claims that people have the right to carry any arms, including hydrogen bombs. Would you go that far? If not, where would you draw the line? Consider the characteristics and uses of bombs, knives, and various types of guns (Edwards mentions three types in paragraph 9).

2. If the Constitution needs to be changed, is it better to amend it (seek approval by convention/legislature of three-fourths of the states) or to interpret it to fit current trends, beliefs, and situations? Compare amending with interpreting: Who has the power to do each, and how much time would each process take?

3. Explosives, machine guns, and military-purpose semiautomatics are all capable of rapid multiple killings. Use of these weapons is highly

restricted for private citizens but is permitted for the military. Under such circumstances, will the people be able to resist government tyranny?

4. In the United States, are we in more danger from tyrants if we don't have guns—or from criminals and mentally ill killers if guns are widely available? In considering the danger of tyranny, you might compare the World War II experiences of Switzerland, where all adult males had to own guns, and the Jewish ghettoes of Germany and Poland, where no one could own guns.

5. Argue that the United States has no rational, comprehensive policy toward weapons control. What evidence can you find that politicians use this issue to divert attention from the really difficult issues involved in crime?

6. Consider that women are often easy targets for crimes of violence. (See "37 Who Saw Murder Didn't Call Police" in Unit Three.) Consider also that the poor and minorities do not get the same police protection as middle-class whites. Argue for or against the idea that law-abiding citizens need to carry guns for self-protection.

7. The National Rifle Association sponsors gun safety classes. However, home accidents with guns are still alarmingly common. Argue for or against the position that guns can be kept safely in the home.

REVISION QUESTIONS

Once you have finished writing your essay, ask yourself the following questions.

1. Is there any statement the reader might not understand?
2. Is there any statement that might offend the reader?
3. Is there anything that's not very convincing?
4. Have I changed the subject and then changed it back again?
5. Have I said the same thing twice?
6. Do I want to try using any feature of style I've seen in the reading selection?

EDITING QUESTIONS

Once you've made changes, ask someone else to read your essay. Change it again as needed. Then read your essay out loud and answer the following questions.

1. Does every sentence make sense?
2. Does every sentence use the kind of language that most people consider "good English" these days? (*Hint:* Imagine a TV announcer reading it.)
3. Do the periods, commas, and other punctuation show the reader how to interpret what I am writing? Does the use of each punctuation mark conform to the rules that readers expect me to follow?
4. Are the words spelled right?

Note that good grammar, punctuation, and spelling usually make your writing clearer—and always improve your image as a competent, educated writer.

If you make changes in your paper, proofread it again!

UNIT
THIRTEEN

Sex Education: What Is the Best Approach?

PREVIEW STEPS FOR UNIT THIRTEEN

In response to questions 1 and 2, try these steps: Write your answers, talk them over with three or four classmates, and then discuss them with the whole class.

1. In your opinion, what is the typical age when young people become sexually active?

2. a. What do teenagers know about sex?

   b. What do teens need to know about sex?

3. a. Read the title of the first essay (page 189). Name the topic. (Who or what is this essay about?)

   b. Now predict the main idea. (What is the main point the author wants to make about this topic?)

   c. Read the first and last paragraphs. Revise your prediction if necessary. (*Note:* The main idea should sum up the smaller ideas of the essay.)

4. Some words from the essay are listed below, accompanied by quotations. Mark any words you do not know and make an educated guess about their meanings using the context supplied by the quotations— and possibly Appendix A, Word Parts, on page 285. You may want to work with a small group of classmates.

STIs "Ignorance Won't Curb *STIs*"

abstinence "The only 100 percent sure way to avoid pregnancy and STIs was *abstinence*."

bling-bling "They . . . had some interesting motivations for telling it the way they did—namely some federal *bling-bling*."

incentives "Religious interests . . . whipped the government into providing schools with some financial *incentives* for teaching 'abstinence-based' sex education."

comp "Legislators think they're saving money . . . by keeping your pants on, so they don't have to *comp* you for *Valtrex* and diapers."

Valtrex See above quotation.

5. Now read the following essay. As you read, jot down any questions that occur to you.

(*Note:* Question 6 appears after the essay.)

Ignorance Won't Curb STIs

Jamie Fetty

In fifth grade, when you knew the sex education unit was coming, you   1
thought you knew it all. In 10th grade, when you had to take health class, you thought you really knew it all.

    Now you're in college, and you really do know all there is to   2
know about sex. Why should you think differently? Most of those classes you did take offered little new or useful information. Your parents probably didn't elaborate too much either, and it's doubtful your place of worship did much of anything in the way of sex education. It's easy to pick it up from your buddies and a few semi-educational porno tapes, right?

It's easy to roam the earth, get laid occasionally, grow old and die   3
all while thinking you know what you need to know about sex.

What that high school health course did harp on, however, was   4
protecting yourself from sexually transmitted infections [also known
as sexually transmitted diseases, or STDs] and unplanned pregnancy.
Your teachers probably told you on many occasions that the only
100 percent sure way to avoid pregnancy and STIs was abstinence.

They weren't wrong, necessarily; they just had some interesting   5
motivations for telling it the way they did—namely some federal
bling-bling.

Religious interests have whipped the government into providing   6
schools with some financial incentives for teaching what's termed
"abstinence-based" sex education. Legislators think they're saving
money in the long run by keeping your pants on, so they don't have to
comp you for Valtrex and diapers.

The problem with this style of sex education is that it relies heav-   7
ily on scare tactics and is itself afraid of revealing too much. You probably remember some of the gory slides of STIs. Here's a little newsflash:
Most of them don't have noticeable symptoms in most people. Herpes
and genital warts may not be curable, but they are treatable; they don't
just fester into little forests on your privates unless you let them.

That's not to say you should feel free to get infected and infect at   8
will. Certainly, AIDS is a force to be reckoned with. But those slides
are an unrealistic representation of what STIs really are and mislead
people to believe they'll always be able to tell if they have one. And as
scary as they were, they didn't stop you having sex, did they?

The same abstinence-based education that showed you those   9
STIs didn't do much in the way of telling you how to protect yourself
from them. Maybe they forgot to mention that different diseases are
spread different ways. Herpes is spread through skin-to-skin contact;
HIV relies more on transfer of fluid. Maybe they didn't add that many
diseases can be transmitted during oral sex or just fooling around
naked. Maybe they didn't say a blessed thing about homosexual sex.

Maybe they passed around some contraceptives, like cervical   10
caps, condoms, and diaphragms. But did they tell you what kind of lu-
bricant to use to keep the condoms from breaking? Did they tell you
where you can go to get birth control pills and condoms cheap, like
Planned Parenthood or your county health department?

The fact is, whether or not people are ever taught all the ins and   11
outs of doing the deed, they're going to do it. And they'll do it in ways

and places and combinations that your teachers, legislators, and religious leaders never imagined.

Educating teenagers on sex before they start having it means a   12
comprehensive effort from not just school and family, but also religion, from which many people draw their sexual values.

Sending young adults into a sexually revolutionized world with   13
about one-tenth of the knowledge they need isn't going to curb the AIDS epidemic or stem unplanned pregnancies. The ignorance will cost everyone more in the long run.

6. State the essay's main idea in your own words. Compare it to your prediction of the main idea. (*Note:* The main idea should sum up the smaller ideas of the essay.)

PREVIEW STEPS FOR "Frequently Asked Questions About Abstinence Education"

1. a. Read the title of the second essay (page 193). Name the topic. (Who or what is this essay about?)

 b. Now predict the main idea. (What is the main point the author wants to make about this topic?)

 c. Read the first and last paragraphs of the essay. Revise your prediction if necessary. (*Note:* The main idea should sum up the smaller ideas of the essay.)

2. What in the author's background may have led it to the main idea? (See author's background, below title.)

3. Some words from the essay are listed below, accompanied by quotations. Mark any words you do not know and make an educated guess about their meanings using the context supplied by the quotations— and possibly Appendix A, Word Parts, on page 285. You may want to work with a small group of classmates.

Note: This essay contains several medical words, but only a few are needed to understand the major ideas. Only key terms are listed here. If you see other words you don't know, just keep on reading.

abstinence education "Frequently Asked Questions About *Abstinence Education*"

norm "Choosing the best alternative in sexual health is the societal *norm.*"

compromised "a *compromised* and confused signal"

discloses "It *discloses* the social and economic costs of adolescent pregnancy."

loaded "asked the following *loaded* question"

sanction "Durex received a *sanction* . . . for . . . *unsubstantiated* and deceptive claims about their condoms."

unsubstantiated See above quotation.

adage as "the old *adage* goes"

inconclusive "Evaluation of ENABL came out showing *inconclusive* results."

credible "hopes to gather *credible data*"

data See above quotation.

assumptions "This charge is so loaded with faulty *assumptions.*"

implies "This question *implies* that abstinence education is all adolescents will receive."

correlation "Studies show that basic knowledge of and access to condoms by adolescents have low *correlation* with consistent and correct use."

invincibility "Adolescents . . . make choices that reflect an attitude of *invincibility*."

paradigm shift "calling for a *paradigm shift* in the best medical, emotional, and economic interest of America"

4. At the end of the Preview, you may want to go over any new features of style that occur in the following reading selection. You will need to know the terms *jargon* and *metaphor*. For help, see Appendix B, Guide to Literary Terms (page 288), with accompanying exercises on individual features.

5. Before reading "Frequently Asked Questions About Abstinence Education," turn to pages 199–201 and skim the Reading Questions. Then read the essay to find answers to these questions. As you read, jot down any questions that occur to you.

Frequently Asked Questions About Abstinence Education

National Coalition for Abstinence Education

The National Coalition for Abstinence Education (NCAE), begun in 1997, includes 60 independent national, state, and local organizations dedicated to abstinence-centered education and to abstinence before marriage. Member organizations include state abstinence coalitions, abstinence-centered curriculum providers, family advocates, policy councils, research groups, and crisis pregnancy centers.

Reprinted courtesy of the National Coalition for Abstinence Education.

[The National Coalition for Abstinence Education was created specifi-   1
cally to monitor a new federally-funded abstinence education program called Title V. Since some people have concerns about possible
drawbacks to abstinence education, some typical questions are given
below, followed by NCAE's answers.]

**Aren't the majority of students sexually active? Won't they have sex no
matter what they're taught?**

Wrong. Not everybody is doing it. In fact, in 1995 the federal Centers   2
for Disease Control found that nearly half of high school students
(48 percent of girls, 46 percent of boys) had never had a sexual experience. In addition, a large percentage of students who have had sex
wish they had remained virgins—and would like to acquire the skills
to become abstinent.

**Don't comprehensive safe-sex education programs promote abstinence
in a much more "balanced" manner?**

Herein lies the key distinction between abstinence-centered sexuality   3
education and comprehensive (abstinence-plus) safe-sex education.
    The message of abstinence-centered sex education is as follows: 4
It is entirely possible for adolescents to remain abstinent. In fact, the
majority of females ages 12 to 19 have never had sex. Health profes-
sionals agree that abstinence is far and away the single most healthy
choice. But to remain abstinent, teens need to be encouraged and
equipped with medically and socially accurate information on the
consequences of sexual promiscuity and with knowledge, character
development, and skills on how to remain abstinent. And abstinence
needs to be presented in a manner which unapologetically states that
choosing the best alternative in sexual health is the societal norm. A
parallel message to abstinence-centered education would be this:
"Don't smoke; it is not healthy for all the following reasons—and here
are a number of skills to help you avoid smoking."
    The message of comprehensive safe-sex education is as follows: 5
"We'd prefer that you choose abstinence. But if you decide not to
choose abstinence, make sure you use a condom." The parallel
message to comprehensive sex education would be: "We wish you
wouldn't smoke, but if you do, smoke filtered cigarettes—and we will
provide them to you without telling your parents."

The comprehensive safe-sex education message is also known 6
as the "dual message." It sends adolescents a compromised and
confused signal. Further, the "abstinence" component within comprehensive safe-sex programs is treated as just an alternative method
to avoid pregnancy and STDs. The comprehensive safe-sex education message ignores basic human nature—that when given the
option between two alternatives, some people will choose the worse
alternative.

Abstinence-centered sex education, on the other hand, focuses 7
on the root issue by seeking to reduce adolescent sexual activity rather
than inadequately attempting to deal with the consequences after the
fact. It treats abstinence as *the* healthy lifestyle choice—not just
another option.

Isn't it true that abstinence education is "fear-based?"

With one million pregnancies and three million cases of STDs among 8
teens per year, it is a shame that the debate on sexuality education has
been reduced to name-calling.

There are two major problems with dismissing abstinence pro- 9
grams as "fear-based." The first problem deals with defining the terms
we use. What exactly does it mean to be fear-based? Is a program fear-
based if it discloses the social and economic costs of adolescent pregnancy? Is a program fear-based if it truthfully tells teens that condoms
provide little or no protection against certain STDs?

Or is a program fear-based if it simply presents an opposing 10
viewpoint about teen sexuality? A case in point is the slide presenta-
tion produced by the Medical Institute for Sexual Health (MISH).
The Sexuality Information and Education Council of the United
States (SIECUS) labels the MISH material as fear-based. Yet MISH's
statistics come directly from the Centers for Disease Control, the
National Institute for Health, established peer-reviewed medical jour-
nals, and other reputable sources of medical information.

The second problem with the fear-based label is that it assumes 11
there is never a place for legitimate fear. In truth, entire generations
of Americans have avoided various risky behaviors because of the
fear of the consequences. Further, Douglas Kirby in the booklet
No Easy Answers states that "the fear of AIDS may generate greater
receptivity to information about prevention." If conveying truth
about the medical, economic, and social consequences of sexual

promiscuity creates fear in adolescents, then perhaps a little more fear is what we need. Fear is a healthy respect for the consequences of bad decisions.

Didn't a recent study show that most parents are against abstinence education?

Again, the misinformation campaign is hard at work. The Durex Condom Company conducted a telephone survey that asked the following loaded question: "Do you support schools in your district accepting state and federal funds that would prevent them from teaching your children the complete facts about birth control and sexually transmitted diseases?" 12

Here is how Durex spun the results: "More than 82 percent responded that they do not support schools that accept abstinence-only funding." This is not honest research. Durex knows that abstinence programs teach the complete facts about birth control and STDs. They just don't promote condoms. The question Durex asked and the results they reported have nothing to do with each other. 13

What if Durex had asked this question: "Do you support schools in your district accepting federal and state funds that would mandate the promotion of condoms for unmarried teens but prevent schools from teaching your children the complete facts about the failure rates of condoms in protecting against pregnancy and STDs?" 14

Is it any wonder that Durex received a sanction from both the Federal Trade Commission and the National Institute of Child Health and Human Development in 1997 for failure to meet minimum quality standards and unsubstantiated and deceptive claims about their condoms? The TRUTH is that most parents approve of abstinence education. A major survey of 28,000 adults taken by *USA Today* in 1997 found that 56 percent thought the best way to reduce pregnancy is to teach abstinence while only 31 percent thought that the best way is to promote safe sex. 15

Speaking of surveys, NCAE would like to ask readers of this document the following question right now: "As parents, would you want your elected representatives in Washington, your community leaders, your school board members, your governor, and your state health department officials to determine policies impacting the health of your children based on information, opinions, or pressure they receive from the Durex Condom Company or Durex spokesperson Jane Fonda?" 16

Isn't there research to show that abstinence programs don't work?

As the old adage goes, "Figures can lie, and liars can figure." Opponents of abstinence education can find or interpret research to support anything they want to say. An example of this is the analysis of an "abstinence" program entitled ENABL (Education Now and Babies Later) in California. Abstinence-until-marriage advocates had reservations about the program from its inception, because they felt it contained some mixed messages for teens. Abstinence-plus (contraceptive) advocates supported the program—until evaluation of ENABL came out showing inconclusive results. At this point, the safe-sex education advocates distanced themselves from the program and declared abstinence education a failure.

There are credible studies to prove that abstinence programs work. But true abstinence programs, on the whole, have received little or no federal funding for research. Congress realized this situation, which is why Title V funding hopes to gather credible data on abstinence-until-marriage education programs. The REAL question is: will abstinence opponents on many state committees try to sabotage the evaluation process as they have done with the intent of the law?

What about adolescents who, for whatever reason, can't remain abstinent? Isn't it irresponsible to withhold from these teens important information which could save their lives?

This is the biggest charge against abstinence education by its opponents. And this charge is so loaded with faulty assumptions that we must address it point-by-point.

First, this question implies that abstinence education is all adolescents will receive. This is just plain false. We have already established in this document that funding for the safe-sex message remains intact. It is doubtful that a single student will lose access to the contraceptive message directly due to the Title V abstinence funding.

Second, this question implies that abstinence education will not discuss contraceptives, pregnancy, and STDs. Wrong again. The fact is that the Title V funding cannot be used to promote contraceptive use to teens for sex outside of marriage. Abstinence programs do address contraceptives and STDs, but they do so honestly by showing the failure rates for pregnancy and disease prevention.

Third, this question implies that condoms are the answer to   22
pregnancies and STDs. Wrong again. Study after study shows that
adolescents do not use condoms correctly 100 percent of the time.
The Centers for Disease Control states that " 'consistently' means
using a condom every time you have sex—100 percent of the time—
no exceptions." CDC adds that "Used inconsistently, condoms offer
little more protection than when they are not used at all." This fact is
important because studies show that basic knowledge of and access to
condoms by adolescents have low correlation with consistent and
correct use.

Fourth, condoms, even when used correctly, offer little or no   23
protection against human papillomavirus (HPV) and only slightly better protection against chlamydia. Both are among America's fastest-
spreading STDs. HPV is incurable, and both HPV and chlamydia, if
untreated, can lead to serious medical consequences. In fact, genital
cancer caused by HPV has claimed the lives of more females than
AIDS. Further, about 15 percent of female adolescents using condoms get pregnant during the first year of use. So much for the "98
percent effective" claim by the condom industry.

Fifth, NCAE acknowledges that some adolescents will choose to   24
be sexually active no matter how much abstinence is taught. But the
decision to be sexually active is a health decision. Such a decision is too
serious to be promoted or facilitated by school teachers or anyone else
who is not in a position of primary responsibility for the adolescent's
health. It must be made with input from parents, the family's primary-
care physician, a family counselor, and the family's spiritual advisor . . .
people who will strive to move the adolescent back toward truly
healthy behavior.

**With sexual maturity coming at a younger and younger age, and
marriage coming at an older age, is it reasonable to expect people to
remain abstinent until marriage?**

Attacking the Title V Program on the basis of whether or not it is   25
"realistic" to expect adults to remain abstinent until marriage is irrelevant for two reasons. First, the Title V Abstinence Education Program is aimed at adolescents because they are more susceptible to
STDs, have a less developed and more emotionally driven decision-
making capacity, are more influenced by peer pressure, and make
choices that reflect an attitude of invincibility.

Second, and more important, true realism demands we recognize   26
that the sexual revolution has proved to be a disaster for American society. Congress has done just that, calling for a paradigm shift in the best
medical, emotional, and economic interest of America. In this it is following a distinguished precedent: Congress has taken similar bold action before in our history—for example, on drugs, racial equality, and
smoking. It is unfortunate that some people cannot accept the courageous act of Congress and are attempting to sabotage the law.

**Given all of the above answers, why would someone be opposed to the
Title V Abstinence Education Program?**

That's a great question. Frankly, we really don't understand how   27
someone can intellectually oppose the clear message that sexual abstinence among adolescents is the best choice for their physical, educational, and emotional future.

But we do know that an entire industry exists in the U.S. because   28
children are getting pregnant and contracting STDs. This industry
would be financially harmed if adolescents should turn toward
abstinence.

The safe-sex advocates (SIECUS, Planned Parenthood, Jane   29
Fonda, Durex, and their ideological allies) have held a monopoly on
sexuality education since 1971. During their reign, adolescent pregnancies and STDs have reached epidemic levels.

As a society, we can argue about the details of this study or that   30
study or this research or that research. But the reality is that teen pregnancies and STDs have skyrocketed during a time when comprehensive safe-sex education has been the dominant message in America's
classrooms. And on this basis alone, the safe-sex message must be
considered a world-class failure.

**READING QUESTIONS FOR "Frequently Asked Questions About
Abstinence Education"**

Main Idea

1. State the essay's main idea in your own words. Compare it to your
   prediction of the main idea. (*Note:* The main idea should sum up the
   smaller ideas of the essay.)

Organization

2. a. Where in the essay is the main idea found?

    b. Why has the author placed the main idea there?

3. In what order are the paragraphs arranged? (Underline one.) Time/ Least to most important/Most to least important/Simple listing/ Logic: cause and effect/Other logic/Other

Style

4. How formal is the essay? (Circle your choice.)

    [Informal—1—2—3—4—5—6—7—8—9—10—Formal]

    What indicators convinced you? (For a list of possible indicators and two benchmark essays, see Appendix F, The Formality Spectrum, on page 298.)

5. Where do you see the following features of style? List one or two examples of each with their paragraph numbers.

    Features (For definitions, see Appendix B, page 288.)

    a. jargon (statistical)

    b. metaphor

6. What is the abstinence-centered approach (paragraph 4)? How is it different from the abstinence-plus or safe-sex approach (paragraph 5)?

Content

7. Does the author propose any change? If so, what do you think would be the result of such change?

8. Do you agree with the author's main idea? Why or why not?

If you have not already read the essay and answered the Reading Questions, be sure to do so before you proceed.

COMPOSITION QUESTIONS

Listed below are the writing questions. Choose one and write an essay that answers it. (If your instructor is willing, try adapting one of these questions or even writing your own. Be sure to get your instructor's approval—and possibly suggestions for change—before answering your question.)

Whichever question you answer, think of the person who will read your answer. The question may tell who your audience is. If not, think of a person you know and respect—preferably your instructor or a fellow student who will read your essay. Try to convince that person to believe you.

Bring in useful details from the selection(s) you have read and perhaps other incidents you know of. For ideas, review your answers to questions in the Preview and Reading Steps. When you first refer to a reading, give its title (in quotation marks) and the author's full name. Also, give the full name of anyone featured in the article the first time you mention that person. In making any later references, use only the person's last name.

Note: If you are assigned to write one paragraph, think of your answer to the question and list several key points you could make to support your answer. Then choose just one of the points and explain it in detail.

1. Jamie Fetty implies that the typical high school health class uses an abstinence-based, or abstinence-centered, approach, promoting "no sex until marriage" (paragraph 4). By contrast, the National Coalition for Abstinence Education (NCAE) says that since 1971, most high schools have taught abstinence-plus, or safe sex" (paragraph 29)—a message that says, "Better not, but if you're going to do it, do it safely." Since adolescent pregnancies and sexually-transmitted infections (STIs) have increased during this period, what is mostly to blame—the abstinence-centered approach, abstinence-plus instruction, or something else entirely?

2. The National Coalition for Abstinence Education (NCAE) says nearly half of high school students have never had sex (paragraph 2). On the other hand, Jamie Fetty, a college student, says that scary health classes "didn't stop you having sex, did they?" (paragraph 8) and "whether or not people are ever taught all the ins and outs of doing the deed, they're going to do it" (paragraph 11). The two authors seem to be referring to different age levels. Would it be possible to use the abstinence-centered approach to sex education for younger teens and the safe-sex approach for older ones? If so, when should schools change from one to the other? Explain.

3. The National Coalition for Abstinence Education (NCAE) accuses the Durex Condom Company of slanting the questions in a telephone survey to show—falsely—that parents want safe-sex education (paragraphs 12–16). Yet some of its members are writers of abstinence-centered teaching materials who profit from the sale of those materials. Jamie Fetty represents young people, who are "going to do it" (paragraph 11) and therefore want information on how to engage in sex as safely as possible. Parents may resist seeing their children grow up or worry about what the neighbors will think. Since no one is totally neutral, who should choose the schools' approach to sex education? You may want to consider each group's knowledge of young people as well as the group's ability to see and accept other points of view.

4. Consider the role of fear in the two essays. Jamie Fetty indicates that young people fear STIs and unwanted pregnancies but have sex anyway (paragraphs 7 and 8). The National Coalition for Abstinence Education speaks of "legitimate fear" that prompted "entire generations of Americans" to avoid "various risky behaviors because of the

fear of the consequences" (paragraph 11). These days, how well does fear work as a deterrent?

5. The National Coalition for Abstinence Education (NCAE) says, "Abstinence programs do address contraceptives and STDs, but they do so ... by showing the failure rates" of contraceptives (paragraph 21). Jamie Fetty notes that such programs do not tell how a sexually active person can protect against diseases (paragraph 9) or where to get cheap contraceptives (paragraph 10). The NCAE suggests that once young people learn the dangers of being sexually active, many will return to abstinence (paragraphs 2 and 24). Is this likely? Or will most sexually active teens remain active and therefore need to know about contraception and prevention of STIs?

6. Jamie Fetty suggests that being sexually active is the norm for young people (paragraph 11). However, the National Coalition for Abstinence Education (NCAE) says sex education programs should present abstinence until marriage as the norm (paragraph 4). That is, the NCAE says that whether or not abstinence is the norm, presenting it as the norm is valuable. Do you agree with the NCAE? Why or why not?

REVISION QUESTIONS

Once you have finished writing your essay, ask yourself the following questions.

1. Is there any statement the reader might not understand?
2. Is there any statement that might offend the reader?
3. Is there anything that's not very convincing?
4. Have I changed the subject and then changed back again?
5. Have I said the same thing twice?
6. Do I want to try any feature of style I've seen in the reading selection?

EDITING QUESTIONS

Once you've made changes, ask someone else to read your essay. Change it again as needed. Then read your essay out loud and answer the following questions.

1. Does the sentence make sense?
2. Does every sentence use the kind of language that most people consider "good English" these days? (*Hint:* Imagine a TV announcer reading it.)
3. Do the periods, commas, and other punctuation show the reader how to interpret what I am writing? Does the use of each punctuation mark conform to the rules that readers expect me to follow?
4. Are the words spelled right?

Note that good grammar, punctuation, and spelling usually make your writing clearer—and always improve your image as a competent, educated writer.

If you make changes in your paper, proofread it again!

FOURTEEN

Should High School
Be Required?

PREVIEW STEPS FOR UNIT FOURTEEN

In response to questions 1 and 2, try these steps: Write your answers, talk them over with three or four classmates, and then discuss them with the whole class.

1. List some possible benefits of high school and college education.

2. a. Have you known high school students who were attending classes but not really taking part—who had dropped out in spirit? If so, what are some possible reasons for their lack of interest?

  b. Think of some ways this problem could be solved. Try listing all the possible solutions you can think of, no matter how workable they seem.

3. a. Read the title of the first essay (page 207). Name the topic. (Who or what is this essay about?)

  b. Now predict the main idea. (What is the main point the author wants to make about this topic?)

  c. Read the first and last paragraphs. Revise your prediction if necessary. (*Note:* The main idea should sum up the smaller ideas of the essay.)

4. Some words from the essay are listed below, accompanied by quotations. Mark any words you do not know and make an educated guess

about their meanings using the context supplied by the quotations—
and possibly Appendix A, Word Parts, on page 285. You may want to
work with a small group of classmates.

tangible "Beyond money there are less *tangible,* but equally important, benefits."

monetary "The payoff—both *monetary* and otherwise—is well worth
it."

5. Now read the following essay. As you read, jot down any questions
that occur to you.

(*Note:* Question 6 appears after the essay.)

The Value of Higher Education

from Degrees to Succeed

As college costs continue to creep higher, some people have called into   1
question the value of higher education. Is it really worth it to spend
years working towards a degree when that same time could be spent
earning money? It's an interesting question, but the statistics make it
clear: Over time, higher education is well worth the investment.

For instance, take these numbers from the U.S. Census Bureau   2
(1998 data):

Degree Level	Annual Income
No high school diploma	$20,110
High school graduate	$28,307
Associate's degree	$36,392
Bachelor's degree	$50,056
Master's degree	$63,220

Workers with an associate's degree earned nearly 25% more than   3
those with just a high school diploma; that may not sound like much

---

for one year—but over just ten years, that's another $80,000! A bachelor's degree holder will typically earn $600,000 more than a high-school educated worker over his or her lifetime. And professional degree earners (MBAs, PhDs, JDs, MDs, etc.) will earn even more!

And don't forget the perceived value of higher education—most   4
employers, when choosing between a degree-holder and a high-school graduate, will usually choose the college graduate without hesitation.

Beyond money there are less tangible, but equally important,   5
benefits for people with higher-education degrees. As the world and technology change rapidly, more jobs require education beyond high school and, with a college education, you'll be better prepared for a changing work environment. Whereas fifty years ago many workers expected to be in the same career for most of their lives, workers today will face multiple careers in the years ahead—some that don't even exist yet! (Think of today's web designers and where they were 10 years ago.) Odds are also good that higher education will expose you to people, ideas, and topics that you would never encounter in a high-school setting. You can't put a price tag on personal growth.

There's no denying that higher education can be expensive, but   6
the payoff—both monetary and otherwise—is well worth it. Take the plunge and make the most of your educational experience, and your career!

6. State the essay's main idea in your own words. Compare it to your prediction of the main idea. (*Note:* The main idea should sum up the smaller ideas of the essay.)

PREVIEW STEPS FOR "Obsessive Compulsion: The Folly of Mandatory High-School Attendance"

Note: Before dealing with question 1, you may want to check the meanings of *obsessive, compulsion, folly, mandatory, stigma,* and *coercion,* some of which appear in the title.

1. a. Read the title of the second essay (page 211). Name the topic. (Who or what is this essay about?)

b. Now predict the main idea. (What is the main point the author wants to make about this topic?)

c. Read the first and last paragraphs of the essay. Revise your prediction if necessary. (*Note:* The main idea should sum up the smaller ideas of the essay.)

2. What in the author's background may have led him to the main idea? (See author's background, below title.)

3. Some words from the essay are listed below, accompanied by quotations. Mark any words you do not know and make an educated guess about their meanings using the context supplied by the quotations—and possibly Appendix A, Word Parts, on page 285. You may want to work with a small group of classmates.

stigma "The *stigma* of dropping out . . . is so great . . . that it is unthinkable."

compulsory "*Compulsory*-attendance laws forbid students to drop out until they turn 16."

negligible "a *negligible* effect on the dropout rate"

assumption "The evidence . . . seems to support this *assumption*."

coerced "*coerced* high-school education"

peer "It may be *peer* influences."

amenable "students who are *amenable* to education"

secular "*secular* private schools, *parochial* schools, and *charter* schools"

parochial See above quotation.

charter See above quotation.

disproportionately "Internal dropouts contribute *disproportionately* to fights and assaults."

chronic "Some schools in large systems suffer *chronic* violence as the internal dropouts multiply."

diverse "these *diverse* educational settings (suburban, rural, and inner-city)"

jaded "They have a *jaded,* often *cavalier* attitude toward education and its importance."

cavalier See above quotation.

criminologists "a study of California youths conducted by *criminologists*"

impoverished "Those who do not complete high school are doomed to live an economically and culturally *impoverished* life."

egocentric "McDonald's is ... successful at training *egocentric* teenagers."

revocable "Deciding not to complete high school is a *revocable* choice."

GED "The former governor of New Jersey ... dropped out of school at 17 [and] ... realized that his lack of a diploma was a handicap, [so he] took the *GED* exam."

4. At the end of the Preview, you may want to go over any new features of style that occur in the following reading selection. You will need to know the terms *allusion* and *metaphor.* For help, see Appendix B, Guide to Literary Terms (page 288), with accompanying exercises on individual features.
5. Before reading "Obsessive Compulsion," turn to pages 214–215 and skim the Reading Questions. Then read the essay to find answers to these questions. As you read, jot down any questions that occur to you.

Obsessive Compulsion: The Folly of Mandatory High-School Attendance

Jackson Toby

After earning a doctorate from Harvard University, Jackson Toby (1925–) spent 50 years as a professor of sociology at Rutgers University and directed its Institute for Criminological Research for 26 of those years. Known for his unconventional views, he has published more than 40 opinion pieces in major newspapers and newsmagazines.

Note: Toby presents his proposal by listing four "facts" and three "myths" (ideas he says are not true).

In all the commentary on the murders at Columbine High School in Littleton, Colorado, an obvious question has gone unraised: Why, if Eric Harris and Dylan Klebold were miserable at school, didn't they simply drop out? Why did they feel trapped? The answer is apparently that the stigma of dropping out of high school is so great in middle-class suburbs that it is unthinkable. 1

In all states, compulsory-attendance laws forbid students to drop out until they turn 16 and sometimes until they turn 18 or even older. States have also imposed penalties on dropouts and their families, including reduced welfare benefits. West Virginia began in 1988 to revoke the driver's licenses of minors who drop out of school, and other states have since adopted this approach, even though it has had a negligible effect on the dropout rate in West Virginia. 2

Why is dropping out regarded as a terrible mistake? First, it is assumed to be a personal mistake because, in a complex, information-oriented society, a high-school education is needed to avoid unemployment. The evidence about the comparative earnings of people with various levels of education seems to support this assumption. Second, it is assumed to be a social mistake. 3

Chester E. Finn, Jr., the education analyst and former Reagan-administration official, describes education as "something that a 4 decently functioning society obliges people to get a certain amount of, even if they don't really want to."

But the case for coerced high-school education—so rarely   5
questioned—really relies on ignoring certain facts and swallowing certain myths. First, the facts:

Fact 1: Some students do not learn what school is supposed to   6
teach them: reading and writing, history and geography, arithmetic, and
science. The reason may be lack of parental encouragement and help, which research has shown to be crucial in motivating children to learn; it may be that students have physical or psychological handicaps; it may be peer influences. Whatever the reasons, kids who don't understand what is going on in class are bored and disruptive when they attend at all. They become internal dropouts, still enrolled but making no effort to learn.

Fact 2: The presence of these internal dropouts discourages   7
teachers. They often wear high-school teachers down to the point that the teachers stop putting forth the effort required to put ideas into the heads of students. One consequence of burnout is enormous teacher-turnover rates, especially in inner-city high schools with large proportions of internal dropouts. But some teachers hold on grimly, taking as many days off as they are entitled to, including "sick" days (known in the trade as "mental-health" days). Of course, burned-out teachers lose effectiveness at teaching students who are in fact amenable to education; that probably is part of the explanation for the greater satisfaction of students and their parents with secular private schools, parochial schools, and charter schools.

Fact 3: Internal dropouts contribute disproportionately to fights and   8
assaults, and probably to thefts, in public high schools. While occasional violence occurs in most schools, some schools in large systems such as those in New York and Washington, D.C., suffer chronic violence as the internal dropouts multiply while the more serious students flee to private or parochial schools or a school system in the suburbs.

Fact 4: In some other industrial countries where high-school en-   9
rollment is voluntary, not compulsory, a significant proportion of young
people enroll and graduate. Japan is particularly noteworthy because its high schools are not only voluntary but also a major expense. Yet a higher percentage of Japanese young people than American ones graduate from high school. The Japanese go to high school, and do much more homework than Americans, because they are convinced by their parents and the cultural values of their society that their futures depend on a good education.

The United States is surely not Japan, so we may not be able to   10
convince as many of our young people to attend and graduate from
school as the Japanese do. But persuasion is possible. We do not compel
college attendance, yet the college-attendance rate in America is still the
highest in the world. Making high school voluntary and the courses
tougher would affect perhaps 5 to 10 percent of students currently enrolled in public high schools. The majority will do whatever they must
to graduate. So why do most people shrink from the conclusion that
compulsory high-school attendance is unnecessary? On to the myths.

[*Note:* The author first labels each italicized statement below as a
myth—untrue—then argues against it.]

Myth 1: Adolescents can be educated whether they like it or not.   11
Actually, education in any meaningful sense depends on a cooperative
relationship between teacher and student. Unmotivated students do
not learn enough to justify the effort to keep them enrolled. Laurence
Steinberg of Temple University, Bradford Brown of the University of
Wisconsin, and Sandford Dornbusch of Stanford University conducted a study of 20,000 students in nine public high schools in
Wisconsin and northern California from 1987 to 1990. They concluded that about 40 percent of the students in these diverse educational settings (suburban, rural, and inner-city) were "disengaged"
from the educational enterprise. Here is how Steinberg put it in his
book *Beyond the Classroom:*

> Disengaged students . . . do only as much as it takes to avoid get-
> ting into trouble. They do not exert much effort in the class-
> room, are easily distracted during class, and expend little energy
> on in-school or out-of-school assignments. They have a jaded,
> often cavalier attitude toward education and its importance to
> their future success or personal development.

Myth 2: The students who will leave school as soon as they can   12
will generate a crime wave. Two studies exploded that myth a generation ago: a national study of adolescents conducted by researchers at
the University of Michigan *(Dropping Out: Problem or Symptom?)*
and a study of California youths conducted by criminologists Delbert
S. Elliot and Harwin L. Ross *(Delinquency and Dropout).* Both studies followed students throughout their high-school years and beyond,
gathering delinquency data covering the entire period. They independently reached the same conclusion: While it is true that high-
school dropouts had a higher crime rate than other students, the

higher delinquency rate preceded their dropping out of school and did not increase after they left.

Myth 3: Those who do not complete high school are doomed to live   13
an economically and culturally impoverished life. What kind of job can a dropout get? How about flipping burgers for the minimum wage? Fast-food restaurants have a reputation for offering dead-end jobs, yet they are actually a major trainer of the poorly educated for jobs that lead into the middle class. McDonald's is more successful at training egocentric teenagers, including dropouts, to become good enough workers to move on to better jobs than most government training programs.

The surprising statistical finding of *Dropping Out,* which looked   14
into the employment experiences of dropouts, is that on average they did at least as well as high-school graduates who did not go on to college. Formal education is not the only path to responsible adulthood. It should also be remembered that deciding not to complete high school is a revocable choice. The former governor of New Jersey, Jim Florio, dropped out of school at 17, joined the Navy, realized that his lack of a diploma was a handicap, took the GED exam, and eventually completed college and law school. Instead of locking the high-school doors to prevent students from leaving, we ought to let those who do leave know that the doors remain open should they wish to return.

The coercion of compulsory education hasn't worked well for a   15
simple reason: Some people do not learn to tolerate school, much less to like it. And some of them engage in desperate coping measures. There was little point in keeping Eric Harris and Dylan Klebold at Columbine High.

READING QUESTIONS FOR "Obsessive Compulsion"

Main Idea

1. State the essay's main idea in your own words. Compare it to your prediction of the main idea. (*Note:* The main idea should sum up the smaller ideas of the essay.)

Organization

2. a. Where in the essay is the main idea found?

b. Why has the author placed the main idea there?

3. In what order are the paragraphs arranged? (Underline one.) Time/ Least to most important/Most to least important/Simple listing/ Logic: cause and effect/Other logic/Other

Style

4. How formal is the essay? (Circle your choice.)

   [Informal—1—2—3—4—5—6—7—8—9—10—Formal]

   What indicators convinced you? (For a list of possible indicators and two benchmark essays, see Appendix F, The Formality Spectrum, on page 298.)

5. Where do you see the following features of style? List one or two examples of each with their paragraph numbers.

   Features (For definitions, see Appendix B, page 288.)

   a. allusion

   b. metaphor

Content

6. Does the author propose any change? If so, what do you think would be the result of such change?

7. Do you agree with the author's main idea? Why or why not?

If you have not already read the essay and answered the Reading Questions, be sure to do so before you proceed.

COMPOSITION QUESTIONS

Listed below are the writing questions. Choose one and write an essay that answers it. (If your instructor is willing, try adapting one of these questions or even writing your own. Be sure to get your instructor's approval—and possibly suggestions for change—before answering your question.)

Whichever question you answer, think of the person who will read your answer. The question may tell who your audience is. If not, think of a person you know and respect—preferably your instructor or a fellow student who will read your essay. Try to convince that person to believe you.

Bring in useful details from the selection(s) you have read and perhaps other incidents you know of. For ideas, review your answers to questions in the Preview and Reading Steps. When you first refer to a reading, give its title (in quotation marks) and the author's full name. Also, give the full name of anyone featured in the article the first time you mention that person. In making any later references, use only the person's last name.

Note: If you are assigned to write one paragraph, think of your answer to the question and list several key points you could make to support your answer. Then choose just one of the points and explain it in detail.

1. "The Value of Higher Education" encourages all students to stay in school. By contrast, Jackson Toby suggests that it would be better to let some students drop out.* He is not concerned about the number, saying that only 5 to 10 percent would actually drop out (paragraph 10). But this percentage might be higher for some groups of students, such as those mentioned in paragraph 6, whose parents don't support education. Would Toby's proposed change be unfair to any of these groups?

2. Jackson Toby says, "McDonald's is more successful at training. . . teenagers . . . than most government training programs" (paragraph 13).

---

*Write "He will drop out" as two words (when using *drop out* as a verb).

However, "The Value of Higher Education" says that high school[*] and college give students a broader education—to prepare them for more than one job in case the job market changes (paragraph 5). Should the schools imitate the McDonald's methods or offer a broader education? Which model is better for potential dropouts?[**]

3. Jackson Toby says students should be free to drop out if school is too difficult. "The Value of Higher Education" implies that everyone should try to complete high school and college. What message should schools be sending to students—quit if school isn't working, or stay and make it work?

4. The 1998 U.S. census says high-school graduates made over $8,000 more than dropouts every year they worked ("The Value of Higher Education," paragraph 2). By contrast, the book *Dropping Out* says dropouts did at least as well as high-school graduates[†] (Jackson Toby, paragraph 14). Toby mentions that this book was written "a generation ago." In your opinion, what is the main reason for such a change in the statistics?

5. "The Value of Higher Education" seems most concerned with what is best for the potential dropout. By contrast, Jackson Toby seems more concerned for teachers and other students, saying they will be better off if troublemakers leave. Toby says troublemakers cause teacher burnout (paragraph 7), as well as fights, assaults, and probably thefts (paragraph 8). How can schools meet the needs of all three groups—potential dropouts, other students, and teachers?

6. "The Value of Higher Education" shows the increased earnings for students who complete high school and college, implying that students drop out because they simply don't realize the benefits of staying in. By

---

[*],[†]You can use the words *high school* in two ways.
Example 1: "They attend high school."
The words *high school* act as a noun (stand for a place). Write them as two separate words.
Example 2: "High school attendance is required."
Example 3: "High-school attendance is required."
Here, the words *high school* act as an adjective (describe something). Either write them as two separate words or join them with a hyphen. Both ways are currently used, so we suggest that you follow your instructor's wishes.
[**]Write "He is a dropout" as one word (when using *dropout* as a noun).

contrast, Jackson Toby gives three possible reasons why students may lose interest in education (paragraph 6). In your opinion, what is the most important reason why students lose interest? What should schools do to help these students succeed in life?

7. "The Value of Higher Education" admits that students who stay in school are giving up money they could be earning if they worked full time (paragraph 1) but says they will make up for the lost earnings later. Jackson Toby says in paragraph 14 that dropouts do at least as well as high-school graduates (though not as well as college graduates), so they may as well drop out if they want to. Do 14-year-olds have the maturity to make such an important long-term decision?

8. "The Value of Higher Education" seems to be aimed at students (and possibly their parents), presenting the advantages of completing high school or even more education. "Obsessive Compulsion" seems to be aimed at school officials, discussing the advantages of getting rid of troublemakers. Who should decide whether a student has the right to drop out of school—the student, the parents, or the school?

9. Jackson Toby says that Japan already has voluntary high-school enrollment with a high graduation rate (paragraph 9). He implies that what works for Japan would work in the United States. Is that a reasonable conclusion? Explain.

REVISION QUESTIONS

Once you have finished writing your essay, ask yourself the following questions.

1. Is there any statement the reader might not understand?
2. Is there any statement that might offend the reader?
3. Is there anything that's not very convincing?
4. Have I changed the subject and then changed back again?
5. Have I said the same thing twice?
6. Do I want to try any feature of style I've seen in the reading selection?

EDITING QUESTIONS

Once you've made changes, ask someone else to read your essay. Change it again as needed. Then read your essay out loud and answer the following questions.

1. Does the sentence make sense?
2. Does every sentence use the kind of language that most people consider "good English" these days? (*Hint:* Imagine a TV announcer reading it.)
3. Do the periods, commas, and other punctuation show the reader how to interpret what I am writing? Does the use of each punctuation mark conform to the rules that readers expect me to follow?
4. Are the words spelled right?

Note that good grammar, punctuation, and spelling usually make your writing clearer—and always improve your image as a competent, educated writer.

If you make changes in your paper, proofread it again!

UNIT
FIFTEEN

Pornography: Free Speech or Harm to Women?

PREVIEW STEPS FOR UNIT FIFTEEN

In response to questions 1 and 2, try these steps: Write your answers, talk them over with three or four classmates, and then discuss them with the whole class.

1. For the next three or four minutes, list as many reasons as you can for legally allowing pornography.

2. For the next three or four minutes, list as many reasons as you can for NOT legally allowing pornography.

3. a. Read the title of the first essay (page 223). Name the topic. (Who or what is this essay about?)

   b. Now predict the main idea. (What is the main point the author wants to make about this topic?)

   c. Read the first and last paragraphs. Revise your prediction if necessary. (*Note:* The main idea should sum up the smaller ideas of the essay.)

4. Some words from the essay are listed below, accompanied by quotations. Mark any words you do not know and make an educated guess about their meanings using the context supplied by the quotations—and possibly Appendix A, Word Parts, on page 285. You may want to work with a small group of classmates.

   misogynistic "It's about a doctor so obsessed with keeping a young woman all to himself that he amputates her legs and arms and keeps what's left of her in a box. Maybe it's art, maybe it's a disgusting, *misogynistic* piece of *claptrap*."

claptrap See above quotation.

legacy "All of us, women and men, have to salute our Founding Fathers and say: Thanks for the *legacy* of freedom you gave us."

5. Now read the following essay. As you read, jot down any questions that occur to you.

(*Note:* Question 6 appears after the essay.)

Why We Must Put Up with Porn

Susan Isaacs

If you and I were sitting together, listening to a little Vivaldi, sipping herbal tea, chatting about men and women, arguing about politics and art, we might get around to what to do about the porn problem—at which point you'd slam down your cup and demand, How can you of all people defend smut-peddling slimeballs who portray women being beaten and raped?   1

Well . . .   2

You're the one (you'd be sure to remind me) who hates any kind of violence against women. You're the one who even gets upset when James Cagney, in *The Public Enemy,* the 1931 classic, smashes a grapefruit into Mae Clarke's face, for heaven's sake!   3

That's right, I'd say.   4

So? Don't you want to protect women? Why not ban books and films that degrade women?   5

Let's have another cup of tea and I'll tell you.   6

The problem is, who is going to decide what is degrading to women? If there were to be a blue-ribbon panel, who would select its   7

---

members? Jerry Falwell of the religious right? Andrea Dworkin, who has written that all sexual intercourse is an expression of men's contempt for women? They certainly do not speak for me. Okay, what about a blue-ribbon panel of, say, Hillary Rodham Clinton, Sandra Day O'Connor, Jackie Joyner-Kersee, Katie Couric, Wendy Wasserstein, and Anne Tyler? A dream team, right?

Sure. But I'll be damned if I'd hand over my right to determine   8
what I see and read to America's best and brightest any more than I would to my husband, my editor, my best friend, or my mother. And you, my tea-sipping companion, and you, out there in Salt Lake City, Sioux City, Jersey City: You also should decide for yourself.

But, you might say next, this sexually explicit garbage eggs peo-   9
ple on to vicious criminal behavior.

The truth is, this remains unproven. While research has pointed   10
to a correlation between both alcohol abuse and dysfunctional families and violent behavior, it has not established the same link between pornography and violence. When serial killer Ted Bundy was trying to get his death sentence commuted in 1989, he claimed that a lifetime of reading pornography made him the monster he was. And why shouldn't he? It was an easy out: It would clear him of responsibility for his evil deeds.

But, you say, proof or no proof, there is so much trash out there   11
and I don't like it! Well, neither do I, but censorship is not the answer. The First Amendment gives you the right to picket a theater or start a letter-writing campaign against any work you consider loathsome. You do not have the right, however, to prevent others from seeing it.

Look, it's rarely easy being a defender of the First Amendment.   12
More often than not, we wind up fighting for the right to burn the flag or burn a cross or say awful racist and sexist things. Or consider a movie like the upcoming *Boxing Helena*. It's about a doctor so obsessed with keeping a young woman all to himself that he amputates her legs and arms and keeps what's left of her in a box. Maybe it's art, maybe it's a disgusting, misogynistic piece of claptrap.

But if we want our great and beloved Constitution to work, we   13
cannot abandon its principles when they don't suit us. To have speech we love, we have to defend speech we hate. Besides, most controversial material is open to more than one interpretation. To some, Robert Mapplethorpe's black-and-white photographs of nude men are breathtaking art; others think them immoral filth. In my own novel, *Almost Paradise,* the heroine, as a child, is sexually abused by her

father. This criminal betrayal colors her life. It was a nightmare for my character, and painful, even sickening, for me to write. Had some zealot been able to ban all references to incest—regardless of context or purpose—my novel would never have gotten written.

We can't hand over to anyone the power to decide what's appro- 14 priate for all. Because a year or a decade from now, someone might want to ban all depictions of career women or day-care centers, using the argument that they undermine family unity. Think that sounds extreme? Don't—historically, censorship has often been the first step toward dictatorship.

That's why we have to stand up for the First Amendment and 15 not be moved, no matter how tempting it is to succumb to a just-this-once mentality. All of us, women and men, have to salute our Founding Fathers and say: Thanks for the legacy of freedom you gave us. And don't worry. We have the strength, the will, and yes, the guts to defend it.

6. State the essay's main idea in your own words. Compare it to your pre-diction of the main idea. (*Note:* The main idea should sum up the smaller ideas of the essay.)

PREVIEW STEPS FOR "Pornography and Civil Liberties"

1. a. Read the title of the second essay (page 228). Name the topic. (Who or what is this essay about?)

   b. Now predict the main idea. (What is the main point the author wants to make about this topic?)

   c. Read the first and last paragraphs of the essay. Revise your predic-tion if necessary. (*Note:* The main idea should sum up the smaller ideas of the essay.)

2. What in the author's background may have led her to the main idea? (See author's background, below title.)

3. Some words from the essay are listed below, accompanied by quotations. Mark any words you do not know and make an educated guess about their meanings using the context supplied by the quotations— and possibly Appendix A, Word Parts, on page 285. You may want to work with a small group of classmates.

objectification "This is not an issue of morality but of power and of sexual *objectification,* sexual *subordination,* sexual violence, and *eroticized* inequality."

subordination See above quotation.

eroticized See above quotation.

insatiable "Women [are] presented as constantly sexually available, *insatiable* and *voracious,* or passive and *servile,* serving men sexually."

voracious See above quotation.

servile See above quotation.

prepubescent "It includes visual records of child sexual abuse (called child pornography) and material promoting *prepubescent* sex."

coercion "We find chilling accounts of sexual violence, rape, and *coercion.*"

fellatio She is "presented in the film as 'liberated' and with insatiable appetite for *fellatio.*"

ordinance "The Council was considering an *ordinance* to add pornography as discrimination against women to existing civil rights statutes."

"johns" "Ex-prostitutes describe being forced by . . . the *'johns'* to copy what they had seen in pornography."

explicit "the sexually *explicit* and violent"

exploitation "Pornography is a systematic practice of *exploitation* and subordination based on sex that *differentially* harms women."

differentially See above quotation.

bigotry "The *bigotry* and contempt [pornography] produces . . . harm women's rights."

precedence "The free speech rights . . . took *precedence* over women's rights."

libertarian left "Women who do speak against pornography are attacked constantly . . . by the sexual liberals and the *libertarian left,* who include the defenders of *sadomasochism* and who define sexual liberation in terms of sexual violence and *sadistic* pornography."

sadomasochism See above quotation.

sadistic See above quotation.

emanating "the misrepresentations and distortions *emanating* from these *constituencies*"

constituencies See above quotation.

religious right "Feminist antipornography campaigners have made alliances with the *religious right.*"

scenarios "in *scenarios* of *degradation,* humiliation, injury, and torture"

degradation See above quotation.

transsexuals "It also applies to children or men or *transsexuals,* and so it covers *pedophilia* and violent and subordinating gay pornography but excludes erotica."

pedophilia See above quotation.

abolition "any more than the *abolition* of slavery ended racism and racial violence"

4. At the end of the Preview, you may want to go over any new features of style that occur in the following reading selection. You will need to know the term *irony of wording*. For help, see Appendix B, Guide to Literary Terms (page 288), with accompanying exercises on individual features.

5. Before reading "Pornography and Civil Liberties," turn to pages 233–234 and skim the Reading Questions. Then read the essay to find answers to these questions. As you read, jot down any questions that occur to you.

Pornography and Civil Liberties

Catherine Itzin

Catherine Itzin (1944–) writes here in a personal capacity as an honorary research fellow in the Violence, Abuse, and Gender Relations Research Unit at the University of Bradford in Bradford, West Yorkshire, England. She is an inspector in the Social Services Inspectorate at the Department of Health and editor/co-author of Pornography: Women, Violence and Civil Liberties, *Oxford University Press, 1993.*

The law does not look at pornography from the position of women   1
and children. If it did, it would see that this is not an issue of morality but of power and of sexual objectification, sexual subordination, sexual violence, and eroticized inequality.

You do not have to look far to find the evidence. In the United   2
Kingdom, the top shelves of newsstands in every neighborhood are stocked with mainstream so-called "adult entertainment" magazines [in which] . . . women [are] presented as constantly sexually available, insatiable and voracious, or passive and servile, serving men sexually. There are forms of technically legal child pornography where women

---

Catherine Itzin is Research Professor and Associate Director of the International Centre for the Study of Violence and Abuse at the University of Sunderland, and Director of the Violence Abuse and Mental Health Programme at the National Institute for Mental Health in England. *Pornography: Women, Violence and Civil Liberties* (1993) edited by Catherine Itzin is available from Oxford University Press.

have their pubic hair shaved and are posed to look like little girls, linking male sexual arousal to children's bodies. There is also sexual violence, with women being humiliated, whipped, and beaten.

Illegal pornography also circulates, sold from under the counter. This pornography features women bound and gagged, raped and tortured. . . . It includes visual records of child sexual abuse (called child pornography) and material promoting prepubescent sex. There is evidence of the existence of "snuff films" in which women and children are sexually murdered on camera.

The market in pornography in the United States is similar— perhaps worse. Indeed, pornography is a multi-billion dollar international industry, the majority of which is run by organized crime in the United States and in the United Kingdom by part of the "respectable" mainstream publishing business. Pornography is also part of the international trade and traffic in women and children for prostitution.

The Harm in Making Pornography

Apart from the harm that is visible in pornography . . . a very substantial body of evidence shows that women and children are harmed through the making and use of pornography.

If we look at the experience of women working within the pornography industry, we find chilling accounts of sexual violence, rape, and coercion. The case of Linda Marchiano—who under the name of Linda Lovelace was the "star" of the 1970s porn film *Deep Throat*—is one of many examples. Linda—presented in the film as "liberated" and with an insatiable appetite for fellatio—was held captive for two years under threat of death, by her boss, Charles Traynor. During the filming, she was hypnotized to suppress the normal gag response. She was tortured when she tried to escape, was never let out of Traynor's sight, and, at gunpoint, suffered innumerable other indignities. When she finally escaped and told her story, it was echoed by that of a great many other women involved in the pornography business.

During hearings held by Minneapolis City Council in 1983 when the Council was considering an ordinance to add pornography as discrimination against women to existing civil rights statutes, ex-prostitutes described being forced by their pimps to be filmed having sex with dogs, or by the "johns" to copy what they had seen in pornography.

In the United Kingdom, a recent article in the *Guardian* . . .   8
includes an interview with a woman who was used throughout
her childhood for the making of pornographic films [involving]
adults, animals, and other children. These examples illustrate some of
the harm experienced by women and children in the making of
pornography. . . .

For purposes of research, pornography has been divided into   9
three categories: the sexually explicit and violent; the sexually explicit
and nonviolent, but subordinating and dehumanizing; and the sexually explicit, nonviolent, and nonsubordinating that is based on mutu-
ality and which can be called "erotica." Research consistently shows
that harmful effects are associated with the first two, but that the
third—erotica—is harmless.

Pornography and the Law

Government inquiries in Canada (1985), the United States (1986),   10
Australia (1988), and New Zealand (1989) have accepted the evidence
of the links between pornography and harm to women and children.
In 1992, the Canadian Supreme Court ruled unanimously that violent,
subordinating, and dehumanizing pornography contributes to sexual
violence and reinforces sexual inequality. The courts in Canada also
have successfully used the three academic research categories [vio-
lent, subordinating, and merely erotic pornography] and the evidence
of harm to prosecute violent and subordinating material and to acquit
sexually explicit material that is nonviolent and nonsubordinating
(including gay and lesbian material).

Even the Federal court in the United States, which in 1985 con-   11
sidered the civil rights ordinance drafted by the lawyer Catharine
MacKinnon and the writer Andrea Dworkin and which was passed
by the Minneapolis and Indianapolis city councils, concluded that
"pornography is a systematic practice of exploitation and subordination based on sex that differentially harms women. The bigotry and
contempt it produces, the acts of aggression it fosters, harm women's
opportunities for equality and rights of all kinds." But the Court then
decided that "this simply demonstrated the power of pornography
as speech" and ruled that the free speech rights of the pornography
industry took precedence over women's rights to be free of sexual
violence and inequality.

The real free speech issue for women is getting access to speech, 12 and the free speech issue in current debates on pornography is being able to speak very much at all against pornography. Women who do speak against pornography are attacked constantly, stereotyped and monsterized, not just by the pornography industry, but also by the sexual liberals and the libertarian left, who include the defenders of sadomasochism and who define sexual liberation in terms of sexual violence and sadistic pornography.

Among the misrepresentations and distortions emanating from 13 these constituencies are that feminist antipornography campaigners have made alliances with the religious right, are sexually repressed, and believe that pornography is the sole cause of women's oppression. This is all demonstrably untrue, as is the suggestion that being against pornography means being for censorship. On the contrary: given the scale of harm to which it contributes, it is clear that pornography is not compatible with the civil liberties of women.

Limiting Pornography without Censorship

So what is the answer? Should there be state censorship of violent and 14 subordinating pornography? I do not think so. Censorship is danger- ous: Freedom of speech matters. And it is now possible to legislate against pornography without censorship, using a harm-based equality approach rather than the obscenity approach that has proven to be unenforceable, inappropriate, and ineffective in dealing with pornog- raphy and has been used to prosecute gay and lesbian material which is not pornography.

One proposal in the United Kingdom is for sex-discrimination 15 legislation that would enable people who could prove they were victims of pornography-related harm to take civil action against the manufacturers and distributors of pornography. This would not ban the publication of pornography, and it would give no power to the state to censor.

Another proposal is to use the U.K. Race Relations Act as a 16 model for legislating against pornography that could be shown to have contributed to the incitement of sexual hatred and violence. In the United Kingdom, race-hatred literature is illegal because of the "identifiable harm" it causes to Black and Jewish people who do not regard the legislation as censorship, but as a guarantee of a measure of some freedom from racial hatred, violence, and discrimination. Why should not the same thing apply to women and pornography?

Take pornography out of the moral realm and place it in the con-   17
text of the evidence of harm and the structures of power and abuse, and you find that it is not impossible to define at all. MacKinnon and Dworkin came up with a workable legal definition at the request of the City Council of Minneapolis. Pornography, they say, is graphic [and] sexually explicit, and it subordinates women. It also presents women in one or more of the following eight conditions of harm:

- dehumanized as sexual objects, things, or commodities;
- as sexual objects who enjoy humiliation or pain;
- as sexual objects who experience sexual pleasure in rape, incest, or other sexual assault; as sexual objects tied up, cut up, or mutilated or bruised, or physically hurt;
- in positions and postures of sexual submission, servility, or display;
- being penetrated by objects or animals;
- in scenarios of degradation, humiliation, injury, and torture;
- shown as filthy or inferior, bleeding, bruised, or hurt in a context that makes these conditions sexual;
- with their body parts (including vaginas, breasts, buttocks, or anuses) exhibited such that women are reduced to those parts.

Although this definition is based upon the treatment of women,   18
it also applies to children or men or transsexuals—and so it covers pedophilia and violent and subordinating gay pornography but excludes erotica.

None of this could guarantee the elimination of sexism and sexual   19
violence any more than the abolition of slavery ended racism and racial violence. But like pornography today, black slavery in the United States was a major international profit-making industry—and it was ended.

People have agreed to forgo certain freedoms because of the   20
damage and harm they do to other people. In the United Kingdom, these include the freedom to steal, to assault, to rape, to murder, to incite racial hatred and discrimination, and to discriminate in employment on the grounds of race or sex.

The freedom to incite sexual hatred, sexual violence, and sex dis-   21
crimination through pornography is another freedom people should agree to forgo to ensure and safeguard the freedom, safety, and civil liberties of women.

READING QUESTIONS FOR "Pornography and Civil Liberties"

Main Idea

1. State the essay's main idea in your own words. Compare it to your prediction of the main idea. (*Note:* The main idea should sum up the smaller ideas of the essay.)

Organization

2. a. Where in the essay is the main idea found?

   b. Why has the author placed the main idea there?

3. In what order are the paragraphs arranged? (Underline one.) Time/ Least to most important/Most to least important/Simple listing/ Logic: cause and effect/Other logic/Other

Style

4. How formal is the essay? (Circle your choice.)

   [Informal—1—2—3—4—5—6—7—8—9—10—Formal]

   What indicators convinced you? (For a list of possible indicators and two benchmark essays, see Appendix F, The Formality Spectrum, on page 298.)

5. Where do you see the following feature of style? List one or two examples with their paragraph numbers.

   Feature (For a definition, see Appendix B, page 288.)

   irony of wording

   Content

6. Susan Isaacs writes that there is no proof that "sexually explicit garbage eggs people on to vicious criminal behavior" (paragraphs 9 and 10). By contrast, Catherine Itzin quotes research to show that when violent or subordinating material is separated from the merely erotic, the first two have harmful effects (paragraph 9). Explain this discrepancy between the authors. Have the courts based their decisions on statements like Isaacs's or statements like Itzin's?

7. Does the author propose any change? If so, what do you think would be the result of such change?

8. Do you agree with the author's main idea? Why or why not?

If you have not already read the essay and answered the Reading Questions, be sure to do so before you proceed.

COMPOSITION QUESTIONS

Listed below are the writing questions. Choose one and write an essay that answers it. (If your instructor is willing, try adapting one of these questions or even writing your own. Be sure to get your instructor's approval—and possibly suggestions for change—before answering your question.)

Whichever question you answer, think of the person who will read your answer. The question may tell who your audience is. If not, think of a person you know and respect—preferably your instructor or a fellow student who will read your essay. Try to convince that person to believe you.

Bring in useful details from the selection(s) you have read and perhaps other incidents you know of. For ideas, review your answers to questions in the Preview and Reading Steps. When you first refer to a reading, give its title (in quotation marks) and the author's full name. Also, give the full name of anyone featured in the article the first time you mention that person. In making any later references, use only the person's last name.

Note: If you are assigned to write one paragraph, think of your answer to the question and list several key points you could make to support your answer. Then choose just one of the points and explain it in detail.

1. In regard to pornography, do you agree more with the U.S. First Amendment as a federal court has interpreted it (Itzin, paragraph 11) or the equality guarantee of Canada's new constitution as the Canadian Supreme Court has interpreted it (Itzin, paragraph 10)? Explain your position.

2. In the view of some people, the new Canadian constitution expands the guarantee of equality at the expense of freedom of expression. Explain why this change in power is either good or bad.

3. When it comes to defending pornography, do you agree more with Susan Isaacs, Jerry Falwell, or Andrea Dworkin? (See paragraph 7 of Isaacs.) Explain how your position is different from the other two positions. (*Note:* If you choose this question, you will need to find examples of Falwell's and Dworkin's writing or speeches elsewhere.)

4. Susan Isaacs argues for free speech. Catherine Itzin calls attention to what she calls "the real free speech issue" (paragraph 12). What does Itzin mean by "the real free speech issue"? If this kind of free speech comes about, how might it affect pornography laws?

5. Consider your answer to reading question 6 after Itzin's essay. In creating policies to deal with pornography, should we treat all sexual materials alike, as Isaacs suggests (paragraphs 9 and 10) or treat different types separately, as Itzin suggests (paragraph 10)? Explain.

6. Both Susan Isaacs (in paragraph 11) and Catherine Itzin (in paragraph 14) are against censoring pornography. However, they both

come up with entirely different conclusions on how to deal with censoring pornography. Compare and contrast their conclusions. Then explain which you prefer and why.

7. Instead of censoring pornography, Catherine Itzin suggests adopting two proposals based on procedures used in the United Kingdom: for "victims of pornography-related harm to take civil action against the manufacturers and distributors of pornography" (paragraph 15) and for "legislating against pornography that could be shown to have contributed to the incitement of sexual hatred and violence" (paragraph 16). Which one of these two procedures do you think would be more successful in the United States? Why?

8. Consider the two procedures mentioned in the previous question. How would the laws passed under the second of these not be censorship? Explain.

9. If you believe in censoring pornography, how would you answer Isaacs's concern that "historically, censorship has often been the first step toward dictatorship" (paragraph 14)?

10. Isaacs argues, "We can't hand over to anyone the power to decide what's appropriate for all" (paragraph 14). She writes that individuals should decide for themselves what is degrading to women. Explain why you agree or disagree with her reasoning.

11. If the U.S. Supreme Court were to rule that a five-person panel had to be set up to determine what is or is not pornographic, identify the five people you would select to serve on this commission. (You may either name individuals or describe types of people.) Explain your standards for choosing panelists and show how each panelist meets these standards.

REVISION QUESTIONS

Once you have finished writing your essay, ask yourself the following questions.

1. Is there any statement the reader might not understand?
2. Is there any statement that might offend the reader?
3. Is there anything that's not very convincing?

4. Have I changed the subject and then changed back again?
5. Have I said the same thing twice?
6. Do I want to try any feature of style I've seen in the reading selection?

EDITING QUESTIONS

Once you've made changes, ask someone else to read your essay. Change it again as needed. Then read your essay out loud and answer the following questions.

1. Does the sentence make sense?
2. Does every sentence use the kind of language that most people consider "good English" these days? (*Hint:* Imagine a TV announcer reading it.)
3. Do the periods, commas, and other punctuation show the reader how to interpret what I am writing? Does the use of each punctuation mark conform to the rules that readers expect me to follow?
4. Are the words spelled right?

Note that good grammar, punctuation, and spelling usually make your writing clearer—and always improve your image as a competent, educated writer.

If you make changes in your paper, proofread it again!

UNIT
SIXTEEN

Is Freedom Worth Dying For?

PREVIEW STEPS FOR UNIT SIXTEEN

In response to questions 1 and 2, try these steps: Write your answers, talk them over with three or four classmates, and then discuss them with the whole class.

1. Do you know of anyone who was injured or killed fighting for the freedom of others? Consider anyone you know, people in the news, anyone your relatives talk about, or even people in movies or books. If so, did this person act under orders from someone else? What difference would that make?

2. Do you know of anyone who has refused or would refuse to go to war, believing that war is morally wrong or that life is more valuable than freedom? What would it take for you to risk your life for someone else's freedom? Under what circumstances would you refuse?

3. a. Read the title of the first essay (page 242). Name the topic. (Who or what is this essay about?)

   b. Now predict the main idea. (What is the main point the author wants to make about this topic?)

   c. Read the first and last paragraphs. Revise your prediction if necessary. (*Note:* The main idea should sum up the smaller ideas of the essay.)

4. Some words from the essay are listed below, accompanied by quotations. Mark any words you do not know and make an educated guess about their meanings using the context supplied by the quotations— and possibly Appendix A, Word Parts, on page 285. You may want to work with a small group of classmates.

precarious "found themselves in a *precarious* position"

sympathized "Most Friends *sympathized* with the cause of freedom because of their own persecutions."

abhorred "They *abhorred* war or violence in any form."

magistrates "They thought their *magistrates* were appointed of God."

servitude "They had . . . freed the Negroes they had held in *servitude.*"

abstention "though not as important as *abstention* from violence"

abolition "Another issue . . . was the *abolition* of slavery."

admonitions "in his powerful *admonitions* among the religious colonists"

mote "to pluck the *mote* out of our brother's eye"

pounds "It cost Pleasants 3,000 *pounds.*"

genteel "Henry had worked hard to raise himself out of *genteel* poverty and into the *gentry.*"

gentry See above quotation.

lamentable "Slavery was 'this *lamentable* Evil' and was 'totally *repugnant.*'"

repugnant See above quotation.

Tories "except for some who had been labeled *Tories*"

5. Now read the following essay. As you read, jot down any questions that occur to you.

(*Note:* Question 6 appears after the essay.)

Quakers and the American Revolution

Jeremiah Benezet

Friends, or Quakers, found themselves in a precarious position during   1
the American Revolution. Although most Friends sympathized with
the cause of freedom because of their own persecutions over the years
on both sides of the ocean, they opposed a war with the Mother
Country for three reasons: First, they abhorred war or violence in any
form. Although they were strong believers in freedom, they considered life more important. Life comes from God and is therefore sacred. Violence breeds death. Second, they thought their magistrates
were appointed of God, and therefore the British King was their di-
vinely assigned political leader. And third, they had recently freed the
Negroes they had held in servitude and thought the colonists hypocritical in calling for their own freedom but not being willing to grant
freedom to their Negro slaves.

    Quakers have always stood against violence. Thus they thought   2
both the British and the American colonists were wrong in fighting
one another. . . .

    Another issue, though not as important as abstention from vio-   3
lence, was the abolition of slavery. Beginning in 1739, the Quakers
made vigorous efforts to rid the American colonies of slavery. . . . In
Virginia, Robert Pleasants led the charge against those Quakers who
had not yet freed their slaves as well as against those non-Quakers he
felt were hypocritical while claiming their own freedom from the chains
of England but keeping their slaves in chains. In his powerful admonitions among the religious colonists, Pleasants would refer to two passages from the seventh chapter of Matthew: to the Saviour's call to cast
out the beam in our own eye in order to see clearly how to pluck the

---

Printed with permission of the author.

mote out of our brother's eye [verses 3–5] and to the Master's golden rule to do unto others as we would have them do unto us [verse 12]. His appeals made a strong impact upon Virginia's non-Quakers. . . .

Though he was Patrick Henry's senior by 14 years, Pleasants had long conversations with the younger statesman and corresponded with him over the years. It was probably the influence of the Quakers that persuaded both Henry and Thomas Jefferson to try getting the slaves freed while each served as Virginia's governor. However, the agricultural South was not willing to concede, and neither of these two patriots gave up their own slaves. Henry apparently felt guilty because sometimes he would spend the hottest of days working in the fields with his slaves. But he also was aware that it had cost Pleasants 3,000 pounds to free his slaves and start paying them and that most Southern Quakers had slid into poverty upon freeing theirs. Henry had worked hard to raise himself out of genteel poverty and into the gentry. . . . He wrote that slavery was "this lamentable Evil" and was "totally repugnant": "as repugnant to humanity as it is inconsistent with the Bible and destructive to Liberty." However, he could not resolve his moral dilemma. Pleasants, in the meantime, warned that if the colonists did not free the slaves voluntarily, the future would bring fatal devastation to America. . . .

After the war, the Quakers never regained their previous political power, especially in Pennsylvania. But because of their strong moral character and efforts to help others during the war, most regained their social status, except for some who had been labeled Tories. . . . The Quakers to this day still stand for non-violence, for the equality of the sexes, and for general respect and love among all peoples.

6. State the essay's main idea in your own words. Compare it to your prediction of the main idea. (*Note:* The main idea should sum up the smaller ideas of the essay.)

PREVIEW STEPS FOR "Give Me Liberty or Give Me Death"

1. a. Read the title of the second essay, a speech (page 246). Name the topic. (Who or what is this essay about?)

    b. Now predict the main idea. (What is the main point the author wants to make about this topic?)

    c. Read the first and last paragraphs of the essay. Revise your prediction if necessary. (*Note:* The main idea should sum up the smaller ideas of the essay.)

2. What in the author's background may have led him to the main idea? (See author's background, below title.)

3. Some words from the essay are listed below, accompanied by quotations. Mark any words you do not know and make an educated guess about their meanings using the context supplied by the quotations—and possibly Appendix A, Word Parts, on page 285. You may want to work with a small group of classmates.

revere "the Majesty of Heaven, which I *revere* above all earthly kings."

arduous "wise men, engaged in a great and *arduous* struggle for liberty"

solace "And judging by the past, I wish to know what there has been . . . to justify those hopes with which gentlemen have been pleased to *solace* themselves."

insidious "Is it that *insidious* smile with which our petition has been lately received?"

comports "Ask yourselves how this gracious reception of our petition *comports* with those warlike preparations which cover our waters and darken our land."

reconciliation "Are fleets and armies necessary to a work of love and *reconciliation?*"

implements "These are the *implements* of war and *subjugation;* the last arguments to which kings resort."

subjugation See above quotation.

martial "What means this *martial array,* if its purpose be not to force us to submission?"

array See above quotation.

forging "those chains which the British ministry have been so long *forging*"

entreaty "Shall we resort to *entreaty* and humble *supplication?*"

supplication See above quotation.

remonstrated "We have *remonstrated;* . . . we have *prostrated* ourselves before the throne, and have *implored* its *interposition* to *arrest* the tyrannical hands of the ministry and Parliament."

prostrated See above quotation.

implored See above quotation.

interposition See above quotation.

arrest See above quotation.

spurned "We have been *spurned,* with contempt, from the foot of the throne!"

basely "if we mean not *basely* to abandon the noble struggle"

formidable "We are weak; unable to cope with so *formidable* an *adversary.*"

adversary See above quotation.

supinely "Shall we acquire the means of effectual resistance by lying *supinely* on our backs and hugging the delusive *phantom* of hope"

phantom See above quotation.

invincible "Three millions of people, armed in the holy cause of liberty, . . . are *invincible* by any force which our enemy can send against us."

vigilant "The battle . . . is not to the strong alone; it is to the *vigilant,* the active, the brave."

election "Besides, sir, we have no *election.*"

extenuate "It is in vain, sir, to *extenuate* the matter."

4. At the end of the Preview, you may want to go over any new features of style that occur in the following reading selection. You will need to know the terms *allusion, irony of wording,* and *metaphor.* For help, see Appendix B, Guide to Literary Terms (page 288), with accompanying exercises on individual features.

5. Before reading "Give Me Liberty or Give Me Death," turn to pages 250–252 and skim the Reading Questions. Then read the essay (speech) to find answers to these questions. As you read, jot down any questions that occur to you.

Give Me Liberty or Give Me Death

Patrick Henry
(Delivered at Richmond, in the Virginia Convention,
on a Resolution to put the Commonwealth
into a State of Defense, March 23d, 1775)

Patrick Henry (1736–1799) was a distinguished lawyer, politician, administrator, and speaker. In 1764, he was elected to the Virginia House of Burgesses (Virginia's legislature before the Revolution). There he introduced a protest against the Stamp Act, a British law requiring Americans to buy and attach expensive stamps to all

---

From Brewer, D. J. (Ed.) (1899). *The World's Best Orations,* official ed. Vol. 7 of 10. St. Louis: Ferd. P. Kaiser. Pp. 2475–2477.

important documents—in effect, a tax. The resolution passed by only one vote. Ten years later, he was elected to the First Continental Congress and again to the Second Continental Congress. (These were two sessions of America's Congress before the Revolution.) Then he became commander-in-chief of Virginia's armed forces and, a few months later, was chosen to serve on the committee to draft the first constitution of Virginia. Henry became its first governor in 1776 and served for five terms, not all consecutive. One man who had heard many of Henry's speeches said that Henry—with his clear voice and perfect articulation—was by far the most powerful speaker he had ever heard. Even though many of his words will be unfamiliar to modern readers, his oratorical style carries his message powerfully.

(*Note:* Try not to let the antique vocabulary bother you; enjoy the style and the rhythm.)

Mr. President:–

No man thinks more highly than I do of the patriotism, as well as abilities, of the very worthy gentlemen who have just addressed the house. But different men often see the same subject in different lights; and, therefore, I hope it will not be thought disrespectful to those gentlemen, if, entertaining as I do opinions of a character very opposite to theirs, I shall speak forth my sentiments freely and without reserve. This is no time for ceremony. The question before the house is one of awful moment to this country. For my own part, I consider it as nothing less than a question of freedom or slavery; and in proportion to the magnitude of the subject ought to be the freedom of the debate. It is only in this way that we can hope to arrive at truth, and fulfill the great responsibility which we hold to God and our country. Should I keep back my opinions at such a time, through fear of giving offense, I should consider myself as guilty of treason towards my country, and of an act of disloyalty toward the Majesty of Heaven, which I revere above all earthly kings.

Mr. President, it is natural to man to indulge in the illusions of hope. We are apt to shut our eyes against a painful truth, and listen to the song of that siren, till she transforms us into beasts. Is this the part of wise men, engaged in a great and arduous struggle for liberty? Are we disposed to be of the number of those, who, having eyes, see not, and having ears, hear not [Mark 8:18, *King James Version*], the things which so nearly concern their temporal salvation? For my part, whatever anguish of spirit it may cost, I am willing to know the whole truth; to know the worst, and to provide for it.

I have but one lamp by which my feet are guided, and that is the lamp of experience. I know of no way of judging of the future but by the past. And judging by the past, I wish to know what there has been in the conduct of the British ministry for the last ten years to justify those hopes with which gentlemen have been pleased to solace themselves and the house. Is it that insidious smile with which our petition has been lately received? Trust it not, sir; it will prove a snare to your feet. Suffer not yourselves to be betrayed with a kiss [Luke 22:47, 48 *KJV*]. Ask yourselves how this gracious reception of our petition comports with those warlike preparations which cover our waters and darken our land. Are fleets and armies necessary to a work of love and reconciliation? Have we shown ourselves so unwilling to be reconciled, that force must be called in to win back our love? Let us not deceive ourselves, sir. These are the implements of war and subjugation; the last arguments to which kings resort. I ask gentlemen, sir, What means this martial array, if its purpose be not to force us to submission? Can gentlemen assign any other possible motive for it? Has Great Britain any enemy, in this quarter of the world, to call for all this accumulation of navies and armies? No, sir, she has none. They are meant for us: They can be meant for no other. They are sent over to bind and rivet upon us those chains which the British ministry have been so long forging. And what have we to oppose to them? Shall we try argument? Sir, we have been trying that for the last ten years. Have we anything new to offer upon the subject? Nothing. We have held the subject up in every light of which it is capable; but it has been all in vain. Shall we resort to entreaty and humble supplication? What terms shall we find, which have not been already exhausted? Let us not, I beseech you, sir, deceive ourselves longer. Sir, we have done everything that could be done, to avert the storm which is now coming on. We have petitioned; we have remonstrated; we have supplicated; we have prostrated ourselves before the throne, and have implored its interposition to arrest the tyrannical hands of the ministry and Parliament. Our petitions have been slighted; our remonstrances have produced additional violence and insult; our supplications have

3

been disregarded; and we have been spurned, with contempt, from the foot of the throne! In vain, after these things, may we indulge the fond hope of peace and reconciliation. There is no longer any room for hope. If we wish to be free—if we mean to preserve inviolate those inestimable privileges for which we have been so long contending—if we mean not basely to abandon the noble struggle in which we have been so long engaged, and which we have pledged ourselves never to abandon, until the glorious object of our contest shall be obtained—we must fight! I repeat it, sir, we must fight! An appeal to arms and to the God of Hosts is all that is left us!

They tell us, sir, that we are weak; unable to cope with so formi-   4
dable an adversary. But when shall we be stronger? Will it be the next week, or the next year? Will it be when we are totally disarmed, and when a British guard shall be stationed in every house? Shall we gather strength by irresolution and inaction? Shall we acquire the means of effectual resistance by lying supinely on our backs and hugging the delusive phantom of hope, until our enemies shall have bound us hand and foot? Sir, we are not weak, if we make a proper use of those means which the God of nature hath placed in our power. Three millions of people, armed in the holy cause of liberty, and in such a country as that which we possess, are invincible by any force which our enemy can send against us. Besides, sir, we shall not fight our battles alone. There is a just God who presides over the destinies of nations, and who will raise up friends to fight our battles for us. The battle, sir, is not to the strong alone; it is to the vigilant, the active, the brave. Besides, sir, we have no election. If we were base enough to desire it, it is now too late to retire from the contest. There is no retreat, but in submission and slavery! Our chains are forged! Their clanking may be heard on the plains of Boston! The war is inevitable—and let it come! I repeat it, sir, let it come.

It is in vain, sir, to extenuate the matter. Gentlemen may cry,   5
Peace, Peace—but there is no peace [Jeremiah 6:14 *KJV*]. The war is actually begun! The next gale that sweeps from the north will bring to our ears the clash of resounding arms! Our brethren are already in the field! Why stand we here idle? What is it that gentlemen wish? What would they have? Is life so dear, or peace so sweet, as to be purchased at the price of chains and slavery? Forbid it, Almighty God! I know not what course others may take; but as for me, give me liberty or give me death!

READING QUESTIONS FOR "Give Me Liberty or Give Me Death"

Main Idea

1. State the essay's main idea in your own words. Compare it to your prediction of the main idea. (*Note:* The main idea should sum up the smaller ideas of the essay.)

Organization

2. a. Where in the essay is the main idea found?

   b. Why has the author placed the main idea there?

3. In what order are the paragraphs arranged? (Underline one.) Time/ Least to most important/Most to least important/Simple listing/ Logic: cause and effect/Other logic/Other

Style

4. How formal is the essay? (Circle your choice.)

   [Informal—1—2—3—4—5—6—7—8—9—10—Formal]

   What indicators convinced you? (For a list of possible indicators and two benchmark essays, see Appendix F, The Formality Spectrum, on page 298.)

5. Where do you see the following features of style? List one or two examples of each with their paragraph numbers.

   Features (For definitions, see Appendix B, page 288.)

a. allusion

b. irony of wording

c. metaphor

d. rhythms. Cite at least a couple of Henry's magnificent rhythms.

e. semicolons. The conventions or customs of punctuation change over time. Find three uses of the semicolon in the printing of Henry's speech that would not be acceptable in today's writing— three uses where we might use a dash for emphasis instead.

Content

6. Examine the organization of Henry's speech. Summarize what he does in each of the parts or paragraphs.

a. Paragraph 1

b. Paragraph 2

c. Paragraph 3

   d. Paragraph 4

   e. Paragraph 5

7. Does the author propose any change? If so, what do you think would be the result of such change?

8. Do you agree with the author's main idea? Why or why not?

9. Before the United States had a constitution, Henry earnestly called for some form of emancipation for the slaves while serving as Virginia's governor. Why did Henry not specifically mention the slaves in his speech "Give Me Liberty or Give Me Death"?

If you have not already read the essay and answered the Reading Questions, be sure to do so before you proceed.

COMPOSITION QUESTIONS

Listed below are the writing questions. Choose one and write an essay that answers it. (If your instructor is willing, try adapting one of these questions or even writing your own. Be sure to get your instructor's approval—and possibly suggestions for change—before answering your question.)

Whichever question you answer, think of the person who will read your answer. The question may tell who your audience is. If not, think of a person you know and respect—preferably your instructor or a fellow student who will read your essay. Try to convince that person to believe you.

Bring in useful details from the selection(s) you have read and perhaps other incidents you know of. For ideas, review your answers to questions in the Preview and Reading Steps. When you first refer to a reading, give its title (in quotation marks) and the author's full name. Also, give the full name of anyone featured in the article the first time you mention that person. In making any later references, use only the person's last name.

Note: If you are assigned to write one paragraph, think of your answer to the question and list several key points you could make to support your answer. Then choose just one of the points and explain it in detail.

1. The Quakers have always been active in politics. They were on cordial terms with Virginia's political figures of the 1700s, such as George Washington and Patrick Henry. So when Henry said, "But different men often see the same subject in different lights," he may have been including Quakers who attended the 1775 Virginia Convention. The Quakers thought having liberty was secondary to preserving life; Henry would die for liberty. Yet both quote the Bible to back their position. Even though they disagree on the overall question, are both quoting the Scriptures accurately and appropriately to make points in their arguments?

2. Compare the arguments the Quakers and Patrick Henry make on the topic of liberty. Which do you agree with more closely? That is, is freedom worth dying for? Would you be willing to die so that others can be free? Explain your position.

3. Before the war, Quakers in Virginia were beholden to Patrick Henry for getting legislation passed freeing them of military service and war taxes. But once the war started and Quakers throughout the colonies refused to take sides, both the British and the colonists thought them traitors, causing the Friends to lose political power, social status, and just treatment. Would you, like the main body of these Quakers, be able to stand firm with your belief system, even during times of persecution? Explain.

4. Some Quakers were so appalled at how the British army was treating Massachusetts' civilians that they broke away from the main body of Quakers and formed the Free Quakers. Among these dissenters were Nathanael Greene, who already had become a general in Washington's army, and Betsy Ross, who later made the first American

flag. After the war, the Free Quaker movement slowly died out. But while it lasted, some Quakers—even though temporarily—abandoned their central belief that life is more sacred than liberty and adopted Patrick Henry's position. Think of some important belief you have. What would it take, if anything, for you to abandon that belief for the good of others? Explain.

5. While the colonists were distracted by fighting the British, why didn't the slaves do more to fight for their own freedom? Did most slaves agree with the Quakers' belief that life is more sacred than freedom and, therefore, opt to preserve their lives? Or were there other factors that kept them from wholesale rebellion? Explain.

6. Thomas Jefferson, the author of our Declaration of Independence, and Patrick Henry both advocated freeing the slaves; however, both owned slaves. In the 1700s, slave ownership was common in many parts of the country. The philosopher Georg Hegel says that human reason and knowledge are constantly expanding and progressing, so a person's ideas should be judged only by the standards of that person's lifetime. Do you agree? To what extent should we hold Jefferson and Henry accountable for having owned slaves? Justify your position.

7. In March 1963, on the hundredth anniversary of the Emancipation Proclamation, Martin Luther King, Jr., delivered his famous "I Have a Dream" speech at the Lincoln Memorial. Though nearly two hundred years apart, the Henry and King speeches both were stirring calls for freedom. Find a copy of King's speech and compare it to Henry's. Note their many rhythms, their repetition of words, their effective use of long words from Latin, such as those that end in -*tion*. Note their biblical references and their use of figurative language. Both appeal to a power greater than themselves, and both build to a dramatic last line. Then explain how all of these factors, and any others you may have noted, effectively persuade their audiences. To what extent is it legitimate to appeal to the emotions of the audience?

8. In his speech, Patrick Henry is trying to persuade the Virginia Convention to declare war against England. He says, "Give me liberty or give me death!" Henry may mean his statement literally: He may actually be offering to fight in the coming war. Many times, however, those who declare war are not those who would do the fighting. Who should have the power to send people to war? Under what circumstances is it right to send others to their deaths for our beliefs?

REVISION QUESTIONS

Once you have finished writing your essay, ask yourself the following questions.

1. Is there any statement the reader might not understand?
2. Is there any statement that might offend the reader?
3. Is there anything that's not very convincing?
4. Have I changed the subject and then changed it back again?
5. Have I said the same thing twice?
6. Do I want to try any feature of style I've seen in the reading selection?

EDITING QUESTIONS

Once you've made changes, ask someone else to read your essay. Change it again as needed. Then read your essay out loud and answer the following questions.

1. Does the sentence make sense?
2. Does every sentence use the kind of language that most people consider "good English" these days? (*Hint:* Imagine a TV announcer reading it.)
3. Do the periods, commas, and other punctuation show the reader how to interpret what I am writing? Does the use of each punctuation mark conform to the rules that readers expect me to follow?
4. Are the words spelled right?

Note that good grammar, punctuation, and spelling usually make your writing clearer—and always improve your image as a competent, educated writer.

If you make changes in your paper, proofread it again!

UNIT
SEVENTEEN

The Effects of Technology on Society

PREVIEW STEPS FOR UNIT SEVENTEEN

In response to questions 1 and 2, try these steps: Write your answers, talk them over with three or four classmates, and then discuss them with the whole class.

1. What good effects has technology had on your life? Jot down whatever comes to mind for two or three minutes.

2. What bad effects has technology had on your life? Do you think the government should control advancements in technology? Again, jot down whatever comes to mind for two or three minutes.

3. a. Read the title of the first essay (page 259). Name the topic. (Who or what is this essay about?)

   b. Now predict the main idea. (What is the main point the author wants to make about this topic?)

   c. Read the first and last paragraphs. Revise your prediction if necessary. (*Note:* The main idea should sum up the smaller ideas of the essay.)

4. Some words from the essay are listed below, accompanied by quotations. Mark any words you do not know and make an educated guess about their meanings using the context supplied by the quotations—and possibly Appendix A, Word Parts, on page 285. You may want to work with a small group of classmates.

   progressives "We have taken the distinction between *progressives* and *conservatives* so much for granted that it is now hard for us to think about politics in any other terms."

conservatives See above quotation.

status quo "Yet this way of looking at things was invented 200 years ago, at a time when modernization and progress were sweeping away entrenched privilege and challenging the *status quo*."

autonomy "Yet we have not come up with a new political direction that . . . relates to . . . our sense of personal *autonomy*."

paternalistic "Economic planners, urban planners, and social planners take over individuals' personal decisions by redefining them as technical problems that only 'the experts' can deal with. The tone is usually *paternalistic*."

5. Now read the following essay. As you read, jot down any questions that occur to you.

(*Note:* Question 6 appears after the essay.)

A New Declaration of Independence:
How to Win Back Our Freedom
from the Technocrats

Charles Siegel

America is at a crucial turning point. We have taken the distinction   1
between progressives and conservatives so much for granted that it is
now hard for us to think about politics in any other terms. Yet this
way of looking at things was invented 200 years ago, at a time when
modernization and progress were sweeping away entrenched privilege
and challenging the status quo. It is no longer relevant now that modernization and progress are the status quo. . . .

Our problem is not modernization itself but technocratic mod-   2
ernism, the blind faith that technology can do everything better. This
fascination with technology and growth transformed America during
the postwar period when we were the only country with a strong

enough economy to move at full speed toward the technological ideal. Mamie Eisenhower would not serve fresh vegetables in the White House because she considered canned and frozen vegetables more modern. Federal, state, and local governments did all they could to promote the construction of freeways, housing subdivisions, and shopping malls rather than neighborhoods where people could walk. Suburban parents sent their children to nursery schools, where they could benefit from special programs designed by experts in educational psychology.

Without question, modernization has had great successes— 3 among them, curing disease and reducing poverty—but now we can see that the modernist faith has also failed in many ways. For example, we spend more than twice as much on each child's education as we did in 1960 (after correcting for inflation), but standardized tests show that students learn less than they did then. Or consider this: America's per capita national income is about twice what it was in 1960 (after correcting for inflation), but Americans do not feel that they are twice as well off as they were in 1960. In many ways, we feel worse off.

Yet we have not come up with a new political direction that 4 responds to the failures of modernization as it relates to four important aspects of our lives: the physical and social environment of our neighborhoods, our places of business, our families, and our sense of personal autonomy. Instead, we are still calling for more technology to solve the problems caused by technology itself.

We should take the opposite tack. Most environmental and 5 social problems we face today exist only because we have had such faith in technology and economic growth in this century that we've rushed headlong to modernize every activity of life, even in many cases when it is obvious that modernization doesn't work. Rather than applying more expertise and spending more money to solve these problems, we should get at their root by limiting technology and growth. We should use modern technology where it works and get the inappropriate technology out of the way.

Revitalizing Our Neighborhoods

To build workable neighborhoods, we need to rein in the automobile— 6 and the best way to do this is to reduce the speed limit. How low should we go? Consider the impact of reducing the speed limit to

15 miles per hour for private vehicles within the city limits. It would allow people to use cars for local errands but force them to take higher-speed public transportation for longer trips. As a result, automobiles would no longer dominate the environment, and bicycles and small electric vehicles could easily fit into the flow of traffic. Streets would be friendlier to pedestrians, and safe enough for children to play in them. We would also have to limit the scale of development to make room for slower forms of transportation. It is hard to get around on a bicycle or in an electric cart, and virtually impossible to walk anywhere, if you inhabit a landscape of tract housing and shopping malls.

Another possibility would be to cut the speed limit to 30 miles per hour. That would shift long-distance commuting from the freeways to high-speed rail systems. Commercial development would cluster around the rail stations to take advantage of the new customer base; freeway-oriented shopping malls would make way for mixed-use shopping and office complexes (with plenty of parking) at rail stations. Some of the suburban sprawl at the edges of metropolitan areas would also recede because it is totally dependent on high-speed freeway access.

Yet, if the city had a high-speed rail system, this change would still allow everyone to live in a suburban neighborhood. The big differences from today's suburbs would be that people would shop and work in mixed-use complexes, which are far more interesting than shopping malls and office parks, and most commutes would be less grueling. This change would also cut automobile use roughly in half, dramatically reducing the city's environmental problems.

Are these ideas a mere pipe dream? Not necessarily. Cities all over the world are "calming" traffic on residential streets. In the 1980s, Germany began an ambitious experiment that went further, slowing traffic on both residential and arterial streets in areas ranging from a neighborhood in Berlin with 30,000 residents to a small town of 2,300 residents. The government cut the speed limit in half but discovered that the time for the average trip increased by just a bit over 10 percent. Obviously, one result of traffic calming was to shorten the length of the average trip. In addition, noise levels and injuries from automobile accidents dropped dramatically. The German automobile association, which was skeptical about the government's data, conducted its own interviews and found that, after speeds were lowered, 67 percent of motorists and even higher proportions of residents approved of the change. The experiment was so successful, in fact, that it has since been imitated in cities in Denmark, Sweden, the Netherlands, Italy, Switzerland, Austria, and Japan.

Protecting Our Small Businesses

To promote civic life, it would also be useful to phase out chain stores   10
and reduce the overall scale of retail outlets, so that national megastores could not displace locally owned businesses. Some cities already have zoning laws that restrict chains, but it would be more effective to have a national law limiting the number of stores that one company could own—to break up existing chains and reduce the mind-numbing sameness that now blankets most of the United States.

Eliminating chains would increase some costs. Obviously, chains   11
and superstores are more efficient than most independently owned stores because of their vast economies of scale. In some cases— supermarkets, for example—the economic benefits of chains might outweigh their social costs. But in others—most notably book-selling— quality, diversity, and the free flow of ideas are so important that it is urgent to get rid of the chains, even if the costs increase.

Replacing chains with small businesses would lower overall pro-   12
ductivity, but retailing is one of the few industries that can stay small without hurting a country's economic position internationally. Virtually all of Japan's retailing is done by mom-and-pop businesses, but it hasn't prevented Japan from becoming one of the most prosperous countries in the world.

Making Our Families Work

Moving from the storefront to the home front, it is clear that some of   13
our most deep-seated social problems result from the modernization of the family. Few would dispute that there is a "parenting deficit" in America today. Children are suffering not only because families are breaking up but also because, even in intact families, both parents must work full time to keep up financially. The left generally ignores this new problem and continues to push for family policies from early in the century: more money for day care, Head Start, and schooling.

These ideas made sense in the 1950s, when stable families were the norm and most people believed in progressive methods of raising children. But today even the left is disillusioned with them. They support these programs to help cope with family breakdown, but they have no vision of a better future.

By default, this territory now belongs to the conservatives who   14
rhapsodize about "the traditional family" (by which they really mean the early modern family, with a husband who goes to work in a factory or office and a wife who stays home). The conservatives strike a chord with many voters because they don't deny the damage done by the decline of the family during the past few decades, but they can't go any farther than that because they are also champions of economic growth.

The fact that parents no longer have time for their children is the   15
worst possible indictment of the modern economy. Rather than demanding more day care and schooling to help families conform to the economy, the left should be demanding radical changes in the growth economy to make it work for families. One practical approach would be to change the current tax laws—and corporate subsidy programs— which discriminate against parents who take care of their own children. Many parents already get tax credits and subsidies to help pay for day care. Why not give parents who forgo day care equivalent benefits? In many cases, equal benefits would make it possible for parents to cut back their work hours and raise their children on their own.

But larger economic changes are also needed. In 1950, one par-   16
ent working 40 hours a week was enough to support a typical family. If we had been more sensible, we could have used the phenomenal rise of women in the workforce from the 1960s onward to create families supported by two parents, each working 20 hours a week. The original promise of modernization was that higher productivity would give people more leisure, but the economy has not kept this promise.

Restoring Our Personal Autonomy

Technocratic modernism undermines autonomy in the same way that   17
it undermines the neighborhood and the family. Economic planners, urban planners, and social planners take over individuals' personal decisions by redefining them as technical problems that only "the

experts" can deal with. The tone is usually paternalistic. The experts themselves believe they are using modern methods to "help" people, but, in reality, they are controlling people and increasing the feelings of powerlessness and dependence that are pervasive in modern society. To restore personal autonomy, we must limit the ability of technological organizations to control our everyday lives.

18   The most astounding example of the way that we allow bureaucracies to control our lives is our commitment to the idea that the economic system must "help" people by "providing jobs." This idea made sense in the early part of the century when most people needed more income to buy necessities. But now that we no longer have that problem, we need to give people the ability to choose their own standard of living. In a surplus economy, the idea that we must provide jobs for people forces us to promote economic growth, even if most of the products we produce are useless.

19   Not surprisingly, we think about work like consumers. We think in terms of having jobs, not in terms of doing jobs because they are useful. We demand more jobs just as we demand more transportation, education, health care, child care, and more of any "service" that we expect the system to provide. And, in the process, we lose sight of the fact that we are actually demanding to do unnecessary work.

20   It is reasonable to work until you produce what you want, then stop. But, as a culture, we believe in creating demand for products that people don't really want purely to create extra work for ourselves. To put the economy back on a rational basis, to produce the goods and services that people actually want, we need to offer job seekers more flexible work hours. One way would be to give employers tax incentives to create more part-time jobs and accommodate different work schedules without penalizing part-time workers with lower hourly pay, restricted benefits, or fewer promotion opportunities. Federal, state, and local governments should act as a model by offering their own employees work hours that are as flexible as possible.

21   We can't expect employers to take advantage of flexible work hours, though, unless we limit the demands that the consumer economy makes on them. In part, this would involve changing personal behavior—getting people to go beyond the "shop till you drop" mindset that makes Americans spend three to four times as many hours shopping as Europeans do. But it also would require larger political changes, such as rebuilding American cities, where it now is absolutely essential for most families to own two cars.

Humanizing the Economy

We can use the law to control growth if we learn to think about tech- 22
nology in human terms, rather than focusing on the abstractions that
only "the experts" can work with. As long as we think of transportation, land use, and pollution control as "urban problems," we will
surrender to the city planners and let them decide what kinds of
neighborhoods we live in. But if we can focus on the human purpose
of our cities—they are the places where we live—it will become obvious that the people themselves should make the political and personal
decisions that will shape the city's design.

Similarly, as long as we think of unemployment and inflation as 23
"economic problems," we will allow economists to decide what our
standard of living should be. But when we think about the human
purpose of the economy—to produce things that we actually want—
it becomes obvious that workers should get to choose their own work
schedules and standard of living. Planning is useful to control the
business cycles and fine-tune the economy, but this planning should
be subordinate to the human question of what we want to consume,
which individuals should decide for themselves.

The bias of the consumer economy has crippled our politics. 24
Real change will be possible when people act as citizens who use the
law to govern themselves—not as clients demanding more services
from the system and voting for the politicians they think will do the
best job of providing them with more education, more health care,
more transportation, and, most important, more jobs. The moral advantage of limiting technology is that it increases individual freedom
and responsibility, which been eroded by modernization. Someone always objects that limiting technology is unrealistic—for example, that Americans will never vote to lower the speed limit. That may
be true today, but only because people believe that building livable
cities is a technical problem that the planners must solve for them, and
that their role is just to demand services from the planners. People will
act differently if they see that, in order to have decent cities to live in,
well-educated children, and an economy that produces things they
want, they must consume less and do more for themselves.

6. State the essay's main idea in your own words. Compare it to your prediction of the main idea. (*Note:* The main idea should sum up the
   smaller ideas of the essay.)

**PREVIEW STEPS FOR "On the Edge of the Digital Age:
The Historic Moment"**

1. a. Read the title of the second essay (page 269). Name the topic. (Who or what is this essay about?)

   b. Now predict the main idea. (What is the main point the author wants to make about this topic?)

   c. Read the first and last paragraphs of the essay. Revise your prediction if necessary. (*Note:* The main idea should sum up the smaller ideas of the essay.)

2. What in the author's background may have led him to the main idea? (See author's background, below title.)

3. Some words from the essay are listed below, accompanied by quotations. Mark any words you do not know and make an educated guess about their meanings using the context supplied by the quotations— and possibly Appendix A, Word Parts, on page 285. You may want to work with a small group of classmates.

   agrarian "The *agrarian* economy was completely restructured, and social and political institutions transformed to fit the new realities."

precursor "And the Internet is the *precursor* to the information superhighway, which will be the pipeline for the vital flow of the information of the Digital Age."

obsolescence "The failure of our schools is rooted in the *obsolescence* of a system that mass-produces brains in an era in which the world's knowledge doubles every four years."

redundant "Information technologies will make millions of working people *redundant* and send them scattering to retool their skills and seek new work."

hierarchical "The centralized, *hierarchical* organization characteristic of the Industrial Age will shift into the more decentralized organization that will be the hallmark of the Digital Age."

infrastructure "By then your home may have 50 of these tiny computers connected to the information *infrastructure,* much as you now have 50 electric motors tied to the electrical grid powering your refrigerator, washing machine."

ubiquitous "These *ubiquitous* computers finally may have the power to bring a sense of tranquillity back to our lives, allowing us to live in less-crowded surroundings, more integrated with nature."

inauspicious "For a revolution, [the creation of the microprocessor] was a pretty *inauspicious* beginning. At the time, many people didn't see it as much of an improvement over the existing mainframe computers."

quasipublic "But soon they [local area networks] were connecting different companies or institutions through such *quasipublic* computer networks as the Internet."

superfluous "But the white collars, too, were becoming *superfluous* in an office environment pervaded by information technologies."

cadres "You don't need *cadres* of middle managers making reports and shuffling information to the executives when personal computers on networks can do the job."

consummate "Our national government is paralyzed largely because it's a *consummate* product of the Industrial Age."

extraneous "They are trying to define their essential core services and get out of delivering *extraneous* services. They are trying to adopt new technologies and shed unneeded levels of managers, in their case, bureaucrats."

imploded "But what happened in the 1980s, the dawn of the Digital Age? . . . The Soviet Union's entire system completely *imploded* in less than 10 years."

totalitarian "But in a much more fundamental way, that *totalitarian* system could not function in a world of digital technologies and global telecommunications. And so we watched the Soviet empire collapse."

ascendant "The *ascendant* industries are ones in which the United States leads the world: computers, telecommunications, entertainment, media."

Renaissance "The first *Renaissance* came about largely because the printing press enabled all the isolated minds of medieval Europe to finally connect."

synergy "What kind of *synergy* will be created this time around [during the second Renaissance], as all the minds on the planet become wired together through the Net?"

tenured "*Tenured* professors and teachers' unions face not minor pay cuts, but radically new roles."

4. At the end of the Preview, you may want to go over any new features of style that occur in the following reading selection. You will need to know the terms *allusion, metaphor,* and *simile.* For help, see Appendix B, Guide to Literary Terms (page 288), with accompanying exercises on individual features.

5. Before reading "On the Edge of the Digital Age: The Historic Moment," turn to pages 279–280 and skim the Reading Questions. Then read the essay to find answers to these questions. As you read, jot down any questions that occur to you.

On the Edge of the Digital Age:
The Historic Moment

Peter Leyden

Peter Leyden (1959–), now the managing editor of Wired *maga-zine, was the Minneapolis–St. Paul* Star Tribune's *information technologies reporter when he wrote the article below. Having joined the newspaper in 1990, he covered the urban affairs beat before moving to the technologies assignments. He has also worked as a newspaper reporter and as a special correspondent in Asia for* Newsweek *magazine and several newspapers. He has master's degrees in journalism and comparative politics from Columbia University and a degree in intellectual history from Georgetown University.*

We are living through an extraordinary moment in human history.   1

Historians will look back on our times, the 40-year span between   2
1980 and 2020, and classify it among the handful of historical moments when humans reorganized their entire civilization around a new
tool, a new idea.

These decades mark the transition from the Industrial Age, an   3
era organized around the motor, to the Digital Age, an era defined by
the microprocessor—the brains within today's personal computer.

The mid-1990s . . . may come to be viewed as the defining mo-   4
ment when society recognized the enormity of the changes taking
place and began to reorient itself.

The last time humans went through such a wrenching transition   5
was during the Industrial Revolution of the late 18th and 19th cen-
turies. The agrarian economy was completely restructured, and social
and political institutions transformed to fit the new realities.

The trauma was severe: Peasants were driven off their fields and   6
into factories. Industrialists became fabulously rich overnight. Rustic
village life was replaced by an urban one. Political revolutions flared.

Our transition will be every bit as brutal. Once-secure profes-   7
sionals will find their skills obsolete. Washington's government

bureaucracies will see much of their power eroded. Cities will face accelerating population losses.

And when the trauma subsides, the changes in our daily lives will   8
be just as profound as those between a rural peasant and an urban factory worker. It may sound preposterous, but that's the best way to describe the scale of changes that we're facing.

You've heard the talk about how the Digital Revolution will   9
change the way you work and live.

Start believing the hype.   10

Digital Age's Next 10 Years May Be More Traumatic Than the Great Depression

From this historical perspective, much of the confusion of our tumul-   11
tuous times begins to make more sense.

Why is it that our federal government seems paralyzed, our   12
schools dysfunctional, our society fracturing into thousands of sub-groups? Why do we have so much anxiety when the economy is so strong?

And what's driving this boom in computers and telecommunica-   13
tions? Sales of personal computers, CD-ROMs, cellular phones, you name it, are off the charts. Just two years ago, you never heard the word "Internet" or had any concept of e-mail. Today everyone seems to be going online.

Here's one way to think about it: We're at a point in the transition   14
where almost everything associated with the old Industrial Age is falling into dysfunction and everything associated with the new Digital Age is booming.

This boom is just the beginning of the spread of microprocessors—   15
tiny computer chips that will be installed in almost all the tools and ap-pliances that we'll use in our lives, making those tools more intelligent and useful. And the Internet is the precursor to the information super-highway, which will be the pipeline for the vital flow of the information of the Digital Age.

Even our seemingly intractable social and political problems can   16
be reinterpreted in this new light: That gridlock in Washington is more about the inability of our old centralized political institutions to adapt to the decentralized, fast-moving realities of our time. The failure of our schools is rooted in the obsolescence of a system that

mass-produces brains in an era in which the world's knowledge doubles every four years.

The economic anxiety comes from the rapid restructuring of the economy and workplace, which puts everyone's career and livelihood at risk. 17

The early signs of this transitional trauma have been around for the last 15 years, from the displacement of manufacturing workers in the early 1980s to the downsizing of office staffs that started in the early 1990s. 18

And the next 10 years may be the most disruptive and difficult period that any of us have lived through—including those who lived through the Great Depression. We'll see the rise and fall of entire sectors of the economy, the disappearance of whole professions, not just individual jobs. Information technologies will make millions of working people redundant and send them scattering to retool their skills and seek new work. 19

The advent of widespread home shopping will reduce the need for sales clerks. Intermediaries such as travel agents will be cut out of many business transactions when consumers can make their own travel arrangements with airlines and hotels via "intelligent" software agents. 20

Even professional salespeople with specialized skills—like real estate agents—may find their services less in demand when consumers themselves can easily tap into real-estate listings and mortgage information databases. 21

The centralized, hierarchical organization characteristic of the Industrial Age will shift into the more decentralized organization that will be the hallmark of the Digital Age. Look at your own workplace: It's probably already started. "Empowerment" of employees is the watchword as layers of managers are eliminated and decision making is pushed closer to where the actual work gets done. 22

Computers May Have the Power to Make the World a More Placid Place to Live by 2020

By about the year 2020, all this will have largely played itself out. The new digital network will be in place, and we'll have absorbed microprocessors in all their myriad forms into our lives. 23

By then your home may have 50 of these tiny computers connected to the information infrastructure, much as you now have 50 24 electric motors tied to the electrical grid powering your refrigerator, washing machine, dishwasher, blender, right down to the clocks on your wall.

In 25 years, the trauma will have largely subsided and the world could well have become a more placid place to live. These ubiquitous computers finally may have the power to bring a sense of tranquillity back to our lives, allowing us to live in less-crowded surroundings, more integrated with nature. 25

Imagine a world where the bulk of people work out of their homes and don't have to live within a 30-minute drive from their employer. You like the mountains? The ocean? A small middle-American town? Move there. 26

Imagine children gathering in neighborhood schools of no more than a dozen kids where parents can pick them up for lunch. Think about governments relying on the diversity and intelligence of entire communities by letting people debate and vote on all the major issues that affect their lives. 27

Imagine regular folks actively participating in the news coverage of their communities. Imagine those who hate shopping using digital models online and getting tailormade clothes. How about a world where physical money—from dollars to dimes—disappears? 28

Sound far-fetched? It's already begun. We're already seeing the baby steps of trends leading in those directions—whether it's custom-made Levi's jeans, the rise in telecommuting or experiments in electronic direct democracy. 29

Every 18 Months Microprocessors Shrink as Power Doubles, Price Drops

The story really starts in the early 1970s with the creation of the microprocessor. For a revolution, it was a pretty inauspicious beginning. At the time, many people didn't see it as much of an improvement over the existing mainframe computers. 30

However, the integrated circuits of microprocessors were smaller and cheaper than the mainframe computers. The development process was such that, eventually, every 18 months or so the microprocessors could double in power, shrink in size, and drop in price. 31

That has allowed a microprocessor coming out this year to be 50 times more powerful than a 1975 IBM mainframe computer. The 32 computer that used to fill a room now fits in a small video game—and the price has fallen from $10 million to $500.

That same dynamic can be expected to boost the power of today's microprocessors a hundredfold in the coming decade. 33

The 1980s marked the beginning of the introduction of the microprocessor into mass society, primarily through the personal computer. Throughout the decade, personal computers took over the business world, which had the money to invest in the relatively expensive new technologies. 34

By the early 1990s, a crucial development took place: Computers began to get tied together. At first, the connections were made within the same company in what are called LANs, or local area networks. But soon they were connecting different companies or institutions through such quasipublic computer networks as the Internet. 35

The key change was that personal computers went from being calculators to being communicators that allowed people to interact, via electronic mail or bulletin boards, for example. People like to communicate. They don't use the telephone because it's a cool gadget; they use it to speak to other human beings. 36

Increasingly throughout the 1990s, the personal computer came to be seen as a totally new way to communicate. And so it began to leave the confines of the business world and make its breakthrough into the home. 37

If the story of the 1980s was the personal computer, then the story of the 1990s is the Net. The developments are of equal importance because the Digital Age needs both the microprocessors in place and the infrastructure to tie them together. Only when they are tied together does the Digital Age take off. 38

And has it ever taken off. Since 1990, anything to do with computer networks has exploded. The Internet was growing 10 percent per month throughout last year. The World Wide Web, the subset of the Internet that handles multimedia images, grew more than 10 percent per week. 39

Technology Life Cycle Shows That Fastest Growth Is Yet to Come

Technology companies in California's Silicon Valley use a recurring image: a marketing curve that describes the rate at which a market absorbs a new product or a society absorbs a new technology. 40

The curve inches up slowly as trendsetters buy the new technol-   41
ogy. Then it jumps at a steep angle as more people buy in. That steep
growth continues until most people in the society own the technology,
and then the curve flattens at the top. That absorption rate has
occurred again and again in the history of technologies—television,
radio, you name it.

When you plot the growth of almost anything related to these   42
digital technologies over the last five years, you see the same unmis-
takable curve ramping up. . . .

Any key technology comes to a point when its usefulness be-   43
comes so apparent that its absorption into society is inevitable. It tips
the balance from the iffiness of a gadget to the certainty of a key tool.
All signs say that the microprocessor has passed that point.

This growth is likely to continue for another 25 years. By the   44
year 2020, the 40-year technology adoption life cycle will be complete. An entire generation will have grown up in the Digital Age
and will take it for granted. And that generation will be running the
world. . . .

Microprocessor Is to This Era What Motor Was to Industrial Age

The microprocessor is a very powerful tool. It can perform the calcu-   45
lations of many minds put together, and it can do those calculations at
speeds that humans simply can't achieve. When linked, they become
vastly more powerful.

Like motors, microprocessors have the power to transform.   46
The same decade that marked the introduction of the microprocessor into society also marked the beginnings of some severe economic
dislocation. A strong argument can be made that they're directly
related.

One of the big stories of the early 1980s was the downsizing of   47
the U.S. manufacturing economy—the closing of factories across the
American Rust Belt. At the time, we blamed foreign competition: We
couldn't compete with Japan.

But the much less visible story was the spread of digital tech-   48
nologies into factories. Microprocessors were not only housed in personal computers; they were finding homes in robots and other tools
on shop floors. Information technologies allowed firms to reorganize
work flow more efficiently; advanced telecommunications allowed

whole factories to be moved to foreign lands. It was largely these digital developments that allowed for the huge layoffs.

One of the big stories of the early 1990s was the 1990–92 reces-   49
sion. What made the recession remarkable was that many of those being laid off were middle managers, clerks, and secretaries. Historically, recessions have primarily hit blue-collar workers.

But the white collars, too, were becoming superfluous in an office   50
environment pervaded by information technologies. You don't need cadres of middle managers making reports and shuffling information to the executives when personal computers on networks can do the job. You don't need as many secretaries answering phones when you have voice mail.

We've heard the stories of our era's human tragedies that rival   51
those of the peasants torn from the fields: the blue-collar worker who had spent 30 years on the assembly line only to be thrown out of work for good; the white-collar worker who gave her life to the corporation only to find she now has to strike out on her own as a consultant.

And we have our rags-to-riches stories as well. We have our   52
Andrew Carnegie of the Digital Age: His name is Bill Gates. He went from a bright kid with some good ideas about software to the richest man in the country as the head of Microsoft. He was worth almost $10 billion before he reached age 40.

That kind of dramatic making of fortunes is a pretty good indi-   53
cation that a new wide-open economic system is taking shape, and the rules have yet to be made.

Digitalization Leaves Centralized Government in Gridlock

It's not just the economy that's feeling the trauma. Once the economy   54
changes, our public institutions inevitably come under the same pressures. And for the last 15 years, our political and social institutions have come under increasing stress and fallen into increasing dysfunction.

Take a look at Washington, DC. It's become a standard lament   55
among Americans of all political persuasions that our federal government simply does not work. No one seems to be able to figure a way out of the legislative gridlock and general paralysis.

Here's one way to view it: Our national government is paralyzed   56
largely because it's a consummate product of the Industrial Age. In

fact, our Constitution was hammered out at the very dawn of that age, more than 200 years ago. And modern Washington is a creature of the mass, centralized, bureaucratized society that was the crowning achievement of that age. The logic of that age was to centralize. And the post–World War II Washington establishment and federal government did that very well.

One of the defining features of the emerging Digital Age is decentralization. The spread of powerful microprocessors, tied together through an infrastructure that moves information at the speed of light, tends to empower the extremities of organizations of all kinds.   57

Seen in that light, modern Washington is completely at odds with the conditions of this new world. It's a centralizing government in a decentralizing world.   58

Taking that same historical perspective, many of the major political events of last year make more sense. We're seeing the very beginnings of a changeover from a highly centralized system of government built up since the New Deal in the 1930s to a more decentralized system in tune with the emerging age.   59

For the first time in 60 years, government appears to be fundamentally shifting course. In 1994, the party consistently holding to the philosophy of less government and more decentralized government—the Republicans—captured control of the Congress after decades out of power. The Democrats, the party clearly associated with big activist government, face the prospects of becoming the nation's minority party after controlling Washington and the bureaucracies since the New Deal.   60

That's not to say that voters consciously voted for the party more in tune with the emerging Digital Age. But when you step back from the minutiae of individual issues, it's apparent that our federal government—and all levels of government—are beginning to go through what businesses have been going through for years.   61

They are trying to define their essential core services and get out of delivering extraneous services. They are trying to adopt new technologies and shed unneeded levels of managers, in their case, bureaucrats. And they are trying to push decision-making down to lower levels of their organizations—and ultimately to the voters themselves.   62

Businesses call it "reengineering" the corporation. Politicians call it "reinventing" government. They're the same thing.   63

Digital Age Spurred Soviet Collapse While Playing to American Strengths

To underscore the power of these historical forces, it's worth looking at the fate of the one other industrial superpower of the 20th century. 64

The Soviet Union took a very different path of industrialization than the United States, but it carried off a pretty impressive feat. In 1917, it was a vast nation of peasants. Sixty years later, in the 1970s, it was a highly industrialized nation in a global struggle for control of the world. 65

But what happened in the 1980s, the dawn of the Digital Age? 66

The Soviet Union's entire system completely imploded in less than 10 years. The Soviets had built an extraordinarily centralized economy and bureaucratized society. Their system was an extreme manifestation of the centralizing tendencies of that era. 67

They had no way to cope with an era of instantaneous communication. Faxes and computer networks helped circulate information within that closed society and get word out to the world. But in a much more fundamental way, that totalitarian system could not function in a world of digital technologies and global telecommunications. And so we watched the Soviet empire collapse. 68

Is the United States doomed to share the fate of the Soviet Union? Far from it. Just as the Industrial Revolution was born in England, the most advanced and powerful country at the time, the Digital Revolution is being born in the last remaining superpower, the United States. We're the first country making this transition into the Digital Age. 69

We're way ahead of Japan and Europe in this process. We have a much higher penetration of personal computers in the workplace and the home. We own 40 percent of all the world's personal computers used in business. The next closest country is Japan, with 7 percent. 70

We dominate the world's Internet and early development of the information superhighway: At the start of this year, the United States had almost 26,000 computer networks hooked up to the Internet, compared to about 1,600 each for Japan and Germany. 71

At a conference called the Networked Economy last fall in Washington, DC, the Japanese government representative said Japan considers itself about 10 years behind the United States in building its information superhighway. 72

This Digital Age should play to many of America's strengths.   73
The ascendant industries are ones in which the United States leads the
world: computers, telecommunications, entertainment, media. And in
a deeper sense, the Digital Age will reward qualities that often char-
acterize the American worker: creativity, innovation, autonomy, initia-
tive, and speed.

More importantly, the Digital Age will lend more importance to   74
the individual. Digital technologies can empower individuals in profound ways. And the United States, far more than any other country
in the world, has built its entire economic and social system on the
individual.

Worldwide Synergy Via the Net Could Spur Creativity—
or Even a Second Renaissance

The Digital Age offers immense possibilities: We may see a time when   75
these digital technologies bring about huge productivity increases that
lead to much higher levels of prosperity and a halving of our 40-hour
work week.

We may even see a flowering of human creativity in something like   76
a second Renaissance. The first Renaissance came about largely because
the printing press enabled all the isolated minds of medieval Europe to
finally connect. What kind of synergy will be created this time around,
as all the minds on the planet become wired together through the Net?

Yet getting from here to there will require an ordeal the likes of   77
which we have never experienced.

The corporation that year in and year out has paid your wages   78
and handed you benefits packages—from health plans to pensions—
may not be around for long, or you won't be on for the ride.

Talk of educational reform may be nothing compared to scrap-   79
ping traditional lectures while beginning long-distance, individualized
learning through computers. Tenured professors and teachers' unions
face not minor pay cuts, but radically new roles.

And reinventing government takes on new meaning in this light.   80
We're having a hard enough time trimming back the military. We
haven't even contemplated dismantling the U.S. Postal Service as most
physical mail turns into digital bits.

You think it's confusing and tumultuous now? Just wait for the   81
coming trauma.

READING QUESTIONS FOR "On the Edge of the Digital Age: The Historic Moment"

Main Idea

1. State the essay's main idea in your own words. Compare it to your prediction of the main idea. (*Note:* The main idea should sum up the smaller ideas of the essay.)

Organization

2. a. Where in the essay is the main idea found?

   b. Why has the author placed the main idea there?

3. In what order are the paragraphs arranged? (Underline one.) Time/ Least to most important/Most to least important/Simple listing/ Logic: cause and effect/Other logic/Other

Style

4. How formal is the essay? (Circle your choice.)

   [Informal—1—2—3—4—5—6—7—8—9—10—Formal]

   What indicators convinced you? (For a list of possible indicators and two benchmark essays, see Appendix F, The Formality Spectrum, on page 298.)

5. Where do you see the following features of style? List one or two examples of each with their paragraph numbers.

   Features (For definitions, see Appendix B, page 288.)

a. allusion

b. metaphor

c. simile

Content

6. Does the author propose any change? If so, what do you think would be the result of such a change?

7. Do you agree with the author's main idea? Why or why not?

If you have not already read the essay and answered the Reading Questions, be sure to do so before you proceed.

COMPOSITION QUESTIONS

Listed below are the writing questions. Choose one and write an essay that answers it. (If your instructor is willing, try adapting one of the questions or even writing your own. Be sure to get your instructor's approval—and possibly suggestions for change—before answering your question.)

Whichever question you choose, think of the person who will read your answer. The question may tell who your audience is. If not, think of a person you know and respect—preferably your instructor or a fellow student who will read your essay. Try to convince that person to believe you.

Bring in useful details from the selection(s) you have read and perhaps other incidents you know of. For ideas, review your answers to questions in the Preview and Reading Steps. When you first refer to a reading, give its title (in quotation marks) and the author's full name. Also, give the full name of anyone featured in the article the first time you mention that person. In making any later references, use only the person's last name.

Note: If you are assigned to write one paragraph, think of your answer to the question, and list several key points you could make to support your answer. Then choose just one of the points and explain it in detail.

1. What Siegel and Leyden describe will produce trauma. While Leyden discusses the traumatic effects leading to the Digital Age, Siegel focuses more on the good effects of his proposed changes. Describe the transitional periods for Siegel's plans: (a) lowering highway speed limits to 30 miles per hour, especially in rural areas (paragraph 7); (b) substituting mixed-use complexes for shopping malls (paragraph 7); (c) phasing out chain stores and superstores, thus increasing prices and the cost of living (paragraph 11); (d) getting people to participate more in federal, state, and local governmental planning (paragraphs 15, 18, 22). Which do you think will be the most difficult period?

2. Siegel's plan would raise the cost of goods (paragraph 11). Can the American consumer make a decision in favor of Siegel's plan if that plan cuts into his or her buying power? He says that Japan prospers on less-efficient small businesses instead of superstores. Are Americans willing to accept the enormous cost of living that exists in Japan? Will Americans let factors other than money be the determining ones in making decisions? Explain.

3. Which traumatic experience do you think would be more palatable to you, Siegel's or Leyden's? Why?

4. Leyden predicts a traumatic transition from the Industrial Age to the Digital Age. How do you think this transition will affect you personally?

5. The changes that both Siegel and Leyden describe would help the environment by reducing use of the automobile. Siegel proposes legislating lower speed limits in order to make a market for high-speed rail service (paragraphs 6–9). Leyden suggests letting technology take its course so that most people will work out of their homes and will not need to use cars as much (paragraph 26). Which idea do you favor? Why?

6. Siegel advocates—and Leyden predicts—a decentralization in human lifestyle (Siegel: whole article; Leyden: paragraphs 16, 22, 54 on).

Explain the differences in the way these two men see the decentralization process.

7. The decentralization in both articles will also affect education (Siegel: paragraphs 13, 15, 24; Leyden: paragraphs 16, 27, 76, 79). How do you envision the educational process either for public schools or for colleges 10 to 20 years from now?

8. Both Siegel and Leyden have proposals that would improve children's lives. Siegel's plan would change federal and state laws (paragraph 15); Leyden's plan would have parents working at home with flexible hours (paragraph 26). Compare and contrast the two plans. Which one do you think would improve family life more?

9. Both Siegel and Leyden look forward to more independence for the individual. Of their two approaches for shaping the future, which one do you think will more likely result in this goal?

10. Take one factor in society during the Renaissance and compare and contrast it with what you think that factor will be like in what Leyden calls the second Renaissance.

11. Siegel is concerned that "we think in terms of having jobs, not in terms of doing jobs because they are useful" (paragraph 19). How is that attitude a problem? If people were paid by achievement rather than on a time basis, would this attitude change for the better? Why or why not?

12. In paragraph 29, Leyden talks of "experiments in electronic direct democracy." What is that, and how can it be accomplished?

13. In his last paragraph, Siegel describes what has "crippled our politics." What, according to Siegel, must be done to get our electorate walking on healthy legs? Predict whether Americans will be willing to make this happen.

14. Compare and contrast the politics discussed in Siegel's last paragraph with the centralized/decentralized concepts of politics discussed by Leyden (paragraph 54 on). How do these two men see technology affecting politics differently?

15. Both Siegel (paragraph 1) and Leyden (paragraph 56) write about how a political system that was formed 200 years ago at the beginning of the Industrial Age is hampering progress now. Must we change just

the political ideas of progressive versus conservative or centralization versus decentralization, or must we take larger steps in rewriting the Constitution? Explain.

16. Both Siegel (paragraph 16) and Leyden (paragraph 75) favor cutting the 40-hour work week in half. Whose ideas do you think have the better chance of bringing about a 20-hour work week? Why?

17. According to Leyden, those who know how to use computers will work from home. Robots will be running much of industry. What kind of work will people do if they do not have computer skills? Is the Western world destined to become an even more widely split society of haves and have-nots? What can be done to help the have-nots live a meaningful existence during the Digital Age?

18. In what ways can the ideas of Siegel and Leyden be integrated effectively for a better society?

REVISION QUESTIONS

Once you have finished writing your essay, ask yourself the following questions.

1. Is there any statement the reader might not understand?
2. Is there any statement that might offend the reader?
3. Is there anything that's not very convincing?
4. Have I changed the subject and then changed back again?
5. Have I said the same thing twice?
6. Do I want to try using any feature of style I've seen in the reading selection?

EDITING QUESTIONS

Once you've made changes, ask someone else to read your essay. Change it again as needed. Then read your essay out loud and answer the following questions.

1. Does every sentence make sense?
2. Does every sentence use the kind of language that most people consider "good English" these days? (*Hint:* Imagine a TV announcer reading it.)
3. Do the periods, commas, and other punctuation show the reader how to interpret what I am writing? Does the use of each punctuation mark conform to the rules that readers expect me to follow?
4. Are the words spelled right?

Note that good grammar, punctuation, and spelling usually make your writing clearer—and always improve your image as a competent, educated writer.

If you make changes in your paper, proofread it again!

APPENDIX

A

Word Parts

Following is a list of word parts to be used in defining the meaning of words that may be new to you. Each word part is given with its meaning and an example word in parentheses.

A

a- = without (asexual)
ab- = from (absent)
-able/-ible = capable of (breakable)
ad- = to (adjust)
-al = related to (sexual)
anti- = against (antisocial)
aud- = related to hearing (audible)
auto- = self (automobile)

C

-cern = to perceive (concern)
co- = having something in common (co-workers)
con- = with/together (consult)

D

de- = down/away (depressed) or reverse (deactivate)
deca- = ten (decade)
-duct = carry/lead (conduct)

E

electr- = electric (electricity)
-er = doer (fighter)
-escent = becoming (adolescent)
-ette = small form of something (kitchenette)
ex- = out of (exit) or former (ex-wife)

F

fatu- = foolish (infatuation)

G

-graph = a picture/writing
   (photograph)

H

holo- = whole (holocaust)
hyper- = over (hyperactive)
hypo- = under, hidden
   (hypocrite)

I

-ible/-able = able to (audible)
-ic/-istic/-itic = characteristic of,
   or related to (artistic;
   arthritic)
in- = not (incapable) or into
   (input)
-ist = expert/specialist (artist)
-ity = state of being (purity)

J

-ject = throw (reject)
-jug- = to join, joined (conjugal)

L

lex- = word (dyslexia)
-logy, -logi- = science of
   (anthropology)
luc- = light (lucid)

M

manu- = hand (manual)
micro- = very small (microscope)
mobil- = moving (automobile)
mono- = one (monologue)
mort- = death (morgue)

N

nephr- = kidney (nephritis)
neuro- = nerve (neurotic)
non- = not (nonprofit)
nov- = new (novelty)

O

-ode = way or path (electrode)

P

path = feeling (sympathy) or
   disease (pathology;
   psychopath)
per- = through or throughout
   (pervade)
-phone = sound (telephone)
-poly = to sell (monopoly)
-pos- = to put (compose)
pre- = before (prewar)
-prehend = to grasp (comprehend)
pro- = forward (progress) or
   favoring (proabortion)
proto- = the first of something;
   the parent (prototype)
psycho- = mind (psychology)

R

re- = again (redo)

S

socio- = society (sociology)
-spir- = breath (expire)
sub- = under (submarine)

T

temp- = time (temporary)
-ten = hold (intent, contend)

-tion = action or act of (suction)
  or condition (qualification)

U

un- = not (unhappy)

V

-vade = to go (invade)
vest- = clothes (vest, vesture)

APPENDIX

B

Guide to Literary Terms

Allusion—brief mention of a famous person, event, document, piece of literature, or quotation.

Ex.: "That's a regular James Bond car" (referring to trick gadgets on the movie character's car).

Note: If a person or event is described in the essay, the reference is not an allusion.

Cliché—a tired expression, once colorful but now overused and stale.

Ex.: "Put your shoulder to the wheel," "pretty as a picture"

Connotation—the emotional meaning of a word.

Ex.: The word *childish* reminds us of the unpleasant qualities of a child, who may be self-centered, demanding, and so forth.

Denotation—the dictionary meaning of a word.

Ex.: The word *childish* means "like a child."

Irony—a contradiction.

Irony of wording: wording that is the opposite of what is meant.

Ex.: "a lovely scab"

Irony of situation: a situation that is the opposite of what we would normally expect.

Ex.: Doctors often take poor care of their own health.

Jargon—specialized language that is hard for an outsider to understand (often meant more to impress us than to tell us anything).

Ex.: "multiple contusions" (several bruises)

Metaphor—see *simile.*

Overstatement (also called hyperbole)—saying more than one means.

Ex.: "When Bob yells, he can be heard for miles."

Restraint—a low-keyed, not-too-emotional style.

Ex.: "If we had been called when he first attacked, the woman might not be dead now."

Sentimentality—appeal to the emotions.

Ex.: "If only we had been called when the madman first appeared out of the shadows to grab little Kitty. . . ."

Simile or **metaphor**—a comparison of two unlike things to create an image.

Simile—a comparison using *like, as,* or *than.*

> *Ex.:* "The windows of the empty house looked like blank eyes."

Metaphor—a comparison not using *like, as,* or *than.*

> *Ex.:* "The windows of the empty house stared blankly."

Note: A comparison of two people or things that really are alike is not a simile or a metaphor.

> *Ex.:* "John looks like his sister."

Symbol—one thing that stands for something greater than itself.

Ex.: A traffic light may stand for the law and its authority.

Tone—the writer's attitude toward his or her subject and audience. The tone may be sad, angry, humorous, and so on.

Ex.: The following two statements mean the same but differ in tone:

"I solemnly swear to bring our cause to the attention of the administration" (serious, formal).

"I'll make the prez sit up and take notice if I have to cut off his tie" (humorous, informal).

Understatement—saying less than one means.

Ex.: As a neighbor, Count Dracula was a bit different.

APPENDIX
C

Allusion

A. In each sentence below is at least one allusion. Explain its meaning. (The first two are done for you.)

1. Mark was literally swept off his feet by *the local Arnold Schwartzenegger.* (A strong and forceful man.)

2. Just before the election, the candidate had studied the latest poll for the last time—he had seen the *handwriting on the wall.*

   (Had seen a prediction of defeat. *Note:* Just before Babylon fell, its king saw a hand write a message on his wall. Not understanding it, he called in the prophet Daniel, who told the king that his kingdom was going to fall to the enemy.)

3. Discouraged, the police chief said, "What we need is *Sherlock Holmes.*"

4. When his civics teacher, Miss Johnson, asked Jack if he had thrown the paper airplane, he *pleaded the Fifth Amendment.*

5. From what her teasing friends had told her, Jill thought her blind date was going to be *Dracula;* but when she opened the door and saw a *Tom Cruise,* she felt a lump in her throat.

6. Pete was as cheery as *Walter Matthau.*

7. Andy Rooney named one of his essays *"In and of Ourselves We Trust."* (What famous quotation does this remind you of? What do you think the essay is about?)

8. As Jack walked out of a two-hour examination, he told a friend, "I think I just *met my Waterloo."*

B. (Optional) Write two allusions and explain each.

1.

2.

C. Define *allusion.*

D. Why do people use allusions?

APPENDIX
D

Connotations of Names

A. Match the name to its connotation by placing numbers in the blanks.

Name

1. Ebenezer Scrooge
2. Brenda Starr
3. Morning Glory
4. Daddy Warbucks
5. Rocky

Connotation

_____ a. interested in nature
_____ b. miserly
_____ c. glamorous
_____ d. tough
_____ e. rich

B. Give the connotation(s) you have in mind for each name below.

Name

1. Joe
2. Lola
3. Nellie
4. Brunhilda
5. Brock
6. Junior
7. Your own name

Connotation

_____
_____
_____
_____
_____
_____
_____

C. Suppose you want to change your name to give yourself a new image. Supply a possible name for each image.

Name	**Connotation**
1. _____	tough, popular leader
2. _____	macho cowboy
3. _____	strong, romantic man
4. _____	wealthy woman
5. _____	flinty, aristocratic judge
6. _____	glamorous woman
7. _____	wise doctor

D. (Optional) Give an example of a real name change and the reason.

E. Define *connotation*.

F. In what occupations might people be particularly aware of the connotations of names?

APPENDIX

E

Figures of Speech: Metaphors, Similes, and Clichés

A. Match the colorful word or phrase on the left with the "plain English" version on the right. The first two are done for you.

**Figure of Speech
(Metaphor or Simile)**

                                                        Plain English

1. bulldog   _____   a. energetic person
2. silky   _____   b. blank look
3. ball of fire   _____   c. jumbled words
4. holy worm   __1__   d. football lineman
5. face of corpse three hours old   _____   e. conniving preacher
6. squirming sea of language   _____   f. flowing hair
7. leaves of a willow tree   __2__   g. soft

B. Now write your own plain English version of each figure of speech below.

Figure of Speech (Metaphor or Simile)	Plain English
1. beanpole	_____
2. walrus	_____
3. political polar winds	_____
4. wounded knight	_____
5. "No man is an island."	_____

C. Why do people use figures of speech?

D. Figures of speech may be either metaphors or similes. Inspect the examples below; then state the difference.

Simile: Their french fries taste like cardboard.
Metaphor: Their french fries are made of cardboard.

Simile: Her eyes were as sharp as knives.
Metaphor: Her eyes cut into me.

Simile: The child's hair was softer than silk.
Metaphor: The child's hair was pure silk.

1. Define a *simile*.

2. Define a *metaphor*.

3. Label the following as either "M" (metaphor) or "S" (simile).
   a. His beard was white as snow. ____
   b. I weeded out my mistakes. ____
   c. My room looks like a disaster area. ____

　　　d. If I keep eating five meals a day, I'll be a whale. ___
　　　e. You smoke more than a chimney. ___

E. One problem that some people have with similes is distinguishing them from simple comparisons. Below is a list of sentences, some having similes and some having simple comparisons. Put an "S" before any sentence with a simile (a colorful expression, not meant to be realistic); put an "SC" in front of any with a simple comparison (a real comparison); put "NC" for no comparison.

　　_____ 1. Jack is five inches taller than Jill.

　　_____ 2. After Jack fell down the hill and into the swamp, he looked like Jill's pig.

　　_____ 3. I am as hungry as a man stranded on an island with nothing but coconuts.

　　_____ 4. As the next mayor, I will fight air pollution.

　　_____ 5. Bill felt as strong as any other man.

　　_____ 6. John ran like the wind.

　　_____ 7. Shorty is taller than the Empire State Building.

F. Sometimes a metaphor gives two images at once (for example, "the hand of God leaves footprints"). Thus it is called a *mixed metaphor*. Before each example below, put "M" for metaphor (consistent, meaningful comparison) or "MM" for mixed metaphor (inappropriate, inconsistent comparison).

　　_____ 1. That's just gravy on the cake.

　　_____ 2. After the explosion below deck, the ship suddenly became an anthill with workers scurrying out of every hole.

　　_____ 3. With red in his eyes, the congressman hoofed the dust for several moments, ready to charge the reporter, but finally restrained himself and offered a bullish grin.

　　_____ 4. There's no use locking the door after the horse is stolen.

　　_____ 5. He tried to sell some hot ice.

G. Metaphors and similes are invented to give color and even humor to a message. But like a twice-told joke, they can lose their punch if repeated often. An overused expression is known as a cliché. Mark each expression below with a + (fresh and colorful) or a − (overused). (Your answers may be different from your instructor's and still be all right: An old expression may still be new to you because you have not yet done as much reading.)

_____ 1. She gave him the cold shoulder.

_____ 2. Hurry up. You're slow as molasses.

_____ 3. It's as bright as new nail polish.

_____ 4. I'll leave when hell freezes over.

_____ 5. With that short, dyed hair, she looks like a dandelion.

_____ 6. His eyes are bigger than his stomach.

_____ 7. Wash up. You've got a bad case of ditchdigger's hands.

H. (Optional) Write a metaphor of your own.

APPENDIX

F

The Formality Spectrum: Indicators of Informality and Formality

Informality ⟵⟶	Formality
Humor	Serious tone or mood
Informal wording or slang	Formal vocabulary
• *kid*	• *juvenile*
• *put in jail*	• *incarcerate*
Short sentences and paragraphs overall	Long sentences and paragraphs overall
Use of first person (*I*) or second person (*you*)	Use of third person (*he, she, it, one, they*)
Contractions	Few or no contractions

Below are two sample passages, one very informal and one very formal. First read both quickly and compare them to get an overall impression of their formality. Label one with an "I" for informal and the other with an "F" for formal. Then list some indicators of informality or formality that you notice in each passage.

Equality and Speech

Catharine A. MacKinnon

Canada's new constitution, the Charter of Rights and Freedoms, includes an expansive equality guarantee and a serious entrenchment of freedom of expression. The Supreme Court of Canada's first move was to define equality in a meaningful way—one more substantive than formal, directed toward changing unequal social relations rather than monitoring their equal positioning before the law. The positive spin of the Canadian interpretation holds the law to promoting equality, projecting the law into a more equal future, rather than remaining rigidly neutral in ways that either reinforce existing social inequality or prohibit changing it, as the American constitutional perspective has increasingly done in recent years.

Why We Must Put Up with Porn

Susan Isaacs

If you and I were sitting together, listening to a little Vivaldi, sipping herbal tea, chatting about men and women, arguing about politics and art, we might get around to what to do about the porn problem—at which point you'd slam down your cup and demand, How can you of all people defend smut-peddling slimeballs who portray women being beaten and raped?

Well . . .

You're the one (you'd be sure to remind me) who hates any kind of violence against women. You're the one who even gets upset when James Cagney, in *The Public Enemy,* the 1931 classic, smashes a grapefruit into Mae Clarke's face, for heaven's sake!

That's right, I'd say.

So? Don't you want to protect women? Why not ban books and films that degrade women?

Let's have another cup of tea and I'll tell you.

1. Which passage is more formal? What characteristics give it formality?

2. What characteristics of informality do you see in the other passage?

APPENDIX

G

Irony of Situation

A. Complete the following sentences. The first three are done for you. (If you don't know the facts to complete items 6–10, just create an answer that shows irony.)

1. Your driver-training teacher has <u>hit a tree</u>.

2. The writer F. Scott Fitzgerald couldn't <u>spell</u> very well.

3. A great South American patriot is named <u>O'Higgins</u>.

4. Your English teacher says _____.

5. A college student goes to sleep at _____ in the evening.

6. On *M.A.S.H.,* Hawkeye once considered _____.

7. Monet painted some of his most famous pictures after losing some of his _____.

8. The composer Beethoven was _____.

9. John F. Kennedy, a wealthy president, sponsored laws to help

_____.

10. A famous football player had the hobby of _____
_____.

B. (Optional) Write two sentences showing irony of situation.

1.

2.

C. Define *irony of situation.*

APPENDIX
H

Irony of Wording

Read the student editorial below. Then answer the questions that follow it.

Life Off Campus

Anonymous

Living off campus is a fantastic experience. No Residence Life rules to   1
worry about; no cafeteria meals to choke on; no fumbling for your
I.D. just to get into your dorm.

When you live off campus, you can experience independence   2
and self-respect (hey, I like burnt toast!). And no one ever tells you
what you can or can't do.

But what about the other side of this wonderful living experi-   3
ence? Have you ever tried living with eight girls while one girl thinks
she owns the freezer? What about your roommate's boyfriend or girlfriend who conveniently calls at three o'clock in the morning (and the
phone is next to your room)? Ah, and then there's the favorite roommate who allows you to clean up her dog's gift to the rug since she is
never home to train it.

A student editorial. Published October 13, 1983, in *State* (student newspaper of Frostburg
State University).

Everyone's favorite job is cleaning up. When dishes start hitting   4
the ceiling, everyone invariably denies ever eating at home. If you have
a Felix in your house, you've got it made. If you don't, well, good luck,
Oscar.*

If roommates are great, then the house conditions are even bet-   5
ter. Ever have the bathroom leak right in your room? Or a gas oven
that nearly blasts you every time you light it?

Bet most of you off-campus lovers have the most tasteful wall-   6
paper you've ever seen (yes, even better than mom's). Not to mention
the most decorative (and comfortable) couches. Sway-back mattresses
take some getting used to, but you can learn to mold into a V-position.

Yes, all in all, off-campus living is most enjoyable. I wouldn't   7
trade it for the world!

1. What is the author's *stated* main idea?

2. What is the author's *real* main idea?

3. What details convince you of the real main idea? Note the paragraph
number here and make a check in the margin by each.

4. a. In what places does the author say just the opposite of what's
meant?

   b. How can you tell the author does not mean these words?

---

*An allusion to the play, movie, and television series *The Odd Couple,* featuring Felix Unger
and Oscar Madison.

5. Why do you think the author chose to say one thing and convince you of just the opposite?

6. How would you define *irony of wording?*

APPENDIX

I

Jargon

A. Match the jargon with the plain English word that has the same meaning. The first one is done for you.

	Jargon	**Plain English**
(Business)	1. utilization	_____ a. heroin
(Drug slang)	2. horse	_____ b. back
(Medicine)	3. posterior	_____ c. poor
(Sociology)	4. underprivileged	__1__ d. use
(Teen slang)	5. dissing	_____ e. speaking or acting disrespectfully to (a person)
(Black slang)	6. honky	_____ f. paper copy
(Computers)	7. hard copy	_____ g. white person

B. List three jargon words you know and their plain English versions.

Jargon	**Plain English**
1. _____	_____
2. _____	_____
3. _____	_____

C. How would you define *jargon?* (*Note:* Are all jargon words long?)

D. There are at least three reasons why people use jargon. Name one.

"Little Miss Muffet" is an old nursery rhyme. Below, Russell Baker shows how people from several fields would discuss it in their own jargon. To identify the person's field, fill in the blank with one of the following: editorial writer, psychiatrist, sociologist, militarist (military specialist), child, book reviewer.

Little Miss Muffet

Russell Baker

Little Miss Muffet, as everyone knows, sat on a tuffet eating her curds   1
and whey when along came a spider who sat down beside her and
frightened Miss Muffet away. While everyone knows this, the signifi-
cance of the event had never been analyzed until a conference of
thinkers recently brought their special insights to bear upon it. Following are excerpts from the transcript of their discussion:

____ We are clearly dealing with a prototypical illustration of a highly   2
tensile social structure's tendency to dis- or perhaps even de-structure
itself under the pressures created when optimum minimums do not
obtain among the disadvantaged. Miss Muffet is nutritionally underprivileged, as evidenced by the subliminal diet of curds and whey
upon which she is forced to subsist, while the spider's cultural disad-
vantage is evidenced by such phenomena as legs exceeding standard
norms, odd mating habits, and so forth.

In this instance, spider expectations lead the culturally disad-   3
vantaged to assert demands to share the tuffet with the nutritionally
underprivileged. Due to a communications failure, Miss Muffet assumes without evidence that the spider will not be satisfied to share
her tuffet, but will also insist on eating her curds and perhaps even
her whey. Thus, the failure to preestablish selectively optimum norm

---

Reprinted by permission.

structures diverts potentially optimal minimums from the expectation levels assumed to . . .

____ Second-strike capability, sir! That's what was lacking. If Miss 4 Muffet had developed a second-strike capability instead of squandering her resources on curds and whey, no spider on earth would have dared launch a first strike capable of carrying him right to the heart of her tuffet. I am confident that Miss Muffet had adequate notice from experts that she could not afford both curds and whey and, at the same time, support an early-spider-warning system. Yet curds alone were not good enough for Miss Muffet. She had to have whey, too. Tuffet security must be the first responsibility of every diner. . . .

____ Written on several levels, this searing and sensitive exploration of 5 the arachnid heart illuminates the agony and splendor of Jewish family life with a candor that is at once breathtaking in its simplicity and soul-shattering in its implied ambiguity. Some will doubtless be shocked to see such objects as tuffets and whey discussed without flinching, but hereafter writers too timid to call a curd a curd will no longer. . . .

____ Why has the Government not seen fit to tell the public all it knows 6 about the so-called curds-and-whey affair? It is not enough to suggest that this was merely a random incident involving a lonely spider and a young diner. In today's world, poised as it is on the knife edge of . . .

____ Little Miss Muffet is, of course, neither little nor a miss. These 7 are obviously the self she has created in her own fantasies to escape the reality that she is a gross divorcee whose superego makes it impossible for her to sustain a normal relationship with any man, symbolized by the spider, who, of course, has no existence outside her fantasies. Little Miss Muffet may, in fact, be a man with deeply repressed Oedipal impulses, who sees in the spider the father he would like to kill, and very well may some day unless he admits that what he believes to be a tuffet is, in fact, probably the dining room chandelier, and that the whey he thinks he is eating is, in fact, probably . . .

____ This is about a little girl who gets scared by a spider. (The child 8 was sent home when the conference broke for lunch. It was agreed that he was too immature to subtract anything from the sum of human understanding.)

Answers: Paragraphs 2 and 3: Sociologist; 4: Militarist; 5: Book reviewer; 6: Editorial writer; 7: Psychiatrist; 8: Child.

APPENDIX

J

Symbols

A. Note each symbol on the left. Then at the right, state what that symbol stands for. The first two are done for you. *Note:* if your answers are not the same as other people's, you are not necessarily wrong. It may be that the symbol has a special personal meaning for you.

Symbol	Meaning
1. dove	peace
2. traffic light	the law
3. lion	
4. rainbow	
5. dog	
6. thunderclouds	
7. heart	
8. fire	
9. wind	
10. sun	
11. blue	

B. (Optional) Symbols 7–11, repeated below, appear in well-known songs. Name one song for each word.

7. heart	
8. fire	
9. wind	

10. sun   _____

11. blue   _____

C. A personal symbol means different things to different people. Fill in the blanks below to show the personal meanings of some symbols. The first two are done for you.

A car: To a 16-year-old, a car can mean <u>power and independence</u>. To her parent, a car can mean <u>danger and loss of authority</u>.

To a poor person, a car can mean _____.

A house: To a child, a house can mean _____.

To a parent, a house can mean _____.

(Optional) Add one or two personal symbols and tell what they mean to you.

D. Define a *symbol:*

APPENDIX
K

Spelling List

Here is a place for you to make a personal spelling list, one that will save you much time and effort when you edit. Add to this list after you finish each paper: Write in any words that gave you trouble—even if you find you guessed them right and even if you "really knew better." File them by first letter so you can find them easily.

Even if you use a computer program to correct your spelling, you'll still need this list for problems the computer can't catch: the one-word/two-word problem (the word *maybe* means *possibly,* but *may be* means *might be*) and other words that sound alike but are spelled differently (*their, there, they're*). Record these with their meanings.

As your list builds, it will become a handy reference, that is quicker to use than the dictionary because it is so much shorter.

A

advice
advising
affect = to influence (verb)
all right
a lot (two words)
all together = as a group
altogether = completely
argument
article

B

belief
believe
buy
by

C

cannot
choose (now I choose)
chose (yesterday I chose)
cite = refer to
commitment
committing

D

do
due
doesn't

E

effect = the result (noun)
every day = each day
everyday = ordinary

F

G

H

have (could have, should have,
will have)

I

imply = to hint
infer = to guess
individuals
in turn (two words)
it's = it is (or it has)
its = belonging to it

J

K

knew = past tense of know

L

less = smaller in amount
fewer = lower in number
loose (rhymes with goose) = not
        tight
lose = not win

M

N

necessary
new = not old
now = not then

O

occur
occurred

P

people's ideas
presence
privilege

Q

R

receive

S

T

than = comparison (more than,
       rather than)
then = not now OR
       if . . . then
their = belonging to them
they're = they are
there = in that place OR
       stating a fact (there are three)
today's world
tomorrow
too = also OR
       overly (too much, too small)
two = 2
to = use whenever too and two
       don't fit (to the store/to see)
truly

U

V

view

W

weather = outdoor conditions
whether = comparison (whether
    or not)
we're = we are
were (They were taking the car.)
where = in what place? (Where
    is it?)
while
who's = who is OR
    who has
whose = belongs to
woman/women
writing/writer/written

X

Y

your = belonging to you
you're = you are

Z

APPENDIX
L

Discussion Grading Sheet

Following is one possible grading scheme for class discussion, based in part on the task and maintenance roles described in the introduction.

Section

Date

NAMES

Brought text											
Listened act.											
Cited text											
Gave info/op.											
Asked info/op.											
Started disc.											
Summarized											
Diagnosed											
Evaluated											
Relieved tens.											
GRADE											

A = 4 pts.   D = 1 pt.
B = 3 pts.   F = 0 pt.
C = 2 pts.
NC (No Credit) = Excused abs.

APPENDIX

M

Essay Checklist

Use this checklist to make sure you have all the ingredients of a successful essay.

	Essay				
Title	**1**	**2**	**3**	**4**	**5**
1. Title that shows the issue and is different from the title of the reading—no underlining or quotation marks[†]					
Introduction (Background)					
2. Title of each reading selection from textbook—in quotation marks[*]					
3. Each author's first and last names with first mention of the reading in your text[**]					
4. Thesis/assertion (question to be discussed—or its answer): address key issues from the question					
Body (Evidence)					
5. Develops the thesis					
6. Uses evidence from the reading(s) in the textbook					
7. Analyzes the issues (deals with the issues in detail)					
8. Shows original thought					

Conclusion					
9. Answers the question clearly—uses key words again (reread introduction and conclusion)					
10. Closes the essay—no new material					

†**Title:** Capitalize the first word (and first word after : or ;). Capitalize the last word. Capitalize all middle words, even short ones, except these:

Articles	**Short Joining Words**	**Short Prepositions (2–4 letters)**
a, an, the	and, but, or, nor, so, for, yet	as, at, by, for, from, in, into, near, of, on, over, to, up, with

Referring to the readings

*1. The first time you refer to an essay, give its title and the author's full name.
  Example 1: In the essay "How to Clean Your Apartment," Oscar Madison says that people should just toss things in their closets.

  Example 2: Oscar Madison, the author of "How to Clean Your Apartment," says, "Throw everything in the closet" (p. 55).

*2. Summarize the author's ideas in your own words (see Example 1, above) or use the author's words—**sparingly**—in quotation marks followed by the page number (see Example 2, above).

**3. Place the apostrophes correctly.
  Example 3: The essay by Miguel Braga OR Miguel Braga's essay

  Example 4: Michelle Ritchie's and Georgia Smith's essays (separate essays)

  Example 5: Joan Green and Al Rosen's essay (one essay written jointly)

Coherence or continuity

1. Arrange your ideas in logical sequence.
2. Show how your ideas are related.

- Combine sentences.
- Use transitions (*however/so/for example*).
- Use pronouns. Be sure the reader can tell what they refer to.

Proofreading

1. Go away from your paper for at least 20 minutes, preferably overnight.
2. Proofread on screen; then print out and proofread on paper.
3. To hear your ideas, read your paper forward, preferably out loud.
4. To check for sentence structure, read from back to front, sentence by sentence.
5. Read once through for each type of error you tend to make.

Conferences (These directions may vary; consult your instructor.)

1. The first draft conference focuses on content and organization.
2. The final draft conference also includes grammar, spelling, and punctuation. Be sure to update your spelling and editing checklists afterward. Show them to your instructor right away.
3. To conferences, bring:
   - class text and class handouts, especially the essay checklist.
   - your complete essay, typed double-spaced, with approximately one-inch margins on all four sides. Keep all your prewriting and successive drafts; turn these in with your final copy.

QUALITIES OF AN EFFECTIVE ESSAY

What is effective content?

- answers the question
- formulates concepts thoughtfully
- shows awareness of two sides of an issue
- uses enough details to support main idea(s)
- uses specific examples
- varies the use of examples or evidence
- shows critical thinking (analysis, synthesis, original thought)

- uses sources appropriately
- uses appropriate formality (see Appendix F, in *Controversy*)

What is effective organization?

- arresting introduction
- thoughtful thesis
- well-developed paragraphs
- appropriate conclusion
- overall unity (all parts support the thesis and relate to each other)
- overall coherence (readers can see the relations between thoughts and move easily from one to the next; transitions and consistent tense will help)

What builds an arresting introduction?

- startling statistics
- an anecdote, short story, fable, or personal experience
- a question or series of questions
- history
- the importance of the subject
- song or relevant quotation (from the reading or elsewhere)

What builds an appropriate ending?

- concluding the anecdote
- repeating the thesis or main idea, using different words
- history and future implications
- statement of the importance of the subject
- summary
- a question or series of questions
- a quotation
- a combination of two of the above

APPENDIX

N

Editing Checklist

Handbk Pages	Error	Sentence-level errors
	frag	sentence fragment = incomplete sentence
		Example: "Going along for the ride."
	CS	comma splice = complete sentence $\boxed{,}$ complete sentence
		Example: "I might go, I'm not sure."
	RO	run-on (also called fused sentence) = complete sentence $\boxed{}$ complete sentence
		Example: "I might go I'm not sure."
		To repair CS and RO:
		• $\boxed{;}$ "I might go; I'm not sure."
		• $\boxed{\text{. Cap}}$ "I might go. I'm not sure."
		• $\boxed{\text{, and/or/but (coordinating conjunction)}}$ "I might go, but I'm not sure."
		• $\boxed{\text{though (subordinating conjunction)}}$ "I might go, though I'm not sure."
		Other frequent errors
	ww	wrong word
	sp	spelling error

Handbk Pages	Error	Other frequent errors
	(p. x)	page number needed for quotation
	⬭	omission
	⌄	punctuation needed
	___	underlining needed
	¶	new paragraph needed
	agr	agreement of subject and verb needed
	//	make construction parallel
		Example: "I like swimming and to run."
		To repair: "I like swimming and running."
		or "I like to swim and run."
	shift	unnecessary change in verb tense or number of people

One	More than one
I	we
you	you
he, she, it	they
a person	people
a juvenile	juveniles

From each graded paper—for each error you made—list the *type* of error, write the actual *example* from your paper, and show how to *correct* the error. Then use the list to help proofread the final drafts of your next papers.

NOTES

NOTES